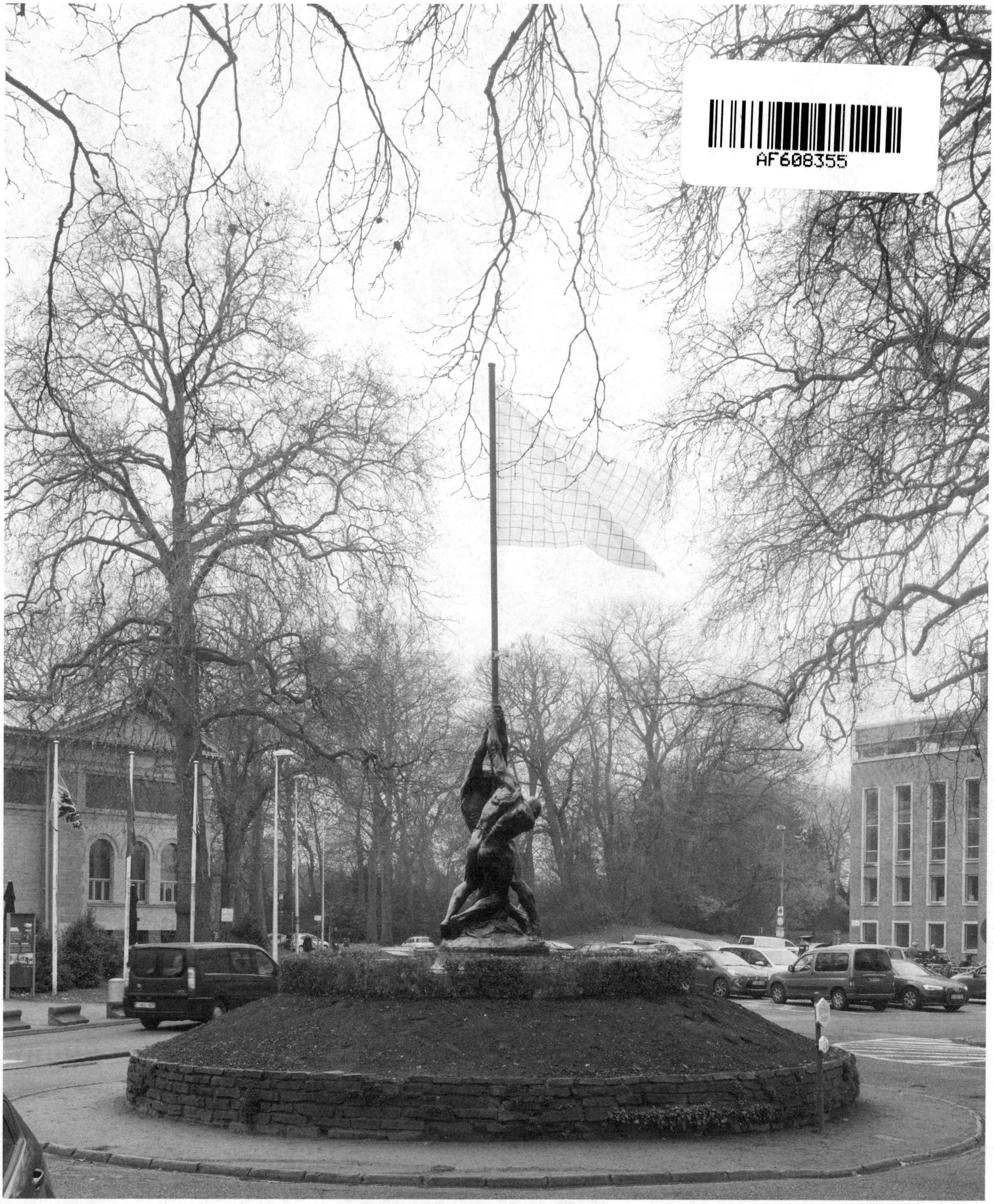

AF608355

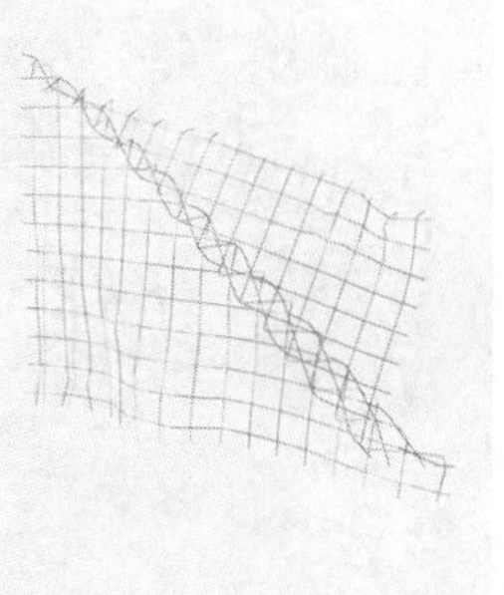

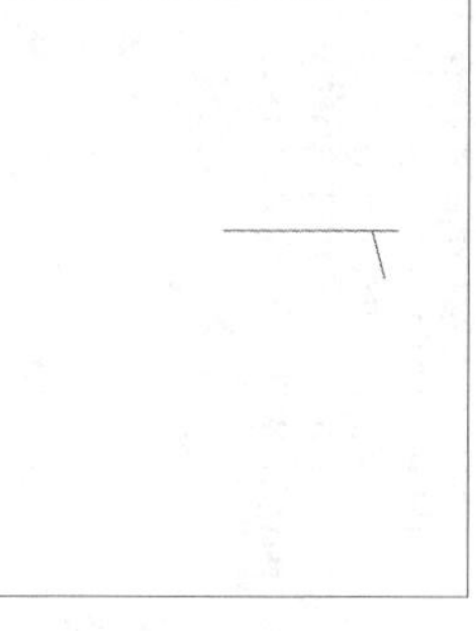

E, 8,64 km/h

[erosion]

Citadel Park lies between the Scheldt and the Lys. It rises from its surroundings. In the park, there are two museums, an animal shelter, a congress hall, man-made caves, ponds, and a velodrome. The wind blows between the trees. Dust is lifted from the soil and flies out of the park.

'Would it be possible to ascribe a kind of prophetic gift or intention to the forces that shaped this landscape?'
'You mean: did the two rivers want to carve out a hill at the edge of what would become the heart of the city?'
'Did they anticipate an elevation on which a park, statues, and museums would be built? As if a physical height might strengthen the symbolic value of the elements that would be displayed on it.'
'Could be, but maybe it's not about the landscape. When depicted in a painting or a photograph, landscapes tend to function as a combination of elements that are outlined against a background. There is a surface – hills, a stormy sea – that supports a composition of trees, buildings, or a battle scene. The surface tends to disappear beneath and behind the landscape. The surface functions as a way to show, make visible, something other than itself. An affect, an event.'
'So it would be futile to ask whether one could find a motivation in this landscape.'
'You would have to take the surface as a forensic surface upon which nothing but the surface itself is being written. You would have to take erosion into consideration. In 1984, the park was officially recognized as a protected landscape for its dendrological, aesthetical, and historical values. To protect a park has many consequences: for example, it implies that erosion – how the land will gradually wear away – is neglected, and human labour will be necessary to maintain it as it is. It is to fix what is mere flux. The question thus becomes: what did nature anticipate before it was designated a protected landscape.'
'OK. So one would have to search the landscape for traces of that anticipation. The question is not only what it wanted to build, but also what it wants to erase. A landscape architect told me that Mount Fuji is slowly crumbling. The authorities are trying to preserve and even reconstruct its famous conical shape. To do so, they are studying old paintings of the mountain. The rock formations they depict become a guideline for the preservation of the mountain. But I wonder if the almost invisible surface structure of those paintings inadvertently moulds Mount Fuji as well, maybe even more so than what they represent. As such, Mount Fuji would not only be shaped by the slopes in Hokusai's drawings, but also inscribed with the texture of the woodblocks used to print them.'
'There are structures, both visible and not, that are an integral part of Citadel Park. In the nineteenth century, a fortress was built. It was conceived as two overlapping grids – two crossed pentagons. This park is not a place of silence and tranquillity, but rather a place where powers are continuously and aggressively trying to reshape it. But those powers themselves have also been altered in the course of history.'
'Winds shape surfaces and surfaces shape winds.'
'Indeed. We should document the surface as an unrelenting chain of events of which the causality cannot be grasped, and strive to reconfigure the narratives that were silenced. We should tell the stories of the surface, circumvent the park it became, and take into account the specks of dust that inconspicuously fly around.'

F#1

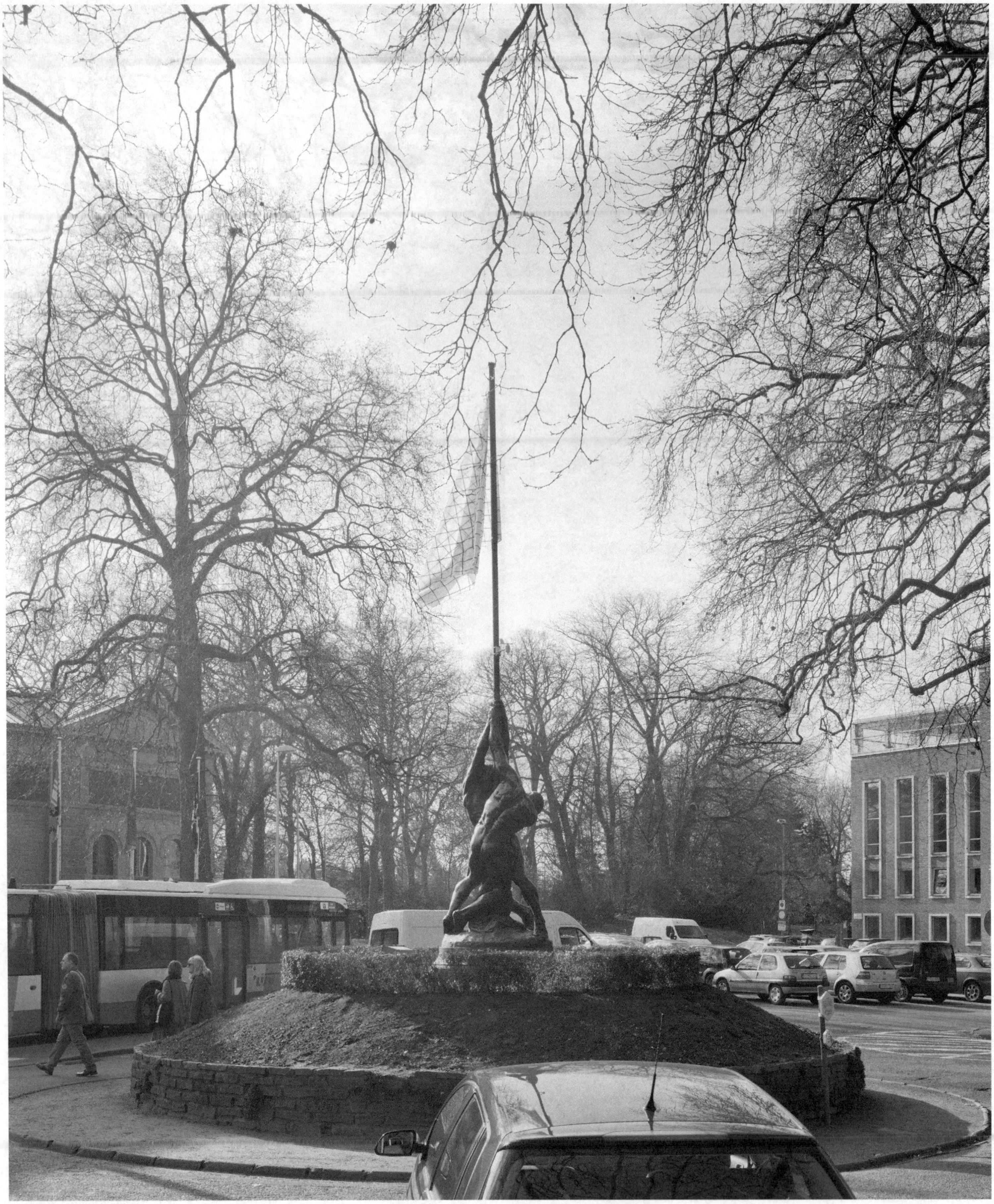

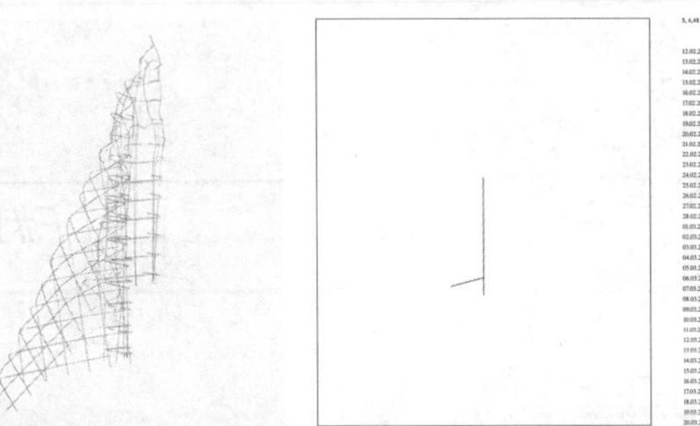

S, 6,48 km/h

[data]

12.02.2017	12:02:50	_44A8205	1/80	8	800	2,4	4,66	E
13.02.2017	#####	#####	#####	#####	#####	#####	#####	#####
14.02.2017	#####	#####	#####	#####	#####	#####	#####	#####
15.02.2017	12:04:09	_44A8280	1/640	8	500	1,8	3,50	S
16.02.2017	#####	#####	#####	#####	#####	#####	#####	#####
17.02.2017	#####	#####	#####	#####	#####	#####	#####	#####
18.02.2017	15:20:13	_44A8446	1/320	8	200	1,7	3,30	SSE
19.02.2017	#####	#####	#####	#####	#####	#####	#####	#####
20.02.2017	#####	#####	#####	#####	#####	#####	#####	#####
21.02.2017	14:05:40	_44A8473	1/250	8	1250	5,1	9,91	WSW
22.02.2017	#####	#####	#####	#####	#####	#####	#####	#####
23.02.2017	#####	#####	#####	#####	#####	#####	#####	#####
24.02.2017	15:52:53	_44A9577	1/200	8	800	1,4	2,72	S
25.02.2017	#####	#####	#####	#####	#####	#####	#####	#####
26.02.2017	#####	#####	#####	#####	#####	#####	#####	#####
27.02.2017	15:23:10	_44A9591	1/125	8	2000	1,4	2,72	NE
28.02.2017	#####	#####	#####	#####	#####	#####	#####	#####
01.03.2017	#####	#####	#####	#####	#####	#####	#####	#####
02.03.2017	11:00:43	_44A0257	1/200	8	640	10,2	19,83	WSW
03.03.2017	#####	#####	#####	#####	#####	#####	#####	#####
04.03.2017	#####	#####	#####	#####	#####	#####	#####	#####
05.03.2017	10:18:47	_44A0320	1/320	8	200	2,5	4,86	ESE
06.03.2017	#####	#####	#####	#####	#####	#####	#####	#####
07.03.2017	#####	#####	#####	#####	#####	#####	#####	#####
08.03.2017	09:27:18	_44A0325	1/200	8	1250	0,6	1,17	SSW
09.03.2017	#####	#####	#####	#####	#####	#####	#####	#####
10.03.2017	#####	#####	#####	#####	#####	#####	#####	#####
11.03.2017	12:12:44	_44A0367	1/250	8	160	0,9	1,75	SSW
12.03.2017	#####	#####	#####	#####	#####	#####	#####	#####
13.03.2017	#####	#####	#####	#####	#####	#####	#####	#####
14.03.2017	11:16:47	_44A0383	1/250	8	400	1,3	2,53	WSW
15.03.2017	#####	#####	#####	#####	#####	#####	#####	#####
16.03.2017	#####	#####	#####	#####	#####	#####	#####	#####
17.03.2017	09:51:38	_44A0427	1/250	8	400	0,7	1,36	WNW
18.03.2017	#####	#####	#####	#####	#####	#####	#####	#####
19.03.2017	#####	#####	#####	#####	#####	#####	#####	#####
20.03.2017	13:07:08	_44A0477	1/200	8	1000	2,8	5,44	W

F#2

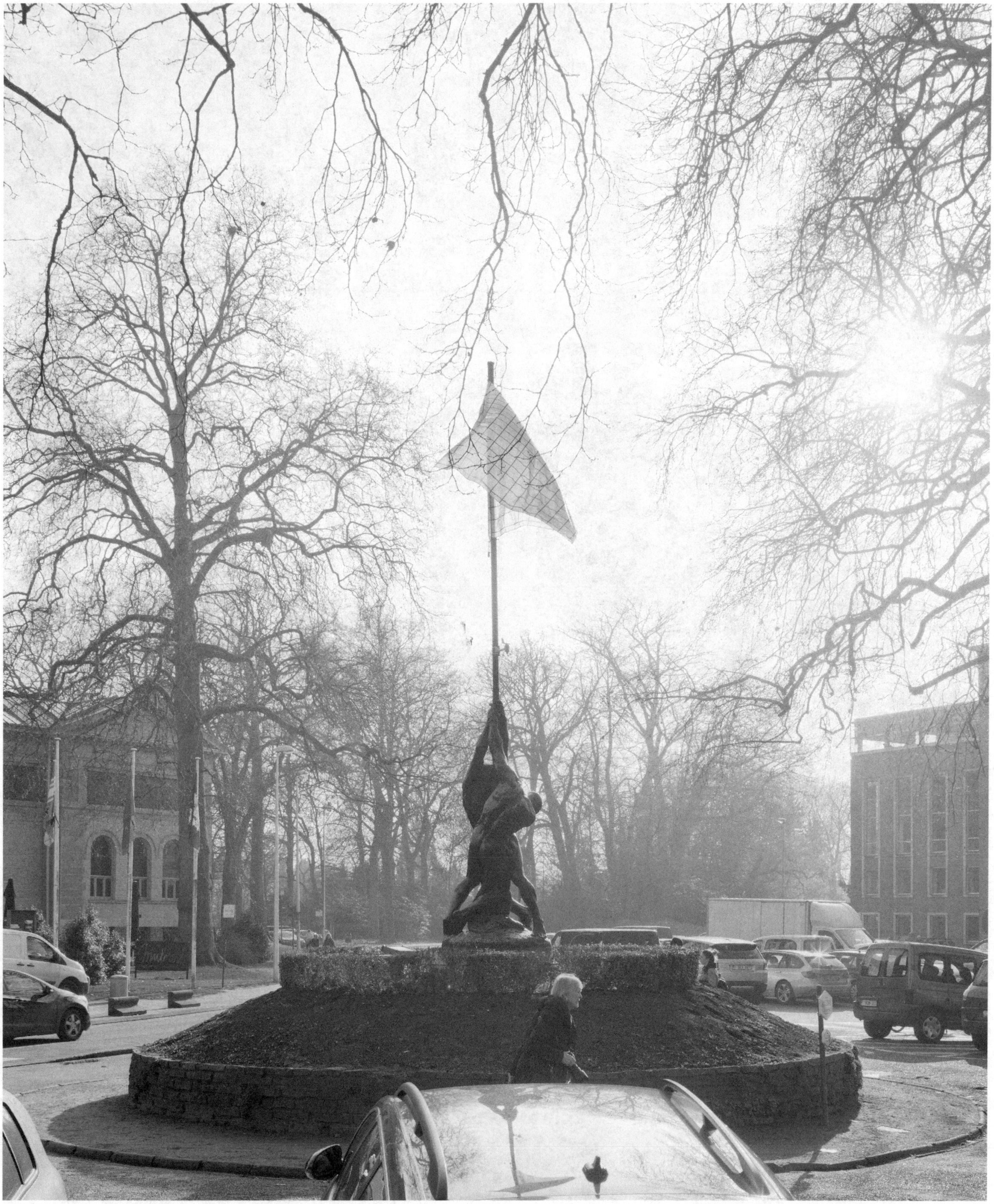

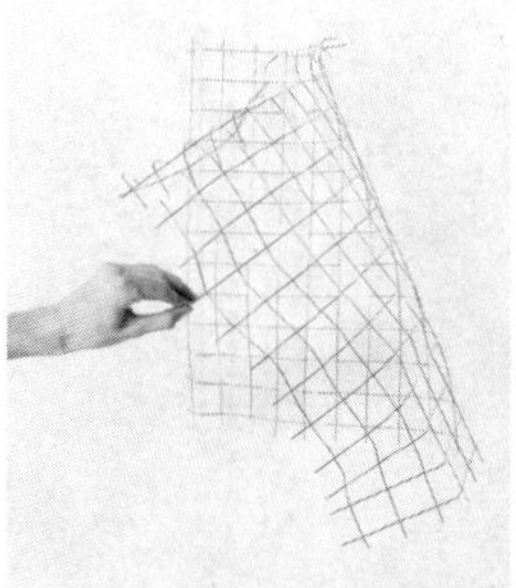

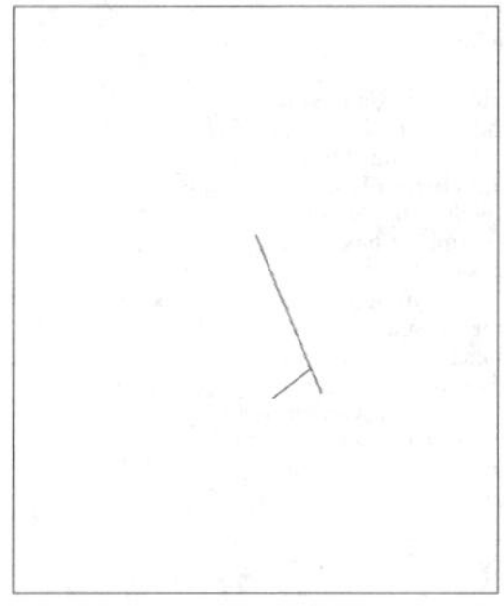

SSE, 6,12 km/h
[a dialogue, every 3d]

The flag is up. We've decided on the point of view from which the photographs will be taken. Both museums are closing and the parking lot empties out.

+3d
A man gets out of a small blue car and walks towards me. He saw me and someone else raising the flag three days ago, asks me what I'm doing.
'We've made a flag. Every third day, someone comes and takes a photograph of it.'
Why every third day?
'Because the flag is up for thirty-nine days, and it had to be divided into equal parts.'
Of course.
He asks me if I have a girlfriend.

+3d
He stays in the car. He waves. Talks to another man who I think was also there the previous session.

+3d
Heavy wind. The sun is setting. The facades of the museums are already lit, and the lights in the park might come on any minute now.
No blue car. But it's late in the evening, everything looks increasingly yellowish, and maybe I was too focused on the flag.

+3d
The parking lot has been sealed off for a bicycle race that finishes in the park. (Two days later, the live broadcast of the race didn't show the flag.) The man says he's from a town, which is thirty minutes from Ghent, that he comes here every day, better than sitting at home alone.

+3d
He says that a French artist (with some kind of Dutch-sounding name) already put up a flag at *De Mastplanters*. He doesn't like contemporary art.
'It's just another flag.'

+3d
Even stronger winds. Bursts of rain. There's a warning telling people to stay out of parks. Branches might fall. The wind's speed is estimated as 8 beaufort. The wind whips the flag. There's a determined jogger in the background.

+3d
He tells me that there's an underground nuclear command bunker in the park. It has supplies, communication channels and can hold up to 50 people. Might be useful one day. Detail: the generator feeding the heating system is outside the safe zone. Maybe they were hoping that the bomb would be dropped during the summer. The Museum of Contemporary Art used it around ten years ago and left lights and moveable walls in there. The fungus eating away at the wood is said to be lethal when inhaled for an extended period of time. If the outside world was radiant and cold, would one think that danger might arise *from within*? As if the park would refuse to tolerate our presence. He says if I got stuck down there, I could still make an exhibition, but the flag would be rather pointless.

+3d
A group of schoolchildren walks from the James Welling exhibition to the one on Francisco Goya. Some of them gaze into the lens, while I read the wind strength from the display, and he watches the flag (I imagine).

+3d
'Can you take the car and move it out of the frame?' I'm not sure if I'm allowed to ask.

+3d
Do both our timings create a system? Like the hands of a clock. A rhythm, perhaps a waltz.

+3d
A breeze.
Not much wind, he says.
Gardeners are planting flowers at the foot of the sculpture.
'No.'

+3d
He asks if it is the last photograph.

[While we were taking down the flag some ten police cars and a tank passed by. There was a speech on immigration given by a politician in a university building nearby. They parked behind the Museum of Fine Arts. Riding backwards, the tank hit a lamppost, which subsequently took on a strange 65° angle. Seven policemen stepped out of their cars and examined the situation. The flag had already been taken down. There was no way for us to document the scene.]

F#3

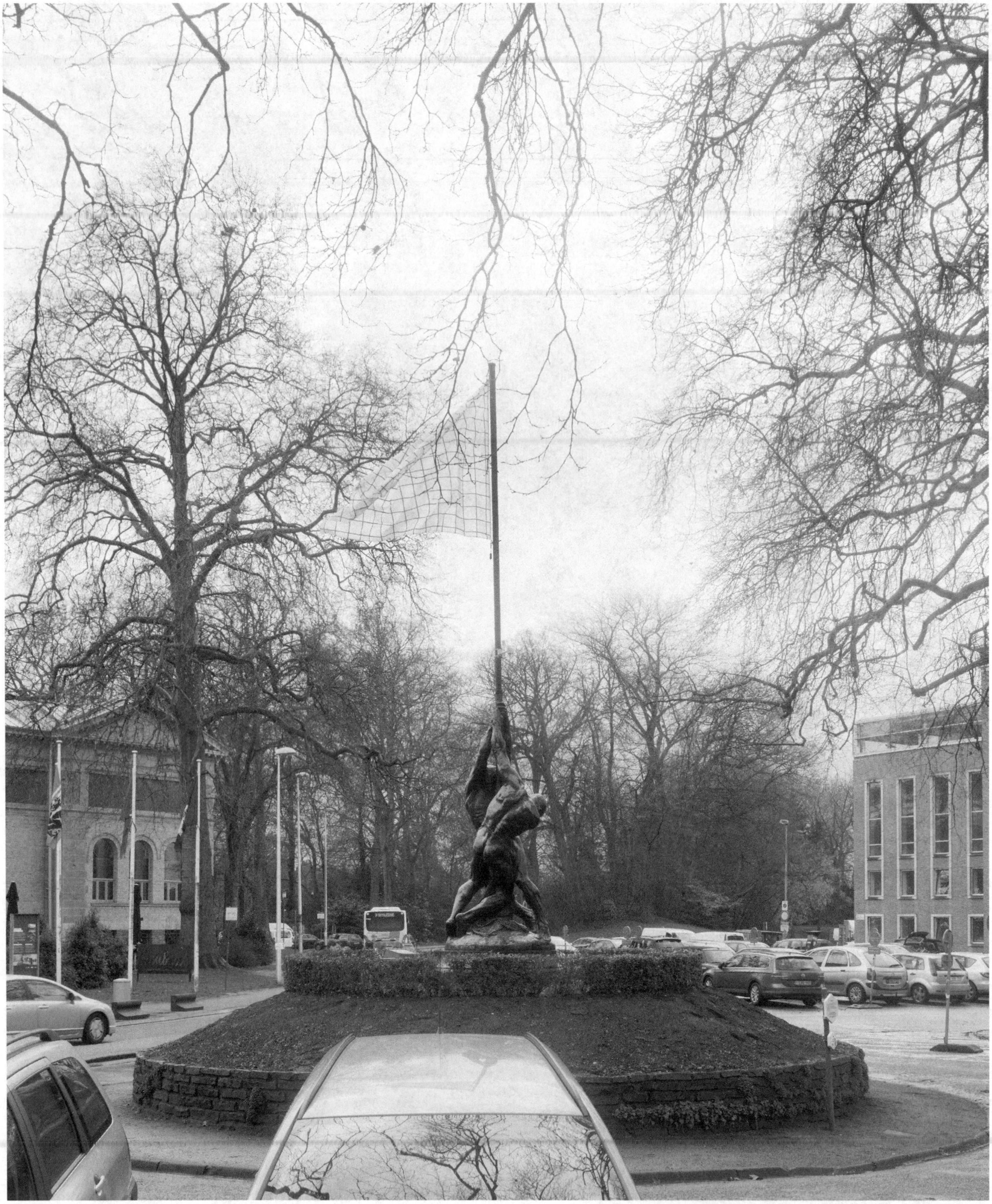

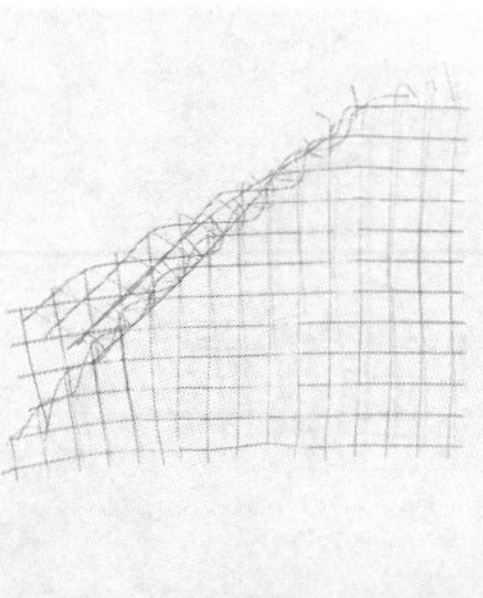

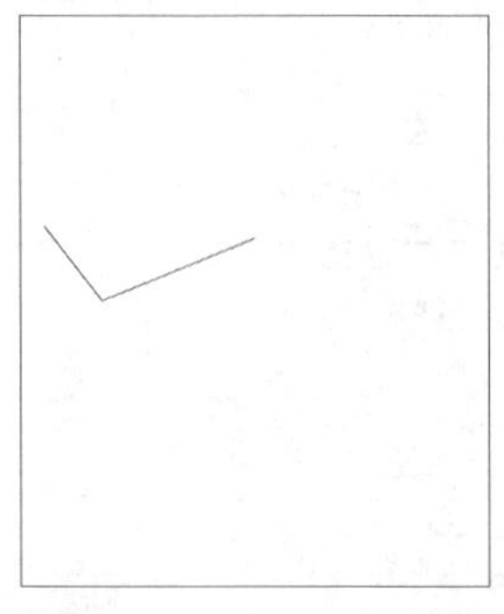

WSW, 18,36 km/h
[grille de lecture]

'Angélique remit le planisphère dans son cabas et sortit des profondeurs du vieux sac une feuille de carton percée d'un certain nombre de trous irrégulièrement disposés. Cet appareil, appelé *grille* en langage cryptographique, devait permettre aux deux amants de correspondre sans danger. Une phrase, écrite au moyen des trous appliqués sur du papier blanc, pouvait être rendue inintelligible par l'adjonction de lettres quelconques, tracées au hasard pour remplir avec ordre les intervalles primitivement ménagés. Seul Velbar saurait retrouver le sens du billet en plaçant sur le texte une grille exactement semblable.'

– Raymond Roussel,
Impressions d'Afrique[1]

F#4

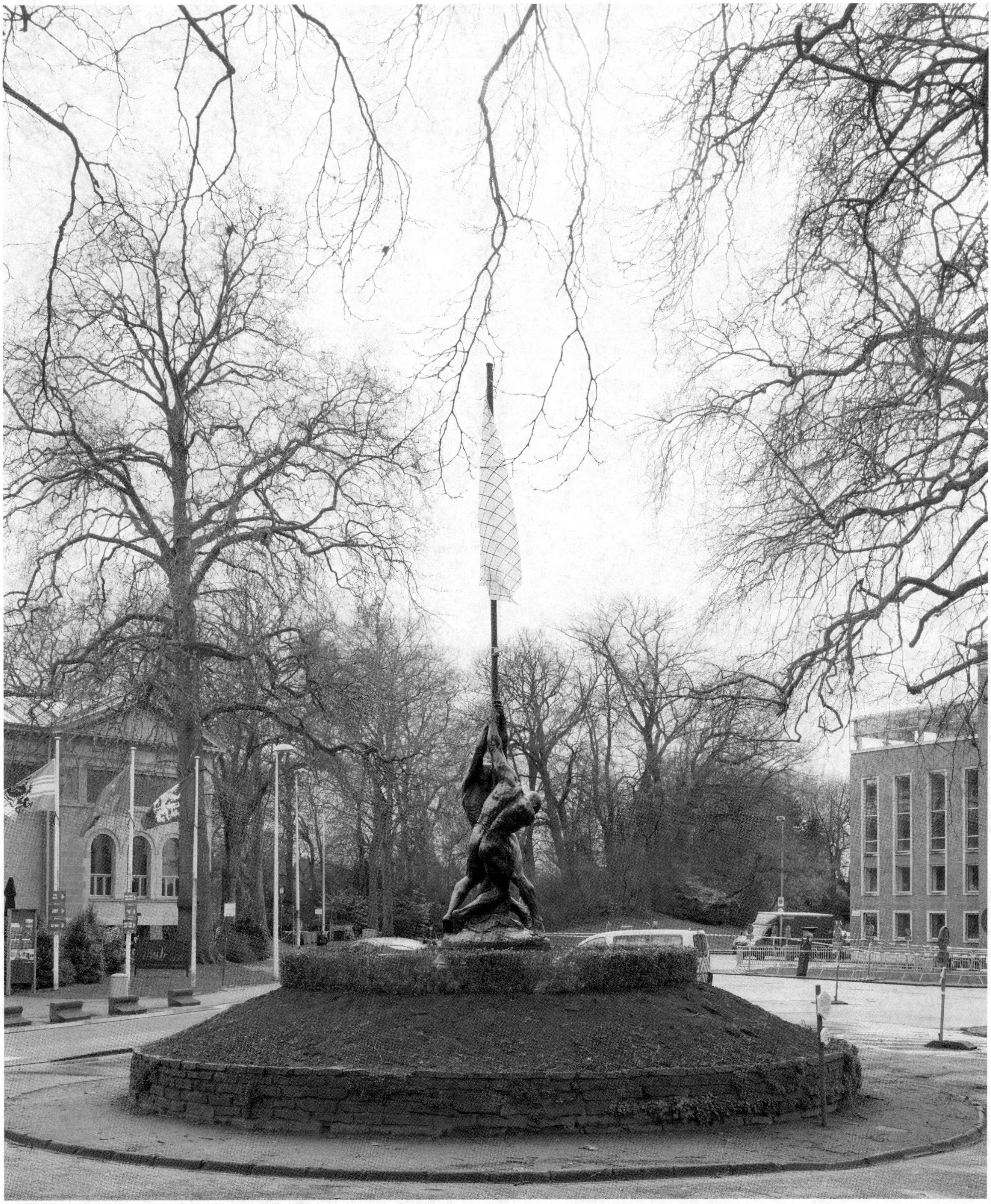

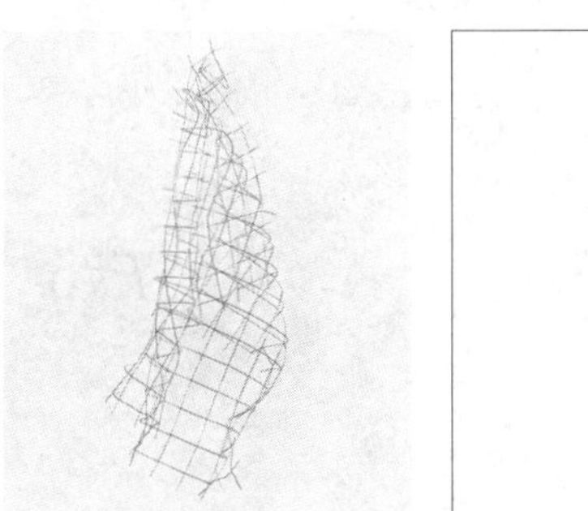

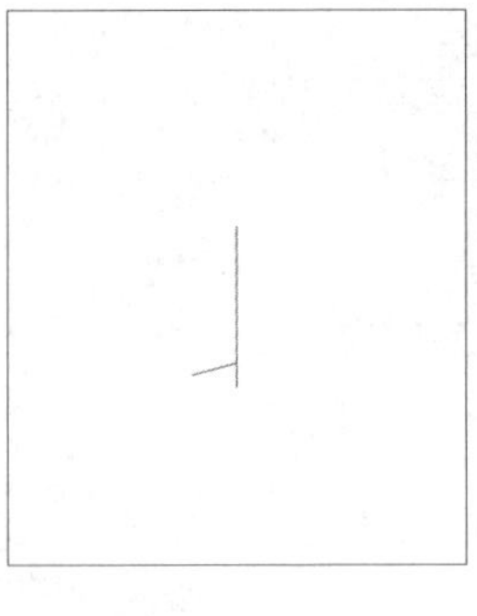

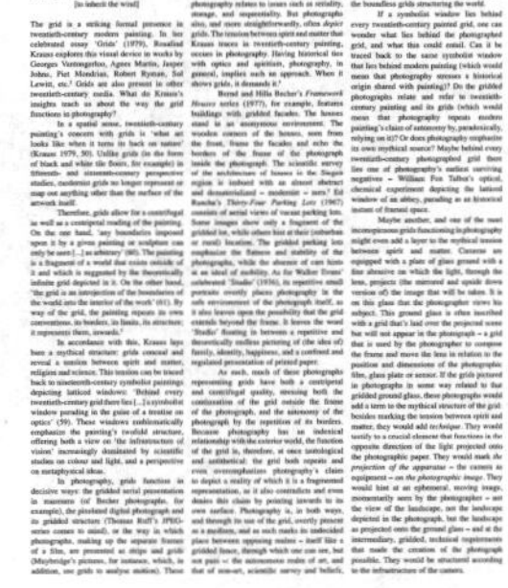

F#5

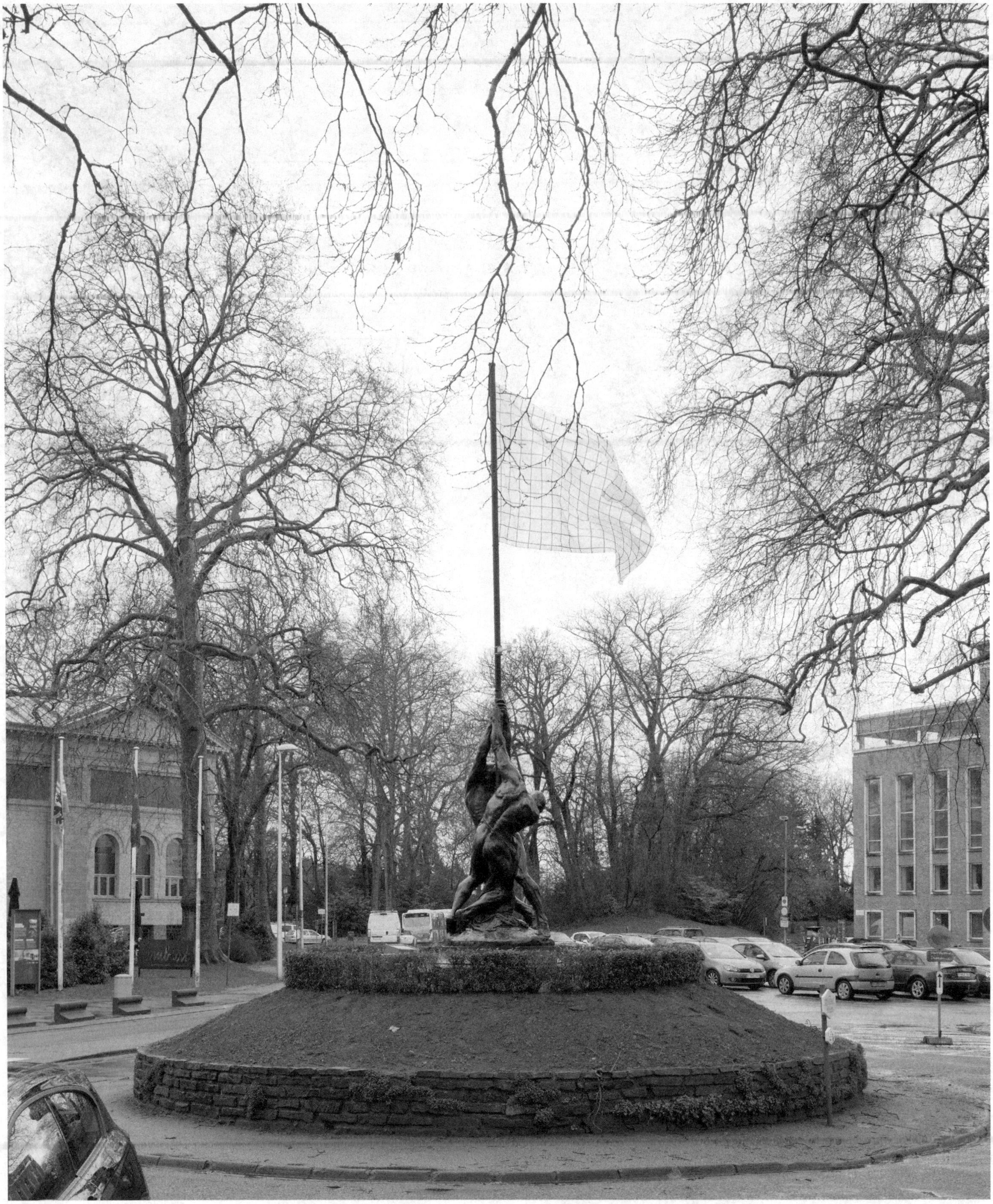

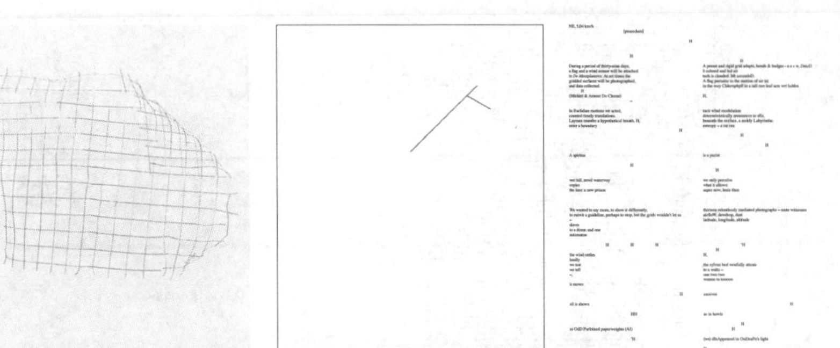

F#6

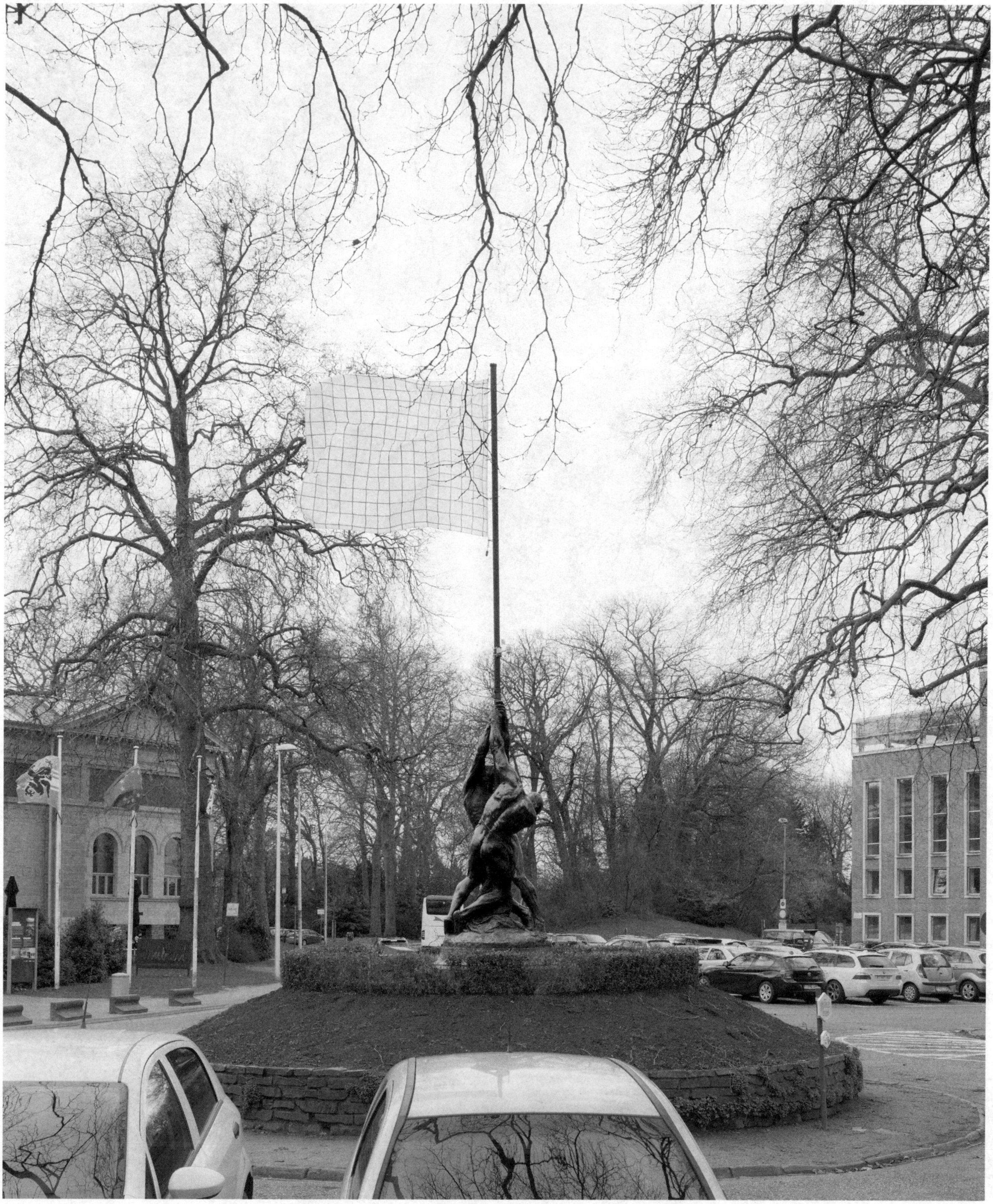

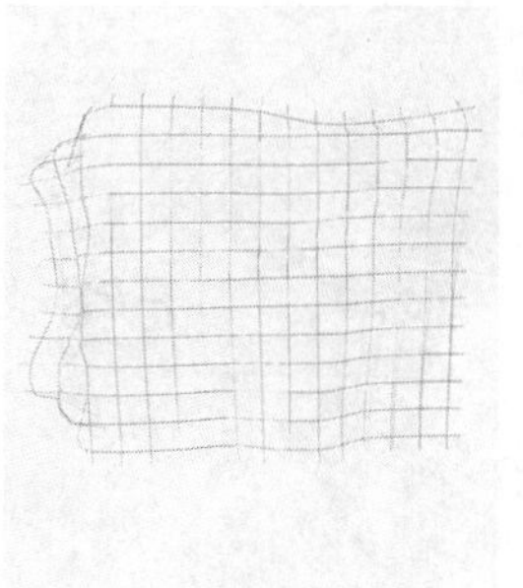

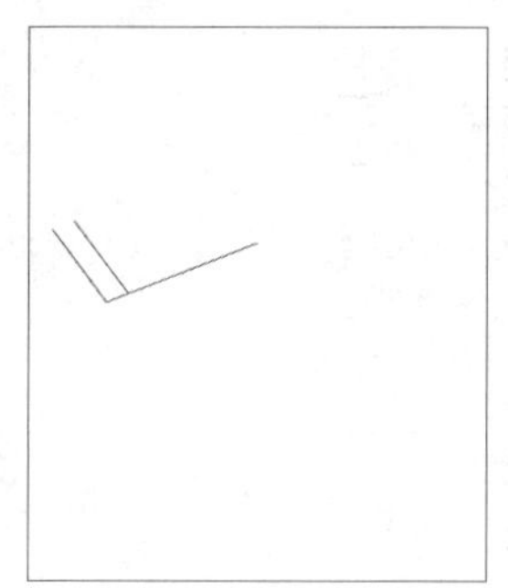

F#7

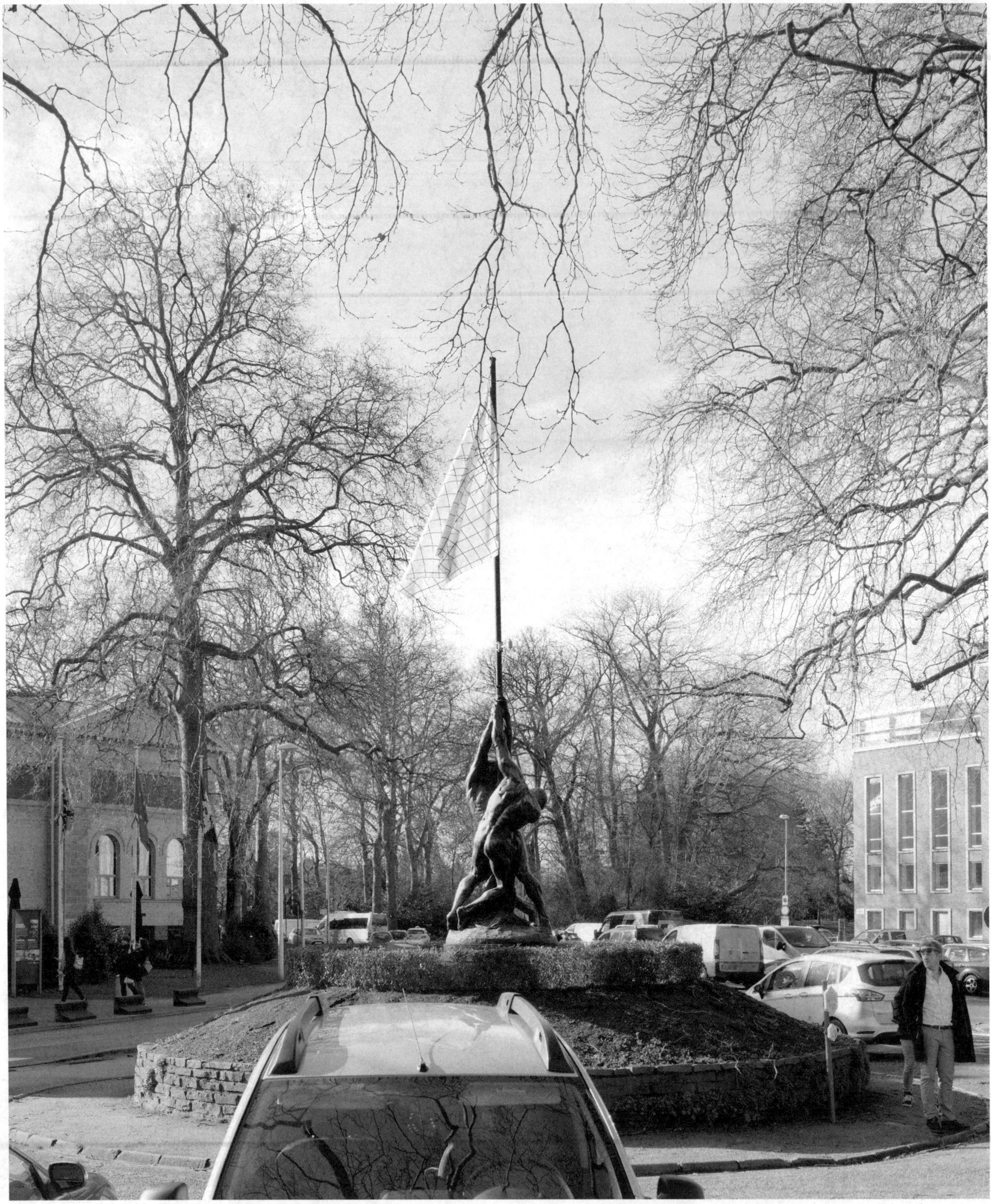

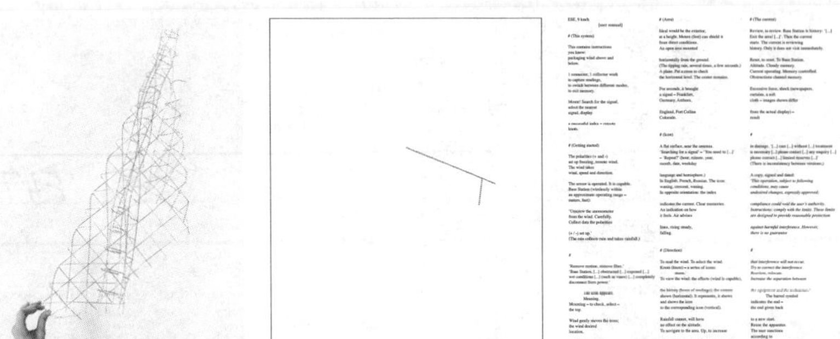

F#8

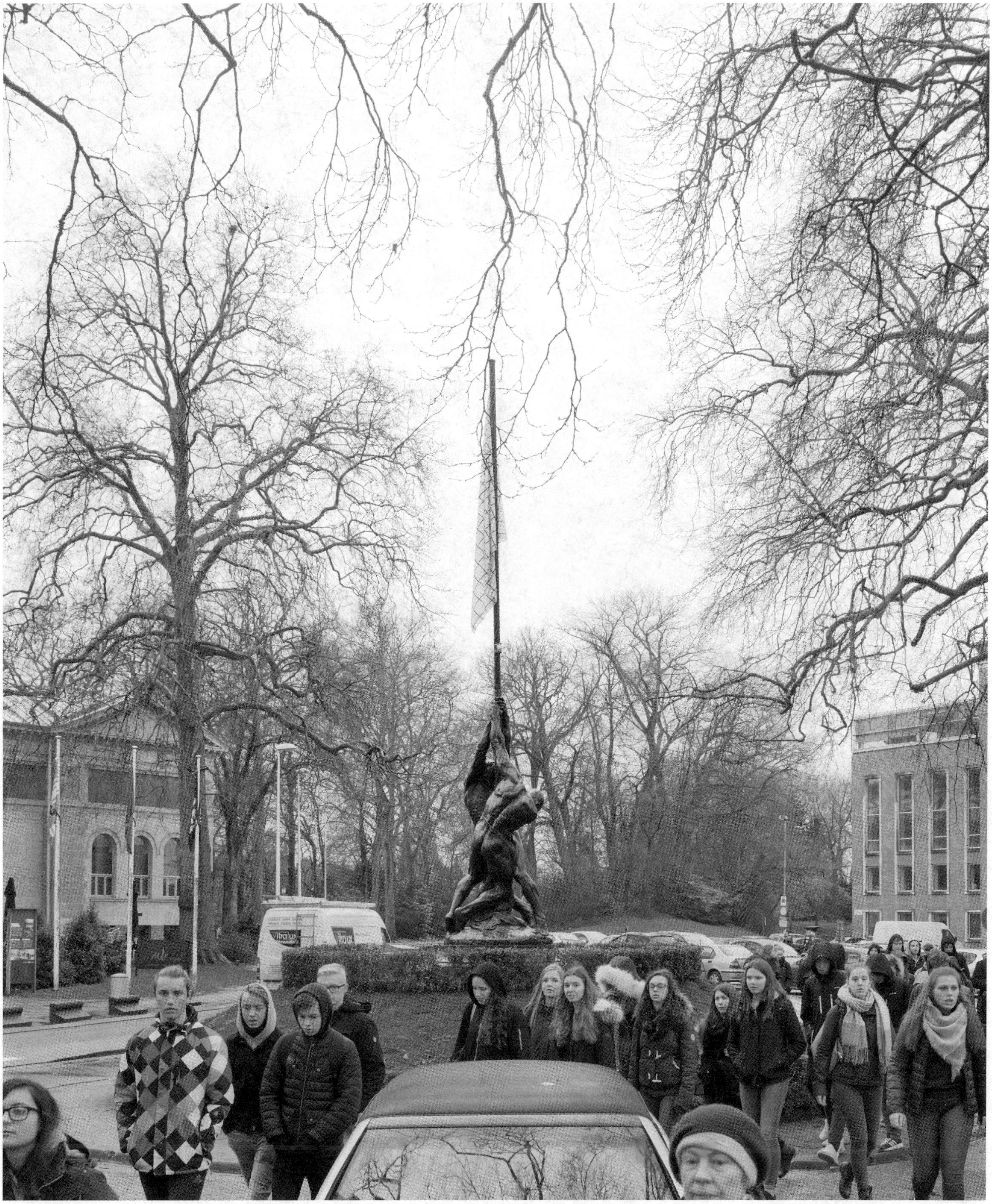

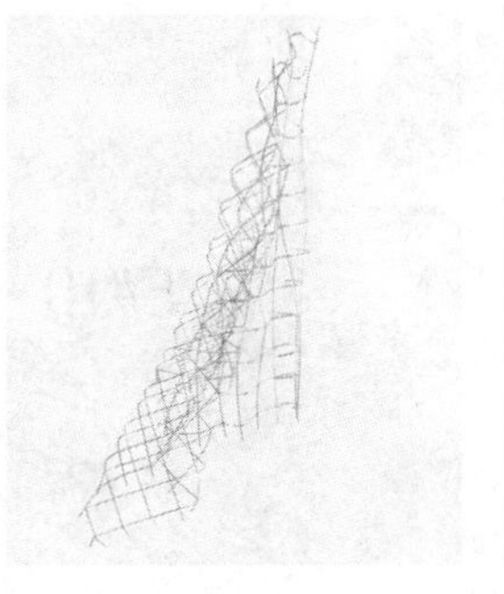

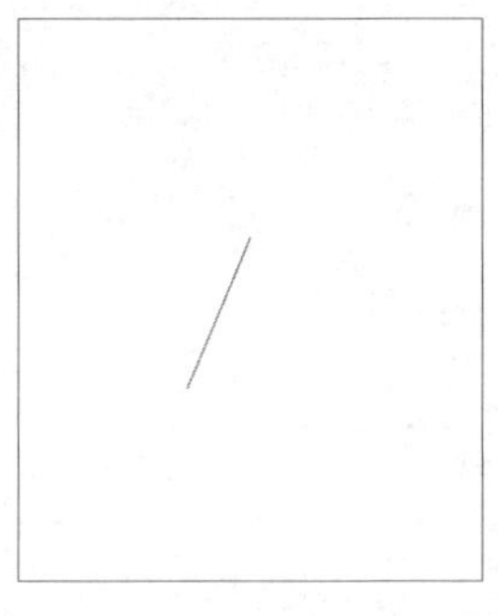

SSW, 2,16 km/h

[document]

According to Eyal Weizman, architecture can be seen and investigated as a documentary form: 'Architecture emerges as a documentary form, not because photographs of it circulate in the public domain but rather because it performs variations on the following three things: it registers the effect of force fields, it contains or stores these forces in material deformations, and, with the help of other mediating technologies and the forum, it transmits this information further' (Weizman 2014, 15).[8] Likewise, a flag can be conceptualized as a document, as a forensic surface. A good example is The Star-Spangled Banner, planted on the moon in 1969. While this flag didn't register – or, according to some, shouldn't have registered – the wind, it did record its environment: after nearly fifty years, the flag has become a Banner, refusing each territorial claim,[9] for in that period of time, the amount of UV-light has bleached and ultimately erased all stars and stripes.

Movement of air affects a gridded flag attached to the pole of *De Mastplanters*. After thirty-nine days, the flag gave a somewhat worn out and polluted appearance. If the specific movements – the different bursts of wind – would have been stored in its fibres, it wasn't capable of transmitting this information; or at least, we lack the expertise to interpret what it perhaps conserves within the confines of its fabric. The anemometer's display gave detailed information, data translated into a graphic shape as wind-barbs. Photographs recorded the movement of the flag. As sculptures, the bent wireframes restored the third dimension that was lost in the photographs, a dimension again lost when they too were photographed.

In this documentary endeavour, every medium used brought opportunities another medium wasn't capable of, as well as inherent limitations. Take photography: the sight is turned into a portable, structured, and simplified record, selecting and applying a frame along with a shift from a multisensory experience to a merely visual and two-dimensional transcript. The photograph – and especially a digital one – is a volatile container of information that you can carry along, put away, muster up, send, and share. But in order to achieve this, the experienced landscape is severely reduced.

'Documentary', as an adjective, describes the way in which a medium is seen as capable – with possibilities and limitations – of recording. But there's more to it. Along the way, each element – text, graph, or image – began to refer to another one, and the documentary became a referential system. As such, the documentary also surfaced as a function in between those media: documentary value was added in the process of the transposition of one medium to another within that system.

The wind-barbs defined the scenography of a virtual exhibition. The photographs of the flag determined how the sculptures had to be bent. And as for the photographs of these sculptures, they not only documented a gridded surface formed by the wind, but also created new shapes. Like a terrain mesh, they began to resemble a top-down view of strange surfaces – unknown islands on which bursts of chaotic wind seemed to have violently moulded strange, unearthly landscapes. The documentary blew through the structure of photography, flag, sculpture, graph, and text. As it registered one medium by means of another, and began tying them together in a relational and referential field, it also instructed the latter by means of the former.

In its contemporary usage, the word 'document' – as a noun or as a verb – signifies something official, a file with information. It is tied to an event or phenomenon that precedes it, which the document registers or records. But etymologically, it has another meaning. It derives from the Latin *docere* – to teach – and *documentum* – a lesson. In between events and phenomena, the document therefore has an ambiguous temporal and causal place. It functions as a record of what happened, *and* as a guideline for the way in which things must happen. To document: to register, to refer, and to instruct, at the same time. As we documented the wind, the wind documented us.

F#9

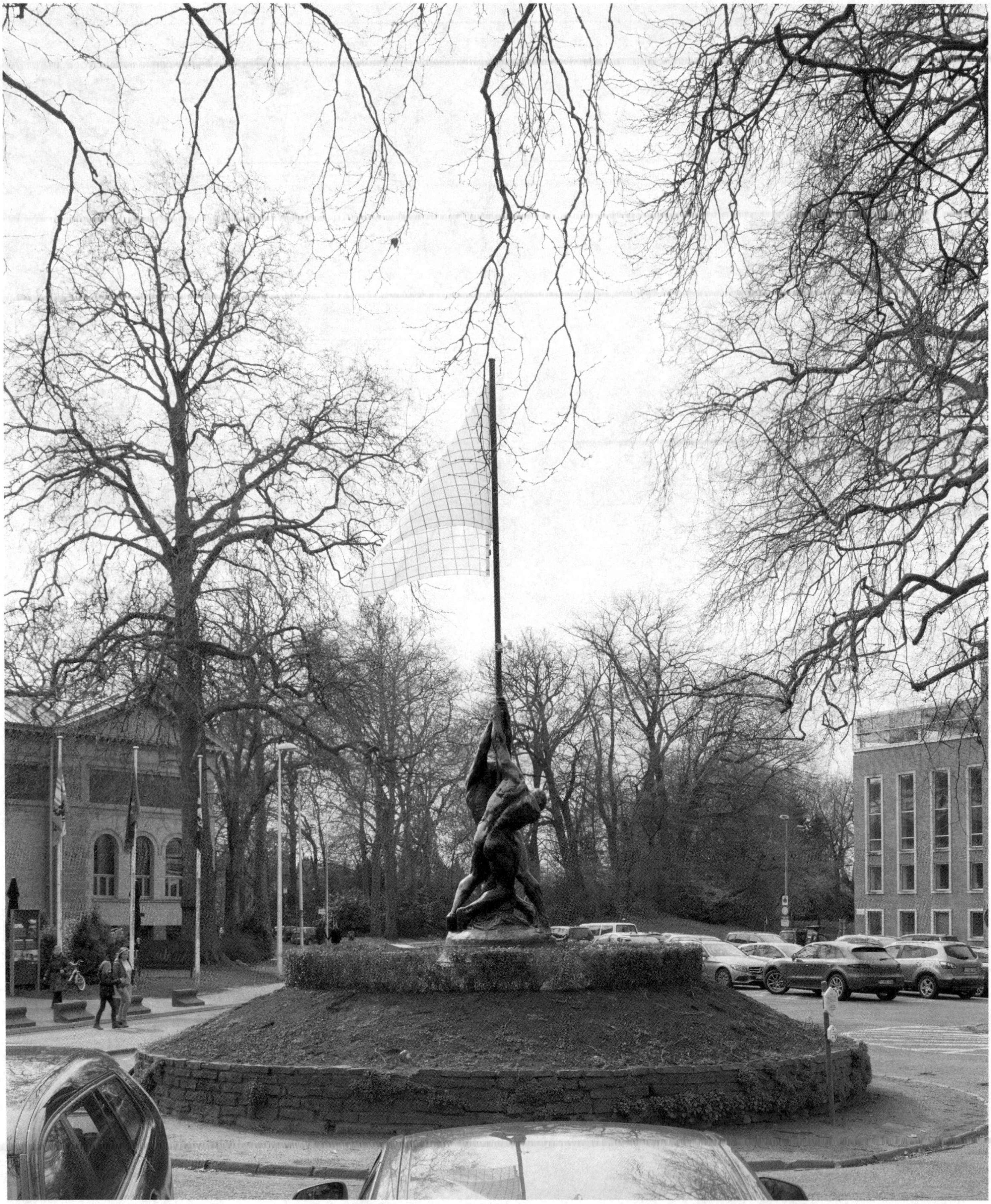

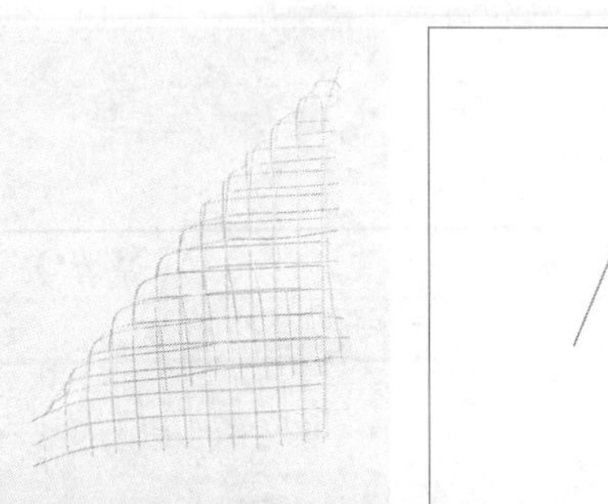

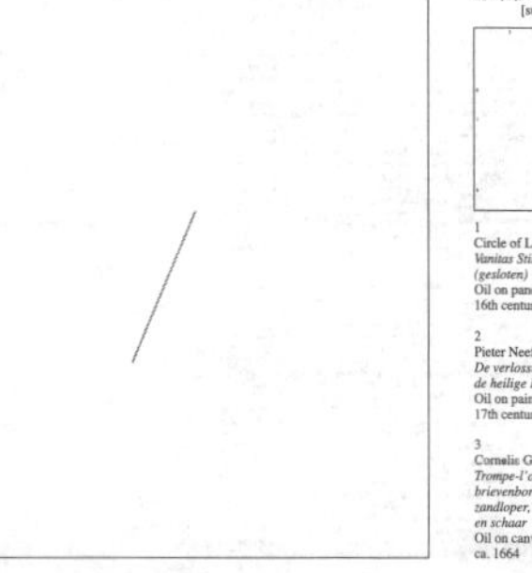

SSW, 3,24 km/h
[surface]

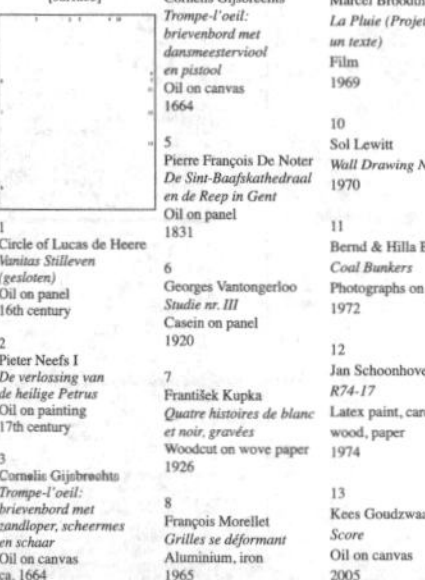

1
Circle of Lucas de Heere
Vanitas Stilleven (gesloten)
Oil on panel
16th century

2
Pieter Neefs I
De verlossing van de heilige Petrus
Oil on painting
17th century

3
Cornelis Gijsbrechts
Trompe-l'oeil: brievenbord met zandloper, scheermes en schaar
Oil on canvas
ca. 1664

4
Cornelis Gijsbrechts
Trompe-l'oeil: brievenbord met dansmeesterviool en pistool
Oil on canvas
1664

5
Pierre François De Noter
De Sint-Baafskathedraal en de Reep in Gent
Oil on panel
1831

6
Georges Vantongerloo
Studie nr. III
Casein on panel
1920

7
František Kupka
Quatre histoires de blanc et noir, gravées
Woodcut on wove paper
1926

8
François Morellet
Grilles se déformant
Aluminium, iron
1965

9
Marcel Broodthaers
La Pluie (Projet pour un texte)
Film
1969

10
Sol Lewitt
Wall Drawing No. 36
1970

11
Bernd & Hilla Becher
Coal Bunkers
Photographs on panel
1972

12
Jan Schoonhoven
R74-17
Latex paint, cardboard, wood, paper
1974

13
Kees Goudzwaard
Score
Oil on canvas
2005

F#10

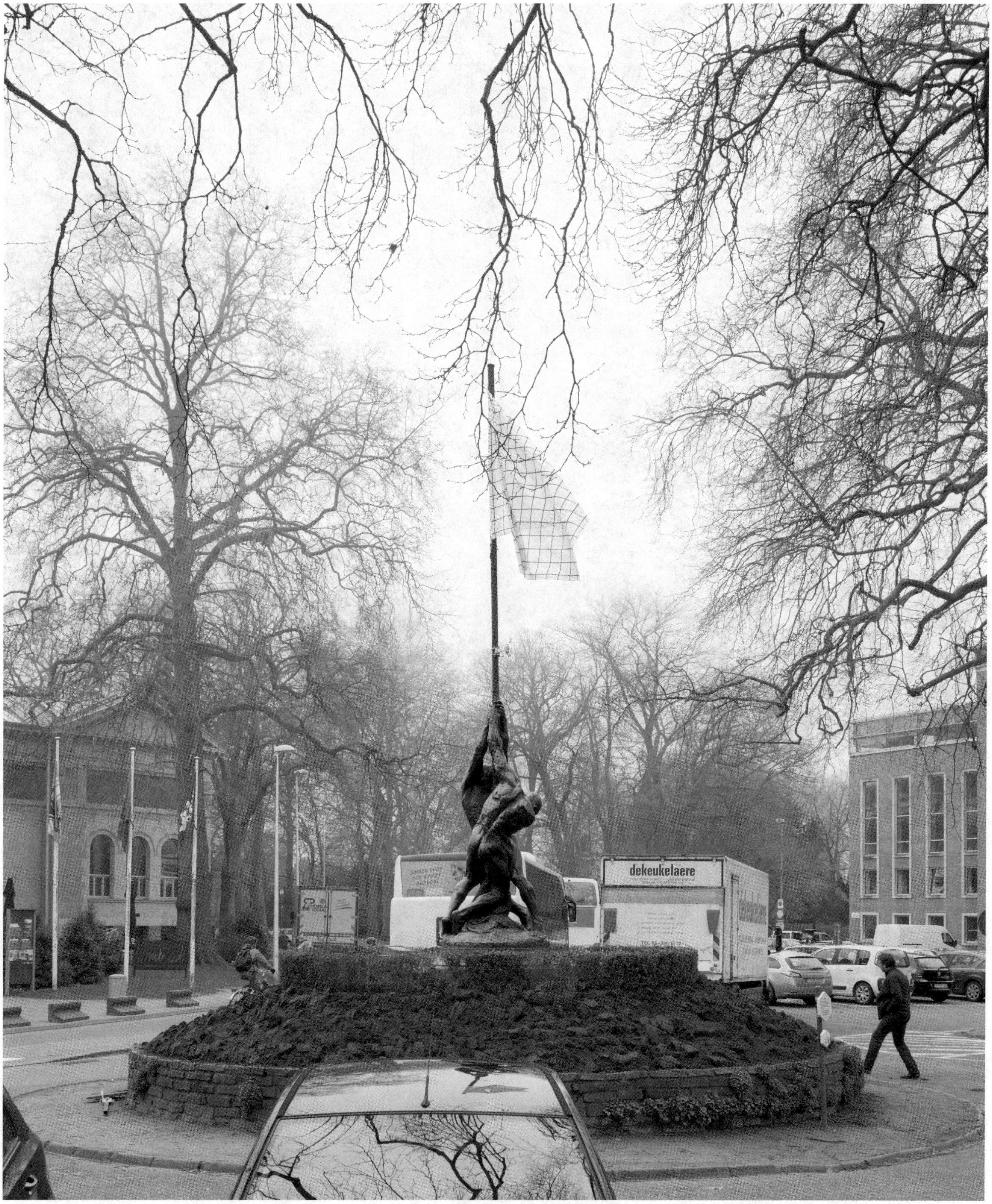

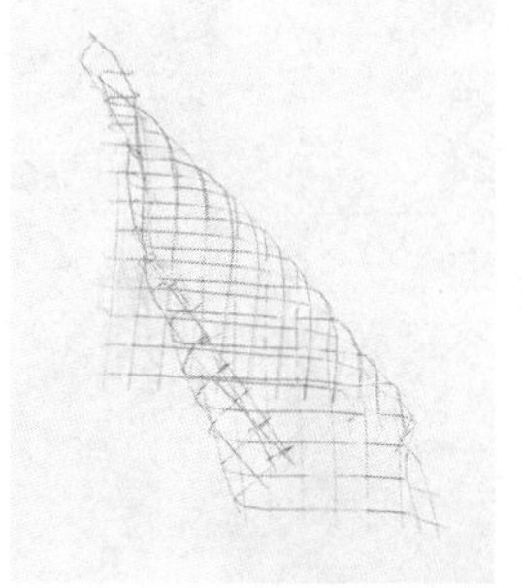

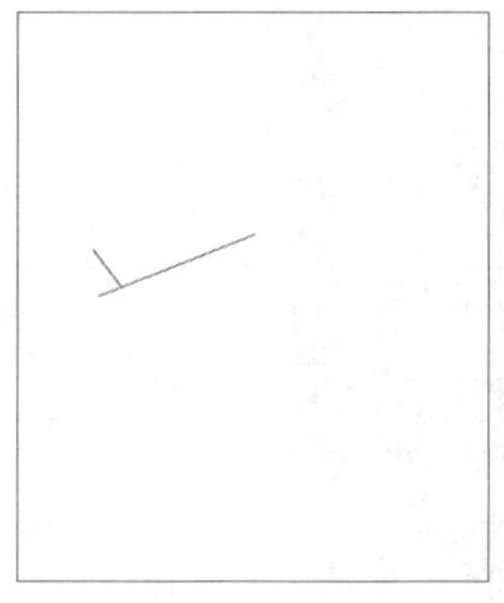

WSW, 4,68 km/h

[penetrating screen]

Miss Hortense Stollnitz became International Amateur Champion Typist in 1916, 'equalling the professional record of 137 words per minute net, and exceeding all previous records with 147 words per minute gross' (Gilbreth & Gilbreth 1917, 36–37). In the same year, she had already won that contest a first time, and the International Novice Champion Typewriter Contest in New York the year before.[10]

Miss Stollnitz can be seen in *fig. 5* in Frank and Lillian Gilbreth's *Applied Motion Study* (1917).[11] A vertical strip of small photographs shows Miss Stollnitz changing the paper of the typewriter she is working on, with only minimal differences between the various shots: while the paper she has finished typing is being rolled out of the typewriter (and seems to fly into the room), she is already taking the next blank paper with her other hand – thereby briefly concealing a clock on the wall behind her. On the same page, *fig. 4* shows Miss Anna Gold, who is also typing, while a second woman is on the other side of the typewriter (and again a clock is between them). Although her face is blurred, her typing fingers are sharp. Miss Gold, the caption states, 'afterwards became National Amateur Champion Typist by winning the contest at Chicago, 1916' (Gilbreth & Gilbreth 1917, 36–37).[12]

'Afterwards': both Miss Gold and Miss Stollnitz were trained by the Gilbreths, who had developed a specific method for improving efficiency in the working environment. In their study, they describe 'the simple photographic process which enables one to record in detail the motions of a handicraft, or a manufacture, so as to bring them by criticism and experiment to their utmost economy of energy and time' (George Iles, in Gilbreth & Gilbreth 1917, ix). To arrive at this 'permanent and practical waste elimination' the Gilbreths attached a small electric light to the moving body part of the worker. As such, this movement created a line of light, which was captured on a photographic plate that was exposed during the time the subject performed the work. This line was called a 'cyclegraph'. To be effective and instructional, the continuous line was broken up: 'the time element was eventually obtained by placing an interrupter in the current, that transformed the white line of the cyclegraph into a series or line of dots and dashes. This made of the cyclegraph a chronocyclegraph' (Gilbreth & Gilbreth 1917, 83–84).

Fig. 7 is a similar strip of photographs displaying a sequence of motions. This 'Automatic Micromotion Study with vertical penetrating screen in the plane of the motions' features a man in a white shirt and black tie. Over his left shoulder: a clock. Each of the eight vertically stacked photographs shows the same composition of the same man in the same room with a white grid superimposed on every image. The chronocyclegraphs rely on what the Gilbreths called the penetrating screen: a sheet of black paper with a white grid on it. That grid is crucial. They superimposed this grid on the factory worker by making a double exposure on the same piece of film. This procedure enabled them to record and analyse the motions of a worker performing a specific task. Motion reveals itself in relation to the rigid grid. The Gilbreths subsequently turned these chronocyclegraphs into three-dimensional, bent wires – sculptures – that functioned as a manual for that specific movement. Manual labour becomes grid becomes manual becomes labour. In *fig. 7*, the penetrating screen indifferently covers the background, the clock, the man's hands, shirt, tie, and face. Beneath the grid, the anonymous worker is folding a white cotton cloth.

In *fig. 6*, the Gilbreths zoom in on Miss Stollnitz's hands ('while writing at her fastest speed'). Only the keyboard and five fingers are visible. The text mentions that these pictures were taken at the rate of 115 exposures per second. With a special apparatus, they 'can be studied as continuous motion at the rate of eight per second' (Gilbreth & Gilbreth 1917, 36–37). The advanced photographing technique used by the Gilbreths has the potential to show more than the amount of words the International Amateur Champion can type in one minute. It reveals the motion in between words. Nonetheless, despite the photographic accuracy, it remains unclear what text Miss Stollnitz was typing. When Miss Stollnitz entered the International Championship Typewriting Contest for professionals in 1921, she typed more words than all the other contestants. However, she ranked seventh because of the number of errors she had made (Hoof 2011, 267).[13]

F#11

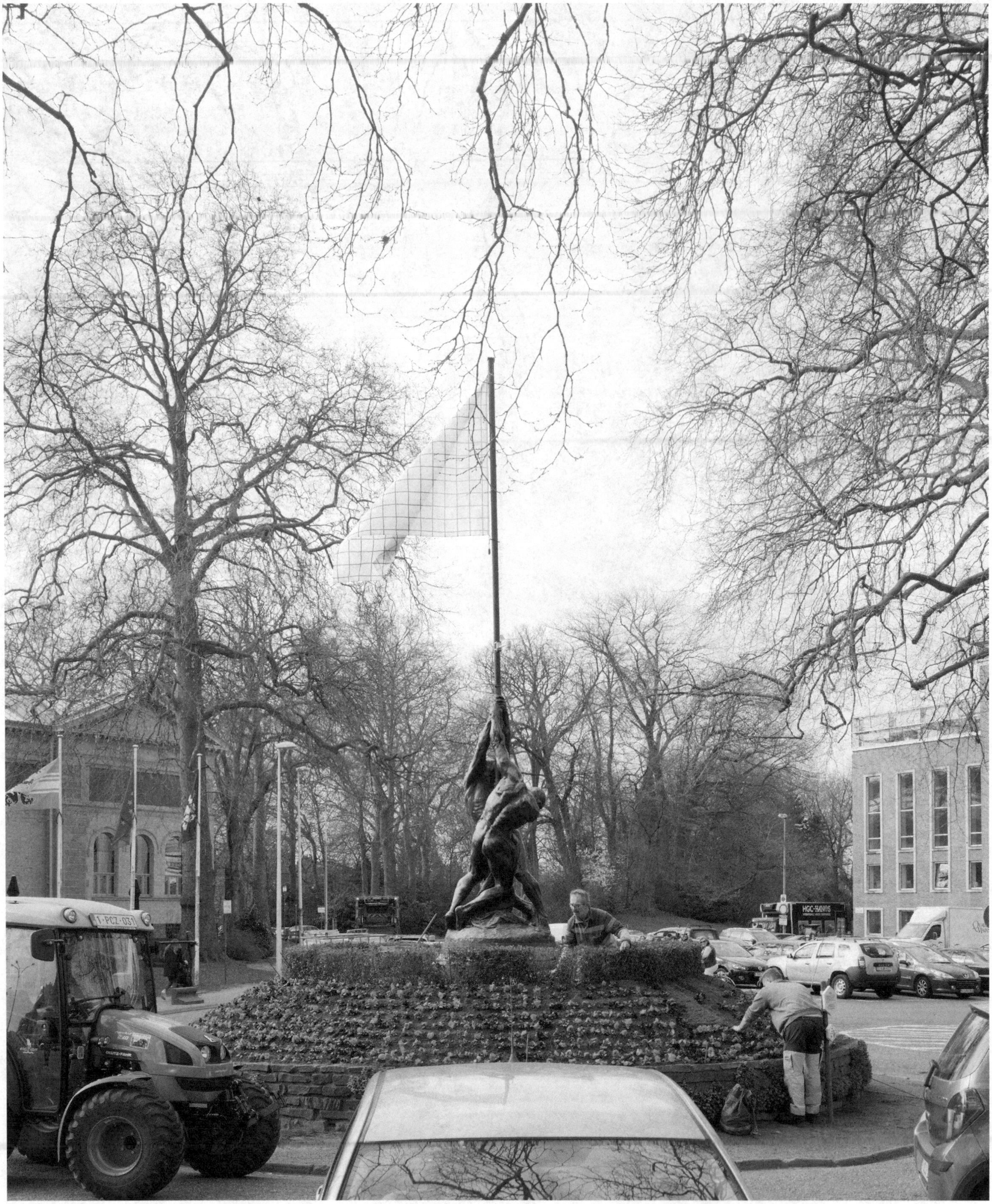

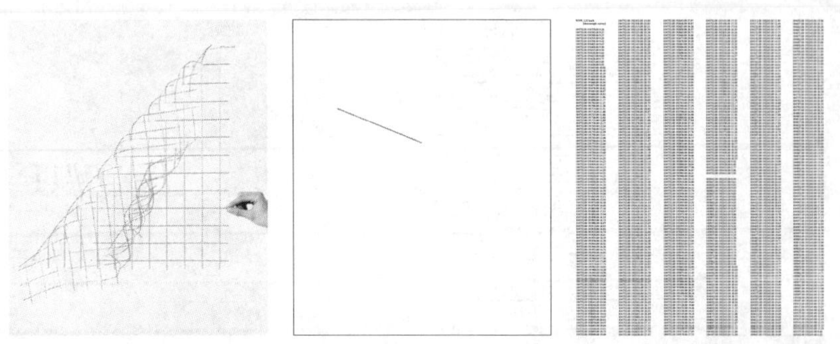

F#12

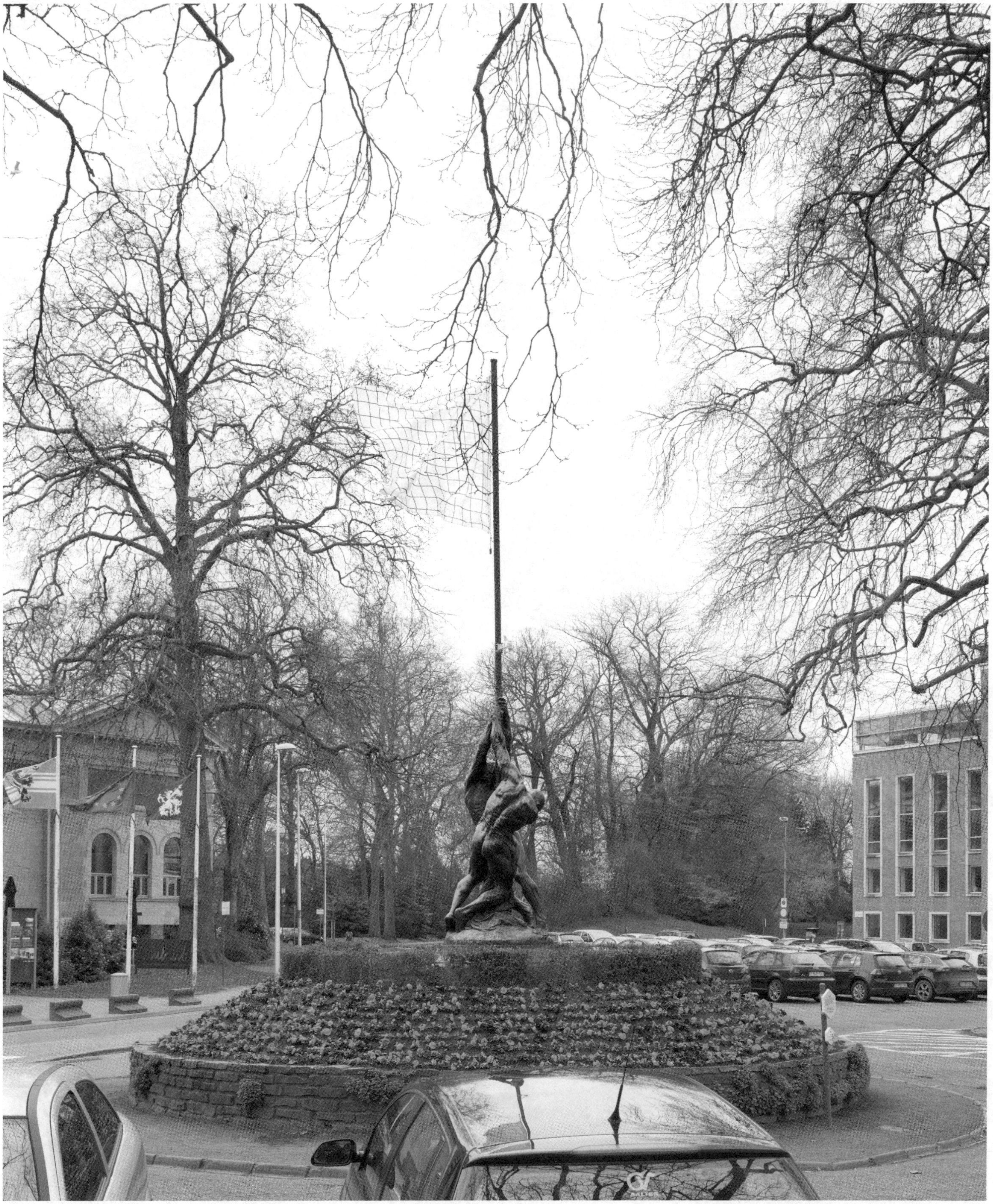

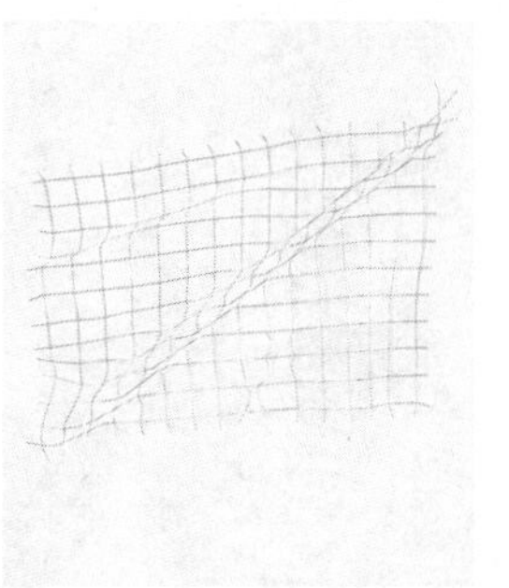

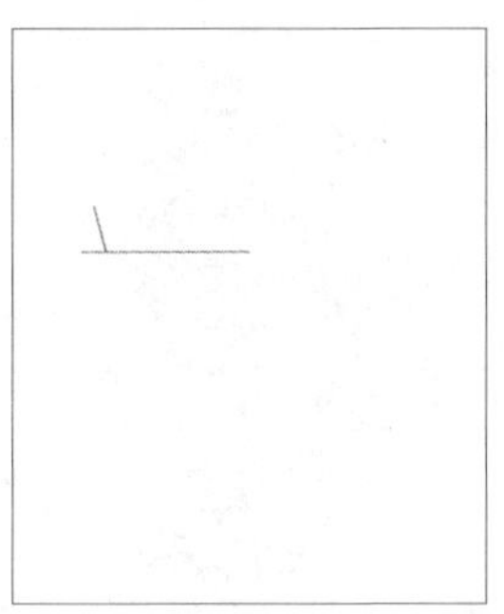

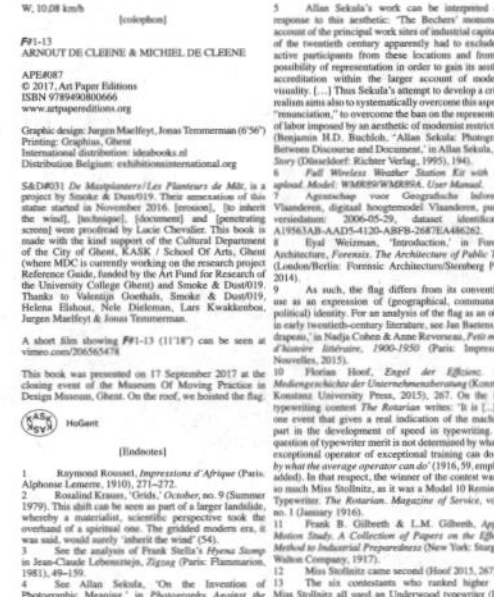

W, 10.08 km/h

[colophon]

F#1-13
ARNOUT DE CLEENE & MICHIEL DE CLEENE

APE#087

© 2017, Art Paper Editions

ISBN 9789490800666
www.artpapereditions.org

Graphic design: Jurgen Maelfeyt, Jonas Temmerman (6'56")
Printing: Graphius, Ghent
International distribution: ideabooks.nl
Distribution Belgium: exhibitionsinternational.org

S&D#031 *De Mastplanters / Les Planteurs de Mât*, is a project by Smoke & Dust/019. Their annexation of this statue started in November 2016. [erosion], [to inherit the wind], [technique], [document] and [penetrating screen] were proofread by Lucie Chevalier. This book is made with the kind support of the Cultural Department of the City of Ghent, KASK / School Of Arts, Ghent (where MDC is currently working on the research project Reference Guide, funded by the Art Fund for Research of the University College Ghent) and Smoke & Dust/019. Thanks to Valentijn Goethals, Smoke & Dust/019, Helena Elshout, Nele Dieleman, Lars Kwakkenbos, Jurgen Maelfeyt & Jonas Temmerman.

A short film showing ***F#***1-13 (11'18") can be seen at vimeo.com/206565478

This book was presented on 17 September 2017 at the closing event of the Museum Of Moving Practice in Design Museum, Ghent. On the roof, we hoisted the flag.

KASK SV HoGent

[Endnotes]

1 Raymond Roussel, *Impressions d'Afrique* (Paris: Alphonse Lemerre, 1910), 271–272.

2 Rosalind Krauss, 'Grids,' *October*, no. 9 (Summer 1979). This shift can be seen as part of a larger landslide, whereby a materialist, scientific perspective took the overhand of a spiritual one. The gridded modern era, it was said, would surely 'inherit the wind' (54).

3 See the analysis of Frank Stella's *Hyena Stomp* in Jean-Claude Lebensztejn, *Zigzag* (Paris: Flammarion, 1981), 49–159.

4 See Allan Sekula, 'On the Invention of Photographic Meaning,' in *Photography Against the Grain* (London: MACK, 2016).

5 Allan Sekula's work can be interpreted as a response to this aesthetic: 'The Bechers' monumental account of the principal work sites of industrial capitalism of the twentieth century apparently had to exclude the active participants from these locations and from the possibility of representation in order to gain its aesthetic accreditation within the larger account of modernist visuality. […] Thus Sekula's attempt to develop a critical realism aims also to systematically overcome this aspect of "renunciation," to overcome the ban on the representation of labor imposed by an aesthetic of modernist restrictions' (Benjamin H.D. Buchloh, 'Allan Sekula: Photography Between Discourse and Document,' in Allan Sekula, *Fish Story* (Düsseldorf: Richter Verlag, 1995), 194).

6 *Full Wireless Weather Station Kit with USB upload. Model: WMR89/WMR89A. User Manual.*

7 Agentschap voor Geografische Informatie Vlaanderen, digitaal hoogtemodel Vlaanderen, punten, versiedatum: 2006-05-29, dataset identification: A19563AB-AAD5-4120-ABFB-2687EA486262.

8 Eyal Weizman, 'Introduction,' in Forensic Architecture, *Forensis. The Architecture of Public Truth* (London/Berlin: Forensic Architecture/Sternberg Press, 2014).

9 As such, the flag differs from its conventional use as an expression of (geographical, communal, or political) identity. For an analysis of the flag as an object in early twentieth-century literature, see Jan Baetens, 'Le drapeau,' in Nadja Cohen & Anne Reverseau, *Petit musée d'histoire littéraire, 1900-1950* (Paris: Impressions Nouvelles, 2015).

10 Florian Hoof, *Engel der Effizienz. Eine Mediengeschichte der Unternehmensberatung* (Konstanz: Konstanz University Press, 2015), 267. On the 1915 typewriting contest *The Rotarian* writes: 'It is […] the one event that gives a real indication of the machine's part in the development of speed in typewriting. The question of typewriter merit is not determined by what the exceptional operator of exceptional training can do, *but by what the average operator can do*' (1916, 59, emphasis added). In that respect, the winner of the contest was not so much Miss Stollnitz, as it was a Model 10 Remington Typewriter. *The Rotarian. Magazine of Service*, vol. 8, no. 1 (January 1916).

11 Frank B. Gilbreth & L.M. Gilbreth, *Applied Motion Study. A Collection of Papers on the Efficient Method to Industrial Preparedness* (New York: Sturgis & Walton Company, 1917).

12 Miss Stollnitz came second (Hoof 2015, 267).

13 The six contestants who ranked higher than Miss Stollnitz all used an Underwood typewriter (Hoof 2015, 267).

F#13

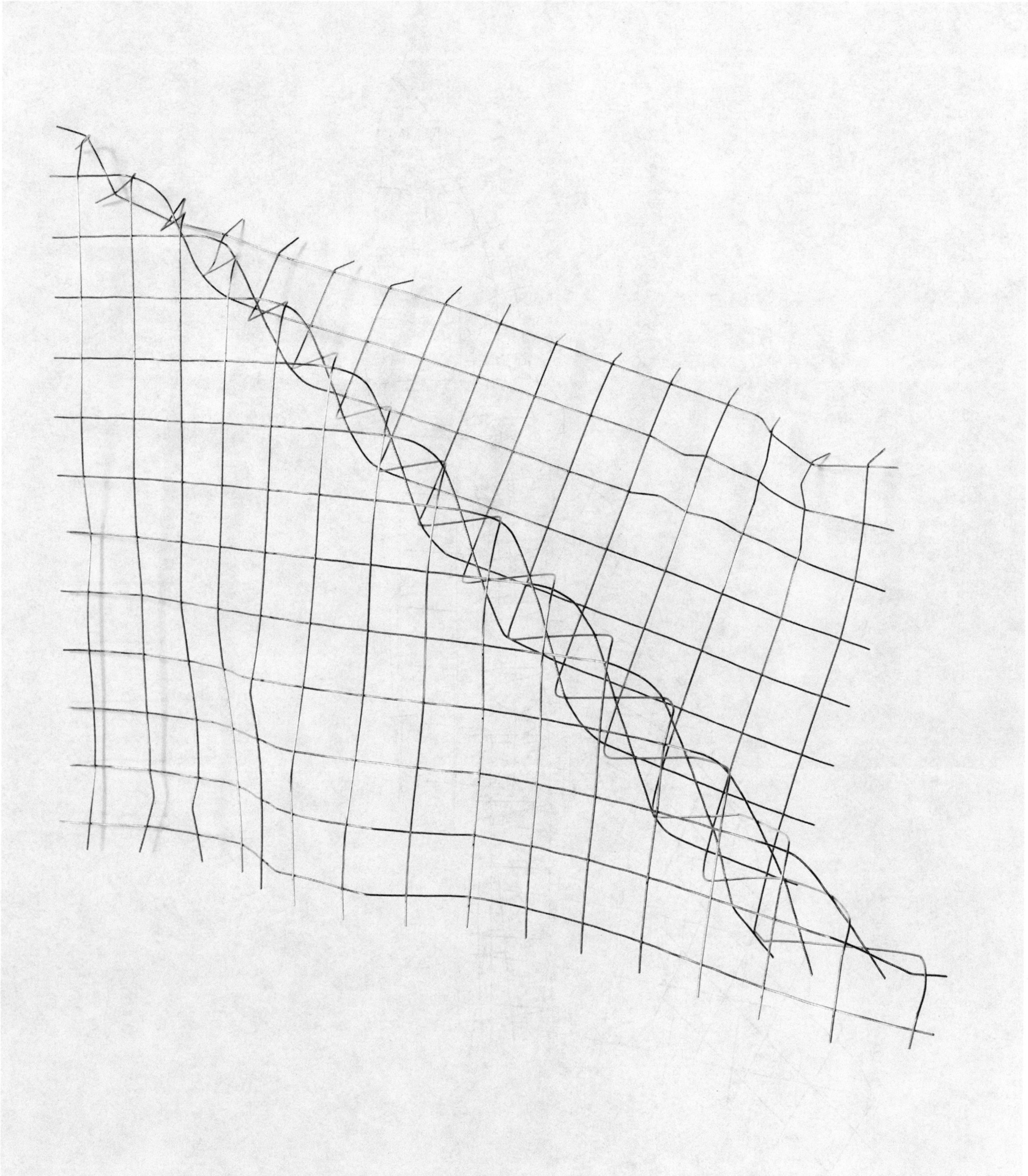

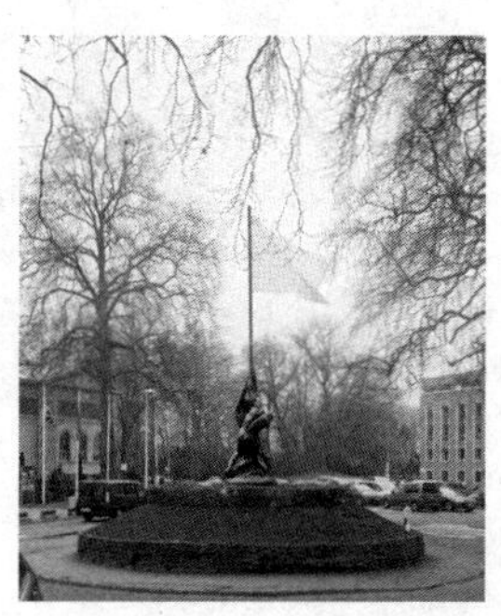

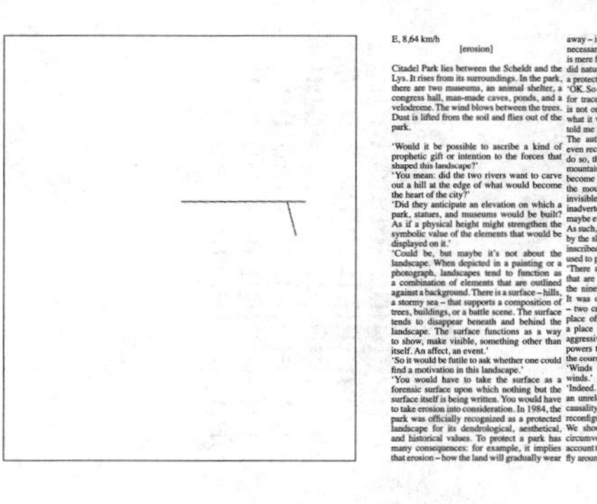

E, 8,64 km/h

[erosion]

Citadel Park lies between the Scheldt and the Lys. It rises from its surroundings. In the park, there are two museums, an animal shelter, a congress hall, man-made caves, ponds, and a velodrome. The wind blows between the trees. Dust is lifted from the soil and flies out of the park.

'Would it be possible to ascribe a kind of prophetic gift or intention to the forces that shaped this landscape?'
'You mean: did the two rivers want to carve out a hill at the edge of what would become the heart of the city?'
'Did they anticipate an elevation on which a park, statues, and museums would be built? As if a physical height might strengthen the symbolic value of the elements that would be displayed on it.'
'Could be, but maybe it's not about the landscape. When depicted in a painting or a photograph, landscapes tend to function as a combination of elements that are outlined against a background. There is a surface – hills, a stormy sea – that supports a composition of trees, buildings, or a battle scene. The surface tends to disappear beneath and behind the landscape. The surface functions as a way to show, make visible, something other than itself. An affect, an event.'
'So it would be futile to ask whether one could find a motivation in this landscape.'
'You would have to take the surface as a forensic surface upon which nothing but the surface itself is being written. You would have to take erosion into consideration. In 1984, the park was officially recognized as a protected landscape for its dendrological, aesthetical, and historical values. To protect a park has many consequences: for example, it implies that erosion – how the land will gradually wear away – is neglected, and human labour will be necessary to maintain it as it is. It is to fix what is mere flux. The question thus becomes: what did nature anticipate before it was designated a protected landscape.'
'OK. So one would have to search the landscape for traces of that anticipation. The question is not only what it wanted to build, but also what it wants to erase. A landscape architect told me that Mount Fuji is slowly crumbling. The authorities are trying to preserve and even reconstruct its famous conical shape. To do so, they are studying old paintings of the mountain. The rock formations they depict become a guideline for the preservation of the mountain. But I wonder if the almost invisible surface structure of those paintings inadvertently moulds Mount Fuji as well, maybe even more so than what they represent. As such, Mount Fuji would not only be shaped by the slopes in Hokusai's drawings, but also inscribed with the texture of the woodblocks used to print them.'
'There are structures, both visible and not, that are an integral part of Citadel Park. In the nineteenth century, a fortress was built. It was conceived as two overlapping grids – two crossed pentagons. This park is not a place of silence and tranquillity, but rather a place where powers are continuously and aggressively trying to reshape it. But those powers themselves have also been altered in the course of history.'
'Winds shape surfaces and surfaces shape winds.'
'Indeed. We should document the surface as an unrelenting chain of events of which the causality cannot be grasped, and strive to reconfigure the narratives that were silenced. We should tell the stories of the surface, circumvent the park it became, and take into account the specks of dust that inconspicuously fly around.'

F#1

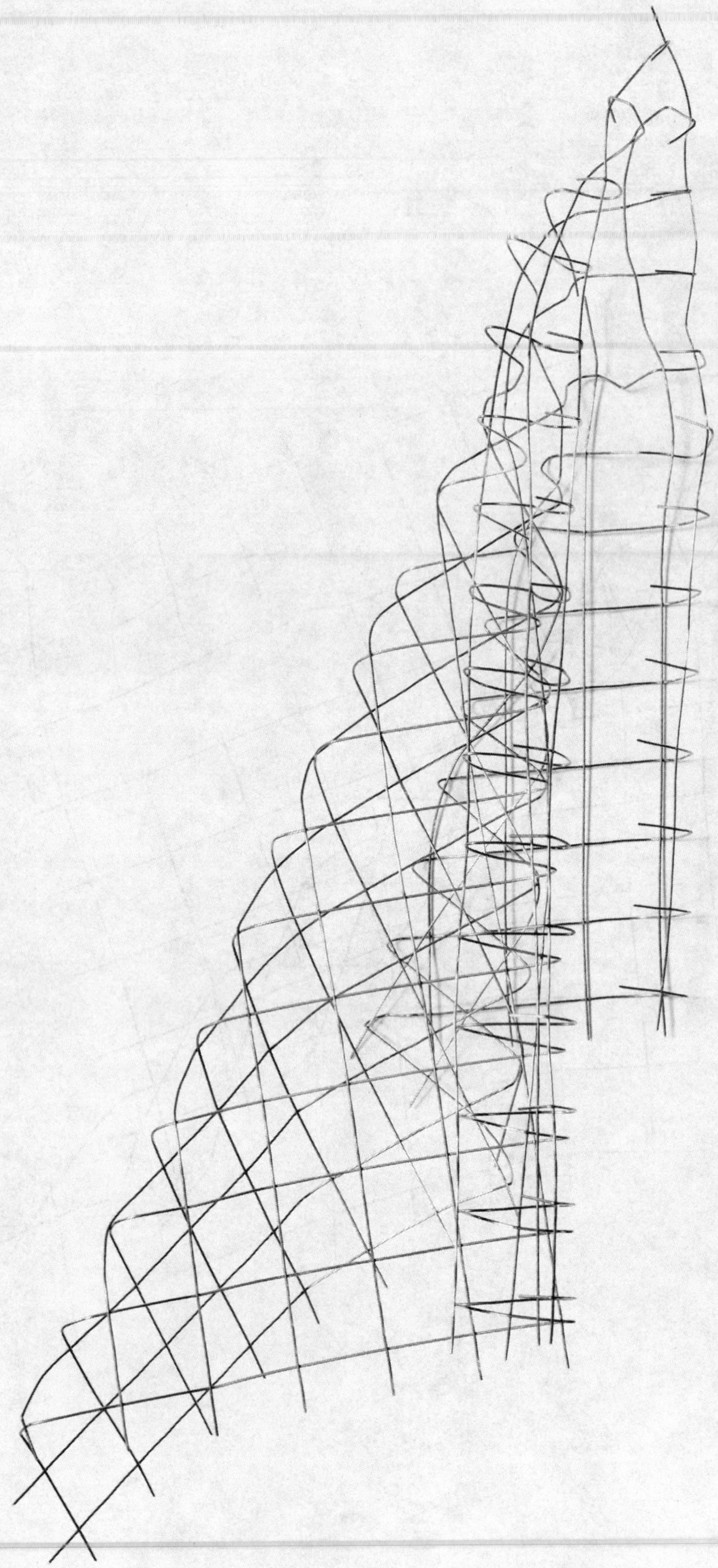

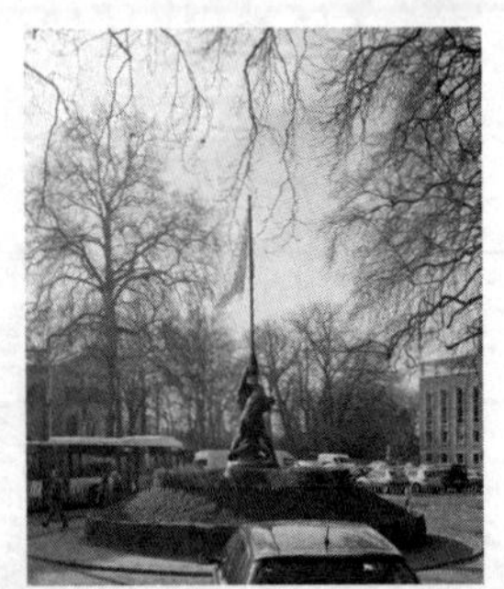

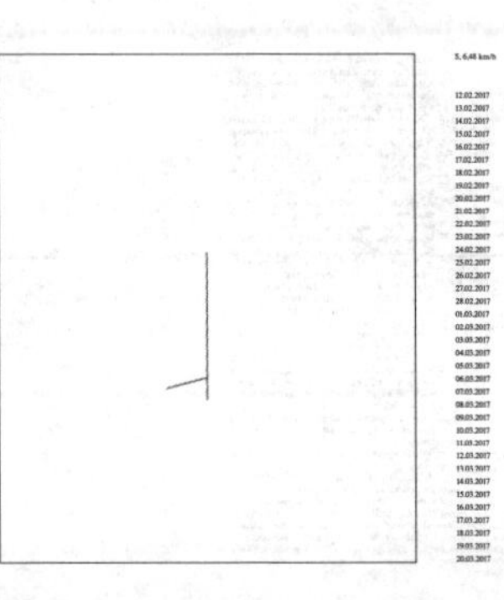

5, 6,48 km/h

[data]

12.02.2017	12:02:50	_44A8205	1/80	8	800	2,4	4,66	E
13.02.2017	#####	#####	#####	#####	#####	#####	#####	#####
14.02.2017	#####	#####	#####	#####	#####	#####	#####	#####
15.02.2017	12:04:09	_44A8280	1/640	8	500	1,8	3,50	S
16.02.2017	#####	#####	#####	#####	#####	#####	#####	#####
17.02.2017	#####	#####	#####	#####	#####	#####	#####	#####
18.02.2017	15:20:13	_44A8446	1/320	8	200	1,7	3,30	SSE
19.02.2017	#####	#####	#####	#####	#####	#####	#####	#####
20.02.2017	#####	#####	#####	#####	#####	#####	#####	#####
21.02.2017	14:05:40	_44A8473	1/250	8	1250	5,1	9,91	WSW
22.02.2017	#####	#####	#####	#####	#####	#####	#####	#####
23.02.2017	#####	#####	#####	#####	#####	#####	#####	#####
24.02.2017	15:52:53	_44A9577	1/200	8	800	1,4	2,72	S
25.02.2017	#####	#####	#####	#####	#####	#####	#####	#####
26.02.2017	#####	#####	#####	#####	#####	#####	#####	#####
27.02.2017	15:23:10	_44A9591	1/125	8	2000	1,4	2,72	NE
28.02.2017	#####	#####	#####	#####	#####	#####	#####	#####
01.03.2017	#####	#####	#####	#####	#####	#####	#####	#####
02.03.2017	11:00:43	_44A0257	1/200	8	640	10,2	19,83	WSW
03.03.2017	#####	#####	#####	#####	#####	#####	#####	#####
04.03.2017	#####	#####	#####	#####	#####	#####	#####	#####
05.03.2017	10:18:47	_44A0320	1/320	8	200	2,5	4,86	ESE
06.03.2017	#####	#####	#####	#####	#####	#####	#####	#####
07.03.2017	#####	#####	#####	#####	#####	#####	#####	#####
08.03.2017	09:27:18	_44A0325	1/200	8	1250	0,6	1,17	SSW
09.03.2017	#####	#####	#####	#####	#####	#####	#####	#####
10.03.2017	#####	#####	#####	#####	#####	#####	#####	#####
11.03.2017	12:12:44	_44A0367	1/250	8	160	0,9	1,75	SSW
12.03.2017	#####	#####	#####	#####	#####	#####	#####	#####
13.03.2017	#####	#####	#####	#####	#####	#####	#####	#####
14.03.2017	11:16:47	_44A0383	1/250	8	400	1,3	2,53	WSW
15.03.2017	#####	#####	#####	#####	#####	#####	#####	#####
16.03.2017	#####	#####	#####	#####	#####	#####	#####	#####
17.03.2017	09:51:38	_44A0427	1/250	8	400	0,7	1,36	WNW
18.03.2017	#####	#####	#####	#####	#####	#####	#####	#####
19.03.2017	#####	#####	#####	#####	#####	#####	#####	#####
20.03.2017	13:07:08	_44A0477	1/200	8	1000	2,8	5,44	W

F#2

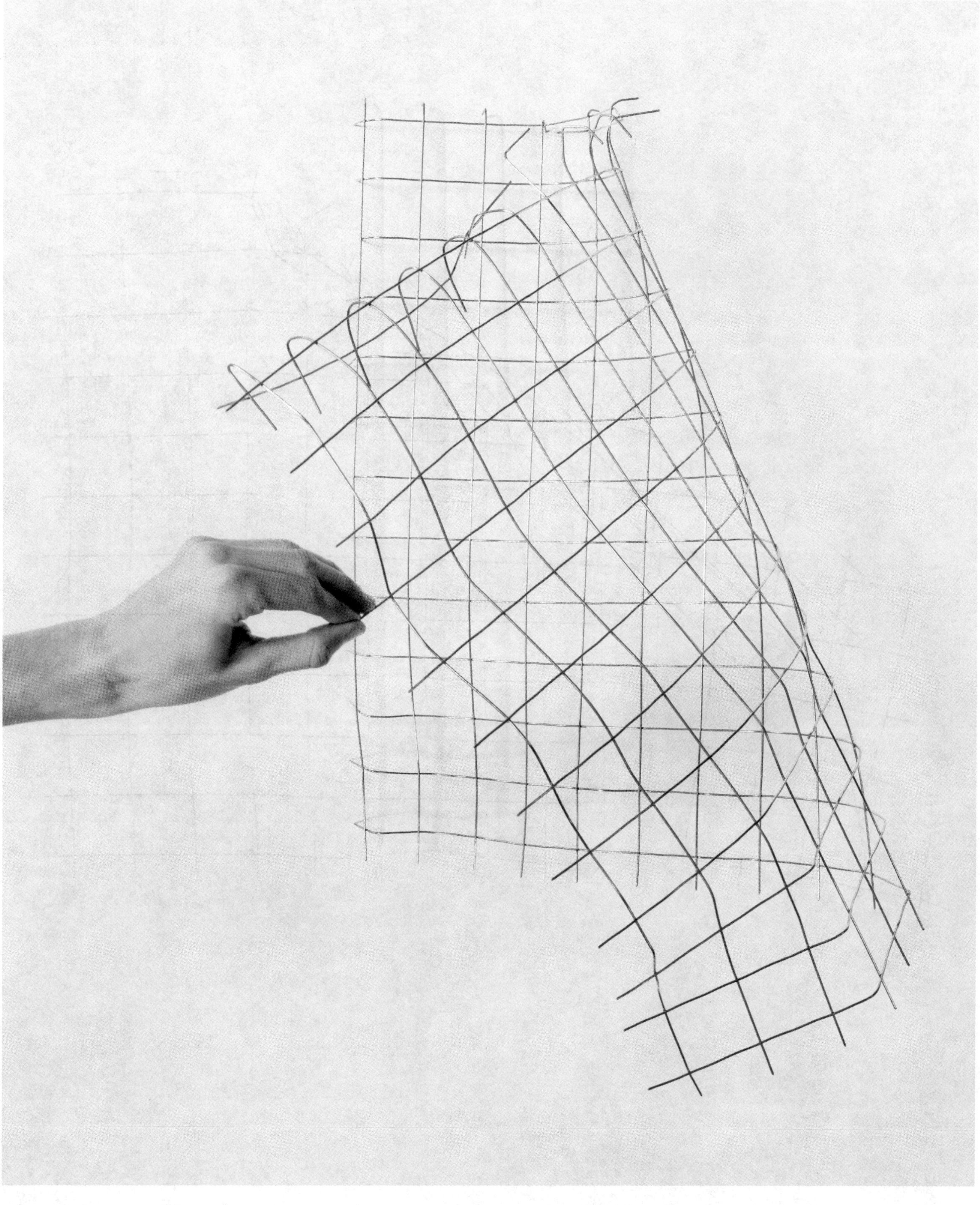

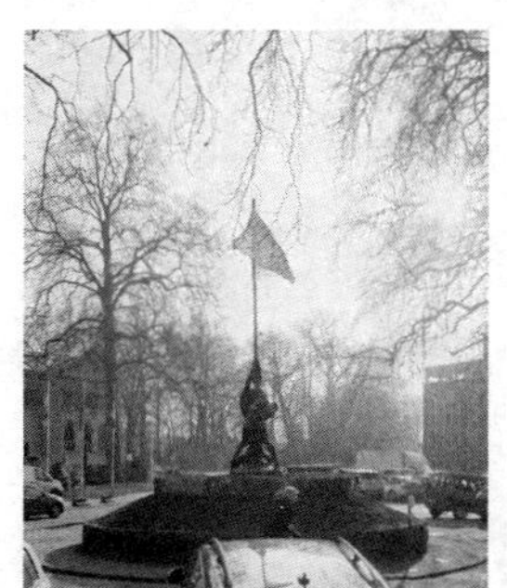

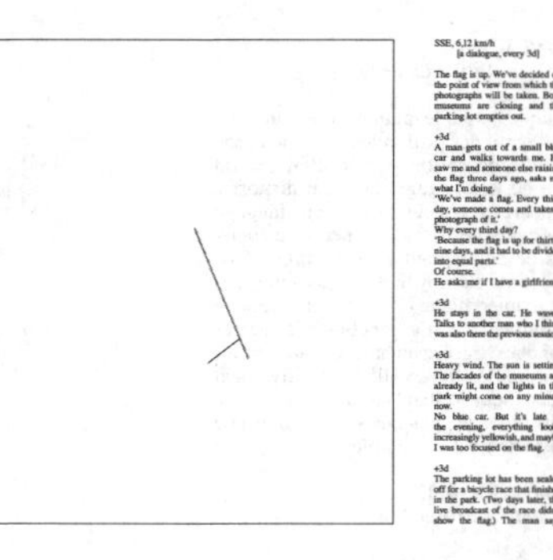

SSE, 6,12 km/h
[a dialogue, every 3d]

The flag is up. We've decided on the point of view from which the photographs will be taken. Both museums are closing and the parking lot empties out.

+3d
A man gets out of a small blue car and walks towards me. He saw me and someone else raising the flag three days ago, asks me what I'm doing.
'We've made a flag. Every third day, someone comes and takes a photograph of it.'
Why every third day?
'Because the flag is up for thirty-nine days, and it had to be divided into equal parts.'
Of course.
He asks me if I have a girlfriend.

+3d
He stays in the car. He waves. Talks to another man who I think was also there the previous session.

+3d
Heavy wind. The sun is setting. The facades of the museums are already lit, and the lights in the park might come on any minute now.
No blue car. But it's late in the evening, everything looks increasingly yellowish, and maybe I was too focused on the flag.

+3d
The parking lot has been sealed off for a bicycle race that finishes in the park. (Two days later, the live broadcast of the race didn't show the flag.) The man says he's from a town, which is thirty minutes from Ghent, that he comes here every day, better than sitting at home alone.

+3d
He says that a French artist (with some kind of Dutch-sounding name) already put up a flag at *De Mastplanters*. He doesn't like contemporary art.
'It's just another flag.'

+3d
Even stronger winds. Bursts of rain. There's a warning telling people to stay out of parks. Branches might fall. The wind's speed is estimated as 8 beaufort. The wind whips the flag. There's a determined jogger in the background.

+3d
He tells me that there's an underground nuclear command bunker in the park. It has supplies, communication channels and can hold up to 50 people. Might be useful one day. Detail: the generator feeding the heating system is outside the safe zone. Maybe they were hoping that the bomb would be dropped during the summer. The Museum of Contemporary Art used it around ten years ago and left lights and moveable walls in there. The fungus eating away at the wood is said to be lethal when inhaled for an extended period of time. If the outside world was radiant and cold, would one think that danger might arise *from within*? As if the park would refuse to tolerate our presence. He says if I got stuck down there, I could still make an exhibition, but the flag would be rather pointless.

+3d
A group of schoolchildren walks from the James Welling exhibition to the one on Francisco Goya. Some of them gaze into the lens, while I read the wind strength from the display, and he watches the flag (I imagine).

+3d
'Can you take the car and move it out of the frame?' I'm not sure if I'm allowed to ask.

+3d
Do both our timings create a system? Like the hands of a clock. A rhythm, perhaps a waltz.

+3d
A breeze.
Not much wind, he says.
Gardeners are planting flowers at the foot of the sculpture.
'No.'

+3d
He asks if it is the last photograph.

[While we were taking down the flag some ten police cars and a tank passed by. There was a speech on immigration given by a politician in a university building nearby. They parked behind the Museum of Fine Arts. Riding backwards, the tank hit a lamppost, which subsequently took on a strange 65° angle. Seven policemen stepped out of their cars and examined the situation. The flag had already been taken down. There was no way for us to document the scene.]

F#3

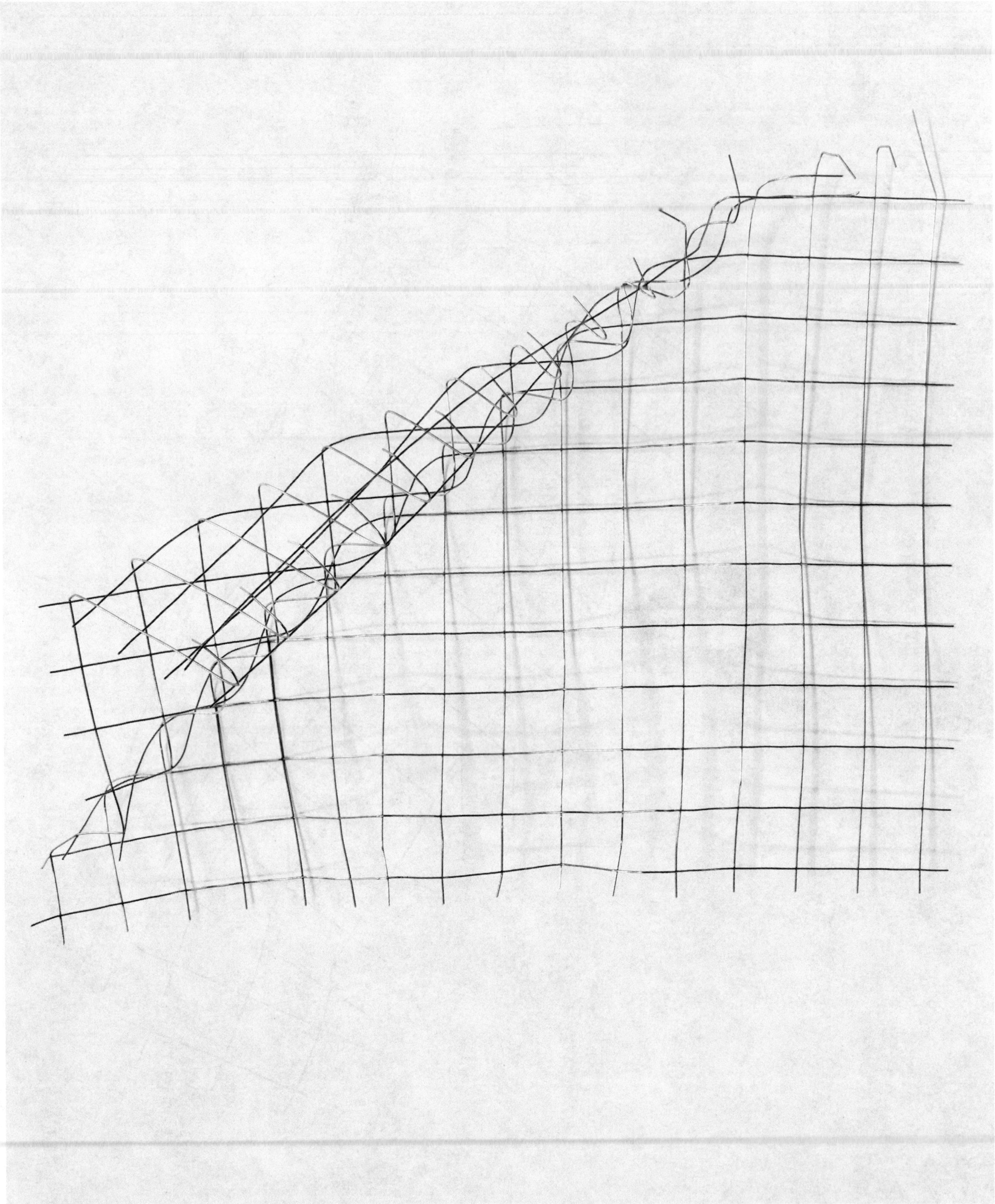

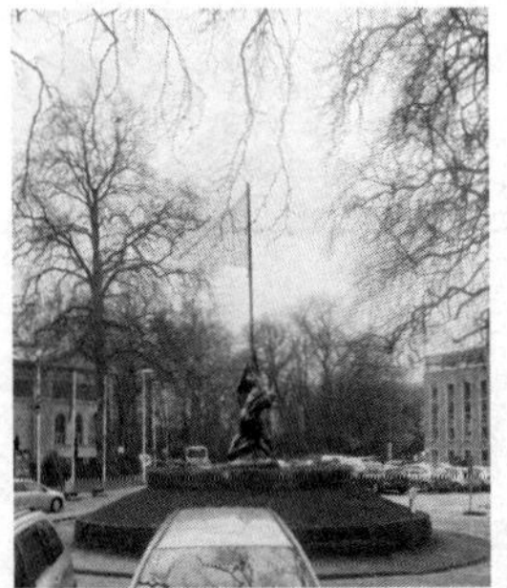

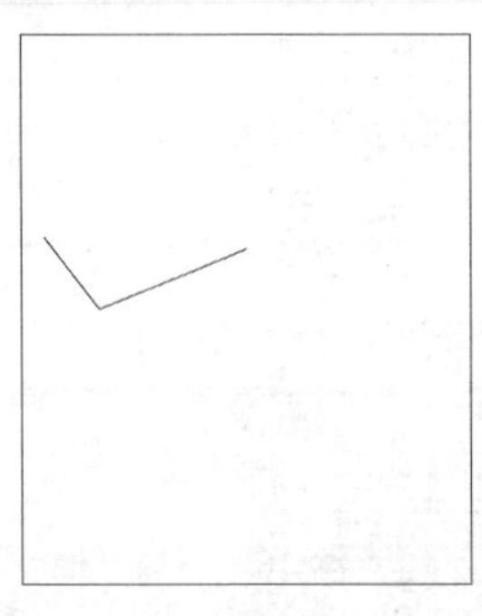

WSW, 18,36 km/h
[grille de lecture]

'Angélique remit le planisphère dans son cabas et sortit des profondeurs du vieux sac une feuille de carton percée d'un certain nombre de trous irrégulièrement disposés. Cet appareil, appelé *grille* en langage cryptographique, devait permettre aux deux amants de correspondre sans danger. Une phrase, écrite au moyen des trous appliqués sur du papier blanc, pouvait être rendue inintelligible par l'adjonction de lettres quelconques, tracées au hasard pour remplir avec ordre les intervalles primitivement ménagés. Seul Velbar saurait retrouver le sens du billet en plaçant sur le texte une grille exactement semblable.'

– Raymond Roussel,
Impressions d'Afrique[1]

F#4

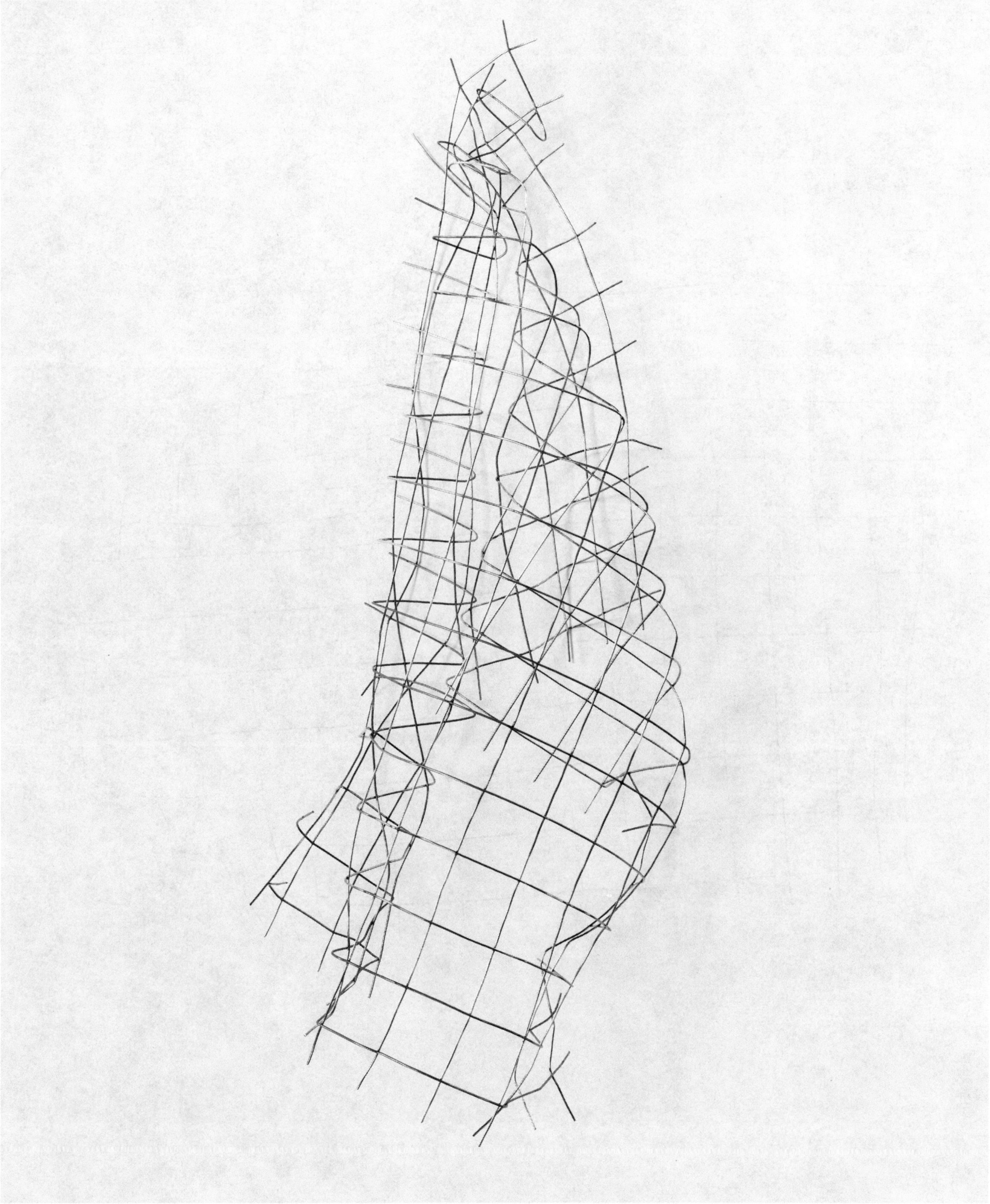

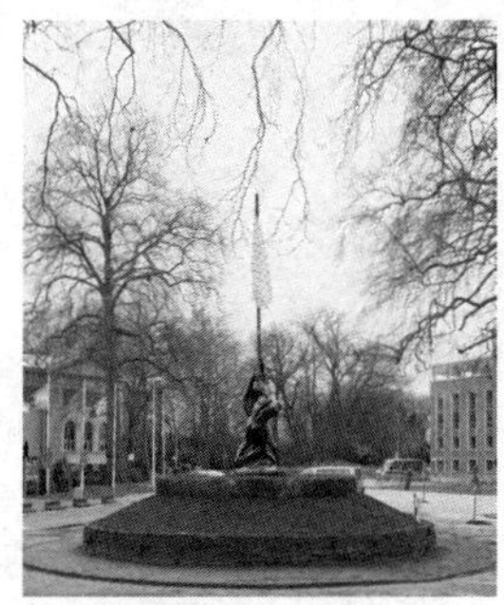

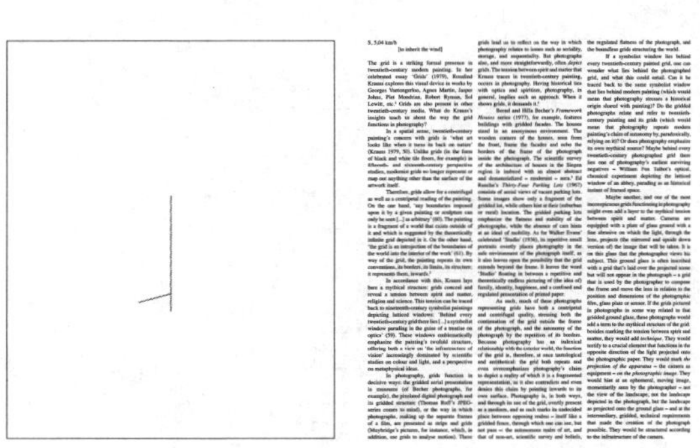

F#5

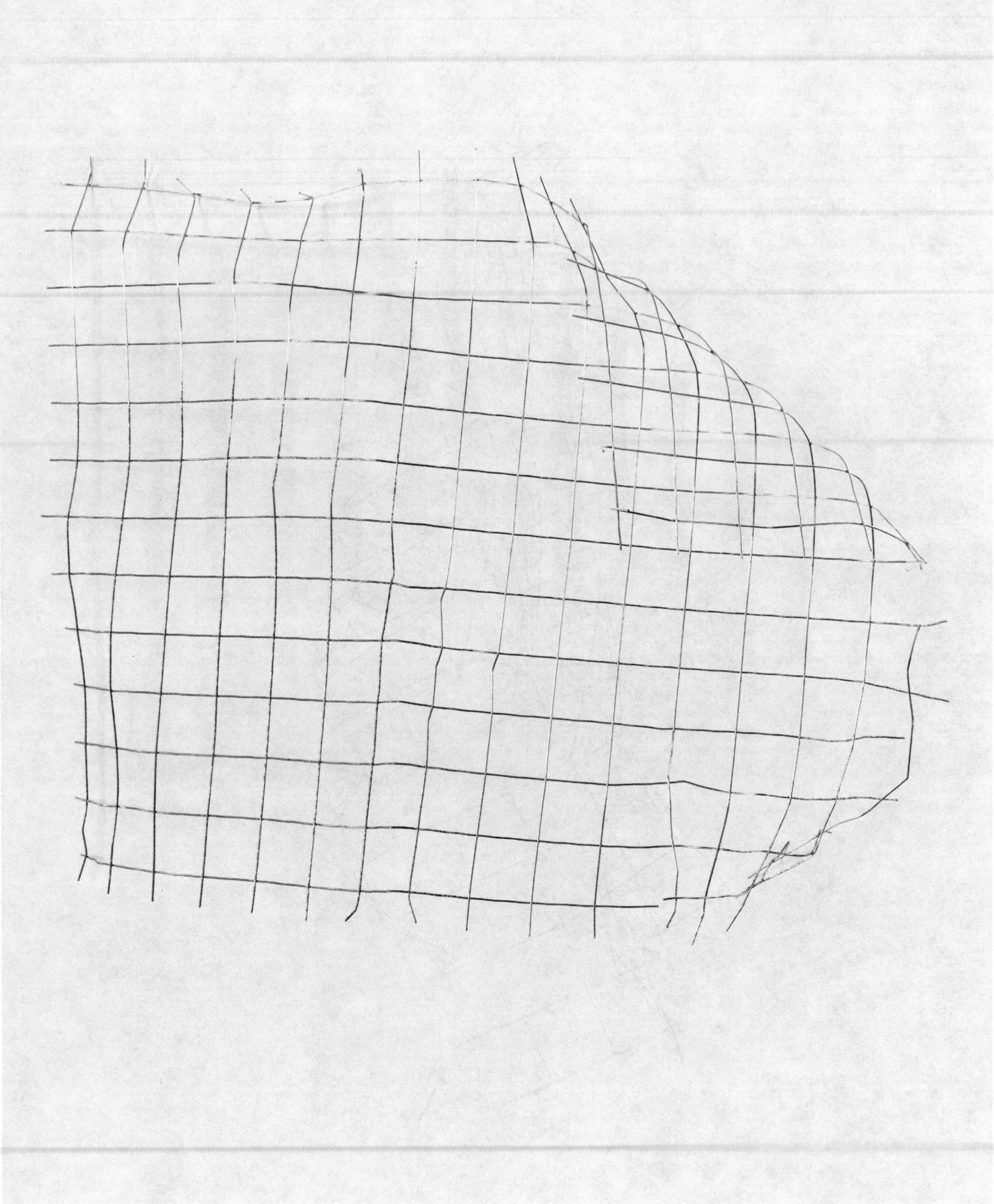

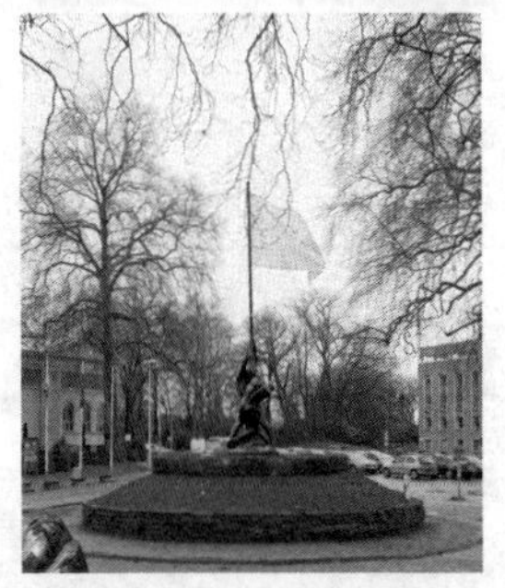

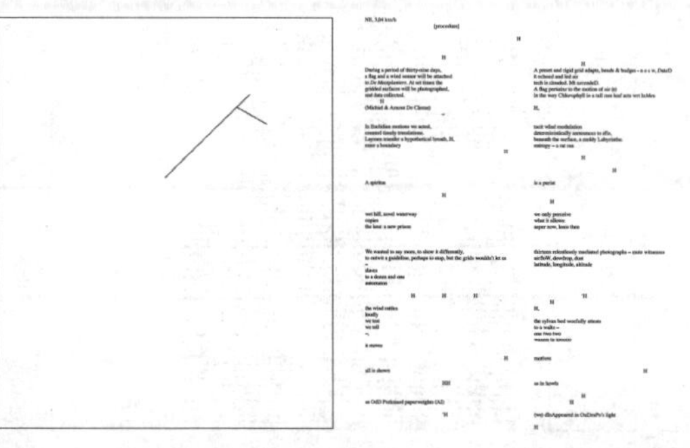

F#6

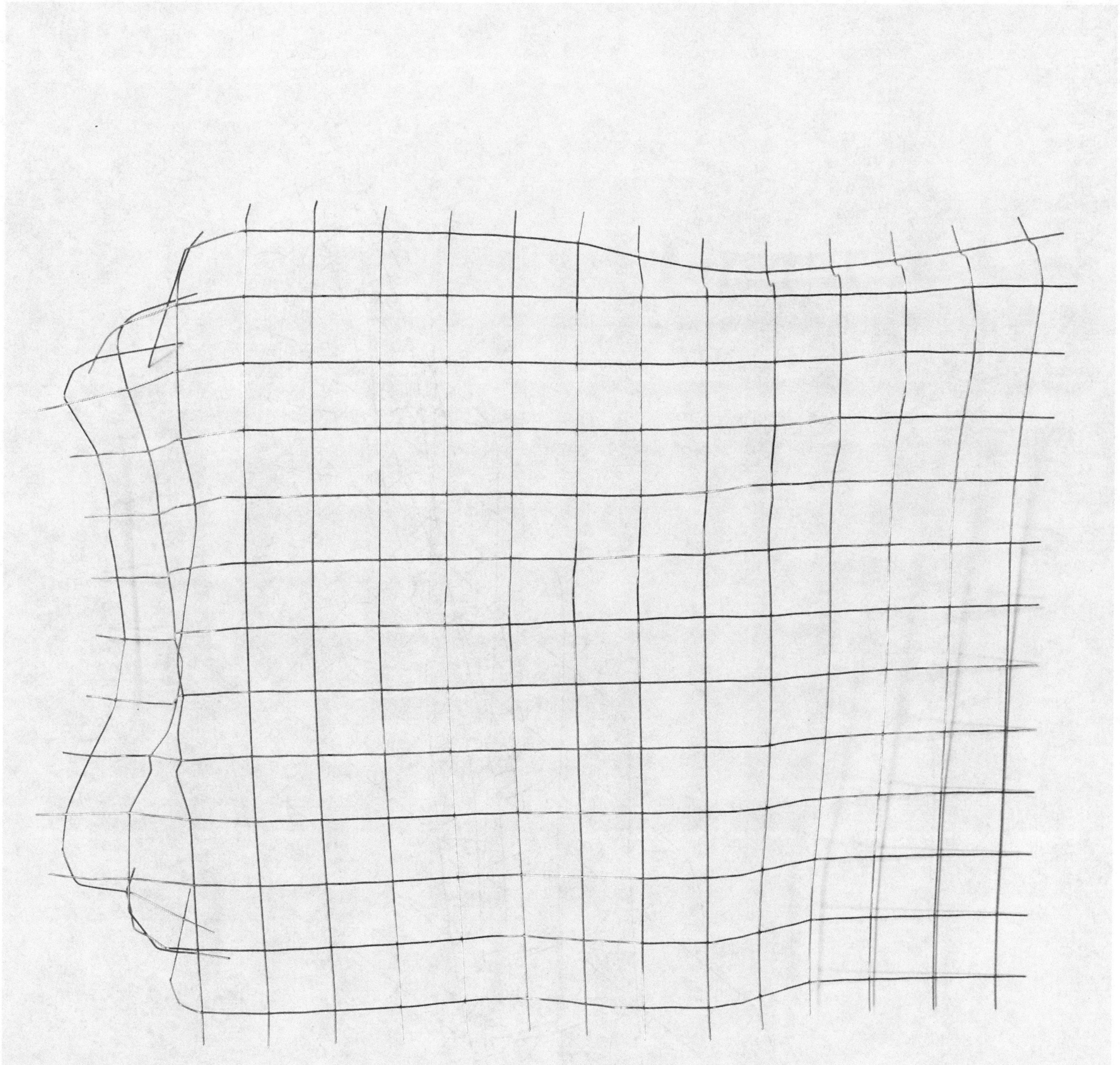

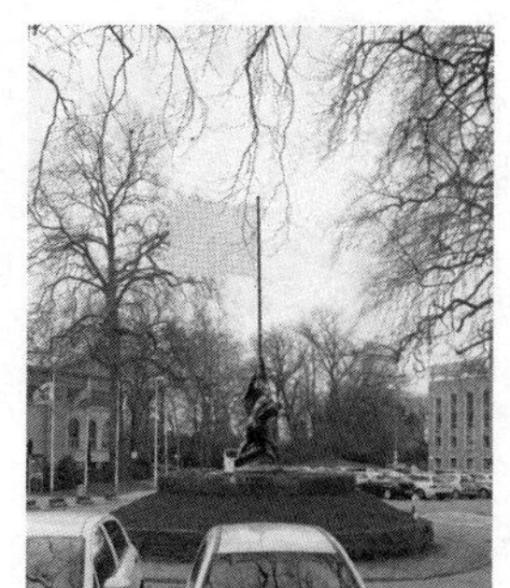

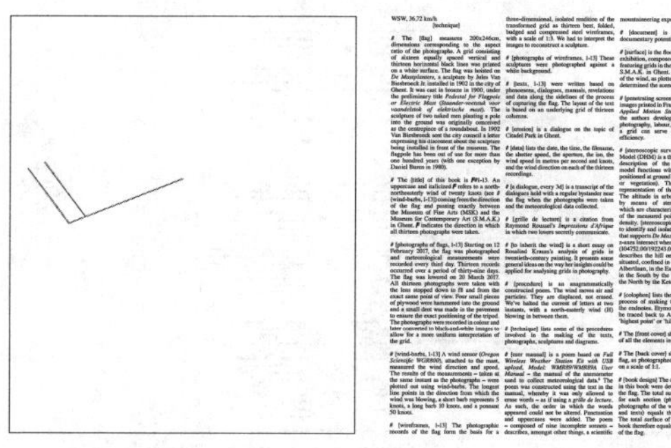

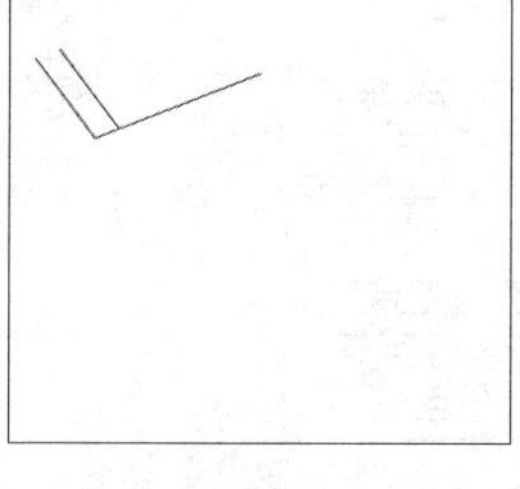

F#7

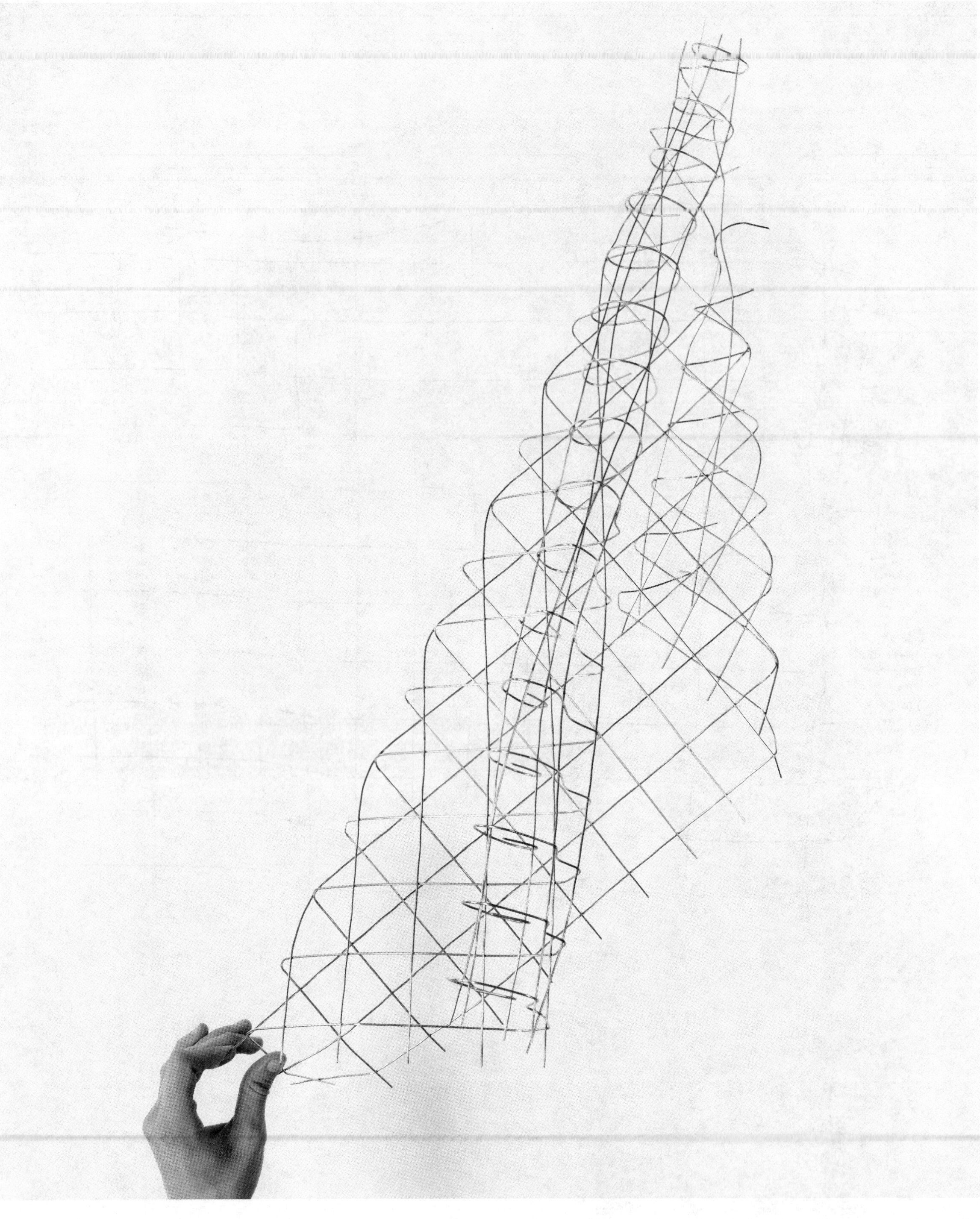

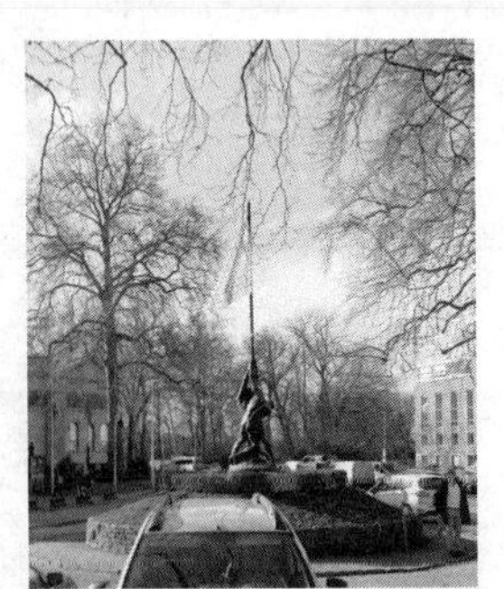

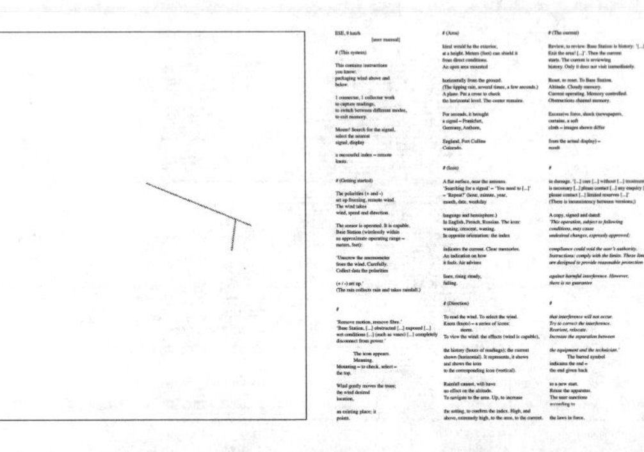

ESE, 8 km/h
[user manual]

(This system)

This contains instructions
you know:
packaging wind above and
below.

1 connector, 1 collector work
to capture readings,
to switch between different modes,
to exit memory.

Mount! Search for the signal,
select the nearest
signal, display

a successful index – remote
knots.

(Getting started)

The polarities (+ and -)
set up freezing, remote wind.
The wind takes
wind, speed and direction.

The sensor is operated. It is capable.
Base Station (wirelessly within
an approximate operating range –
meters, feet):

'Unscrew the anemometer
from the wind. Carefully.
Collect data the polarities

(+ / -) set up.'
(The rain collects rain and takes rainfall.)

#

'Remove motion, remove film.'
'Base Station, [...] obstructed [...] exposed [...]
wet conditions [...] (such as vases) [...] completely
disconnect from power.'

The icon appears.
Meaning.
Mounting – to check, select –
the top.

Wind gently moves the trees;
the wind desired
location,

an existing place; it
points.

(Area)

Ideal would be the exterior,
at a height. Meters (feet) can shield it
from direct conditions.
An open area mounted

horizontally from the ground.
(The tipping rain, several times, a few seconds.)
A plane. Put a cross to check
the horizontal level. The center remains.

For seconds, it brought
a signal – Frankfurt,
Germany, Anthorn,

England, Fort Collins
Colorado.

(Icon)

A flat surface, near the antenna.
'Searching for a signal' – 'You need to [...]'
– 'Repeat?' (hour, minute, year,
month, date, weekday

language and hemisphere.)
In English, French, Russian. The icon:
waxing, crescent, waning.
In opposite orientation: the index

indicates the current. Clear memories.
An indication on how
it feels. Air advises

lines, rising steady,
falling.

(Direction)

To read the wind. To select the wind.
Knots (knots) – a series of icons:
storm.
To view the wind: the effects (wind is capable),

the history (hours of readings); the current
shown (horizontal). It represents, it shows
and shows the icon
to the corresponding icon (vertical).

Rainfall cannot, will have
no effect on the altitude.
To navigate to the area. Up, to increase

the setting, to confirm the index. High, and
above, extremely high, to the area, to the current.

(The current)

Review, to review: Base Station is history: '[...]
Exit the area! [...]'. Then the current
starts. The current is reviewing
history. Only it does not visit immediately.

Reset, to reset. To Base Station.
Altitude. Cloudy memory.
Current operating. Memory controlled.
Obstructions channel memory.

Excessive force, shock (newspapers,
curtains, a soft
cloth – images shown differ

from the actual display) –
result

#

in damage. '[...] care [...] without [...] treatment
is necessary [...] please contact [...] any enquiry [...]
please contact [...] limited reserves [...]'
(There is inconsistency between versions.)

A copy, signed and dated:
'This operation, subject to following
conditions, may cause
undesired changes, expressly approved;

compliance could void the user's authority.
Instructions: comply with the limits. These limits
are designed to provide reasonable protection

against harmful interference. However,
there is no guarantee

#

that interference will not occur.
Try to correct the interference.
Reorient, relocate.
Increase the separation between

the equipment and the technician.'
The barred symbol
indicates the end –
the end given back

to a new start.
Reuse the apparatus.
The user sanctions
according to

the laws in force.

F#8

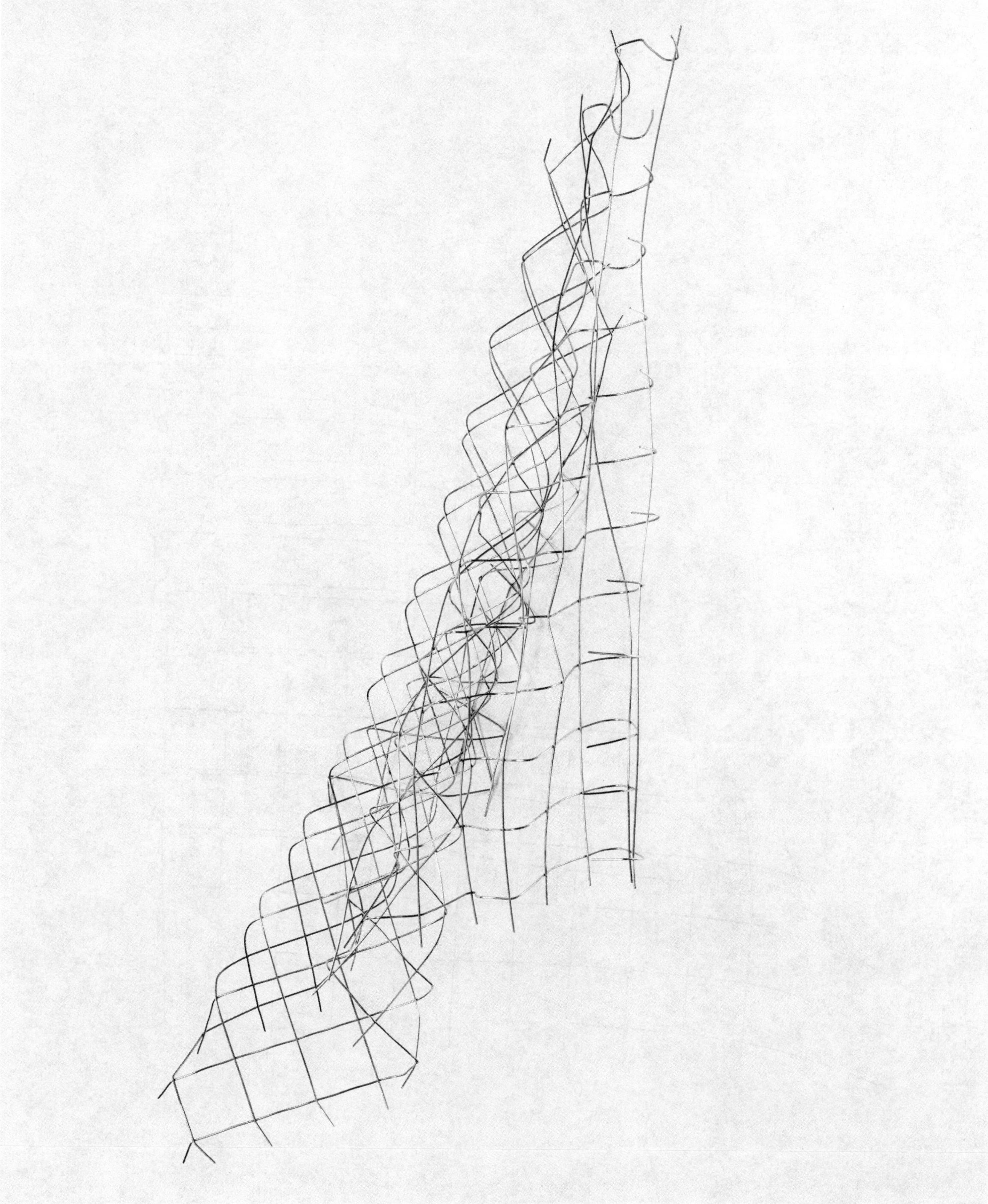

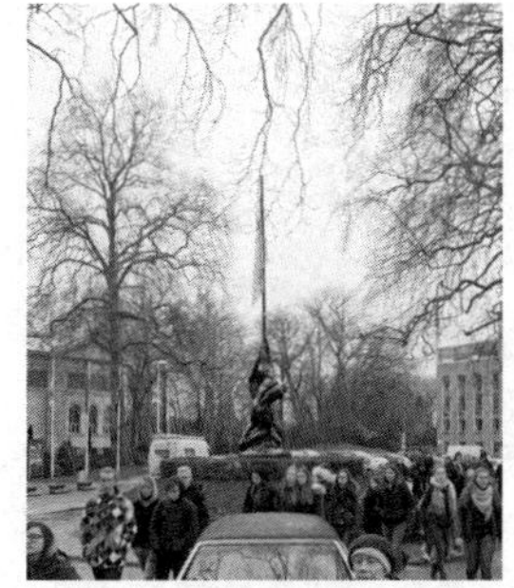

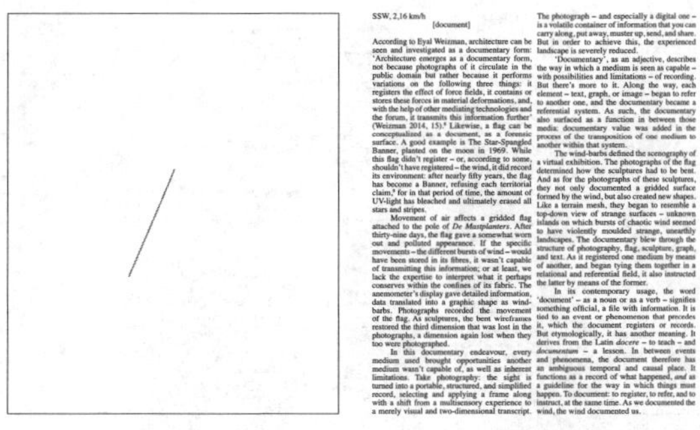

SSW, 2,16 km/h

[document]

According to Eyal Weizman, architecture can be seen and investigated as a documentary form: 'Architecture emerges as a documentary form, not because photographs of it circulate in the public domain but rather because it performs variations on the following three things: it registers the effect of force fields, it contains or stores these forces in material deformations, and, with the help of other mediating technologies and the forum, it transmits this information further' (Weizman 2014, 15).[8] Likewise, a flag can be conceptualized as a document, as a forensic surface. A good example is The Star-Spangled Banner, planted on the moon in 1969. While this flag didn't register – or, according to some, shouldn't have registered – the wind, it did record its environment: after nearly fifty years, the flag has become a Banner, refusing each territorial claim,[9] for in that period of time, the amount of UV-light has bleached and ultimately erased all stars and stripes.

Movement of air affects a gridded flag attached to the pole of *De Mastplanters*. After thirty-nine days, the flag gave a somewhat worn out and polluted appearance. If the specific movements – the different bursts of wind – would have been stored in its fibres, it wasn't capable of transmitting this information; or at least, we lack the expertise to interpret what it perhaps conserves within the confines of its fabric. The anemometer's display gave detailed information, data translated into a graphic shape as wind-barbs. Photographs recorded the movement of the flag. As sculptures, the bent wireframes restored the third dimension that was lost in the photographs, a dimension again lost when they too were photographed.

In this documentary endeavour, every medium used brought opportunities another medium wasn't capable of, as well as inherent limitations. Take photography: the sight is turned into a portable, structured, and simplified record, selecting and applying a frame along with a shift from a multisensory experience to a merely visual and two-dimensional transcript. The photograph – and especially a digital one – is a volatile container of information that you can carry along, put away, muster up, send, and share. But in order to achieve this, the experienced landscape is severely reduced.

'Documentary', as an adjective, describes the way in which a medium is seen as capable – with possibilities and limitations – of recording. But there's more to it. Along the way, each element – text, graph, or image – began to refer to another one, and the documentary became a referential system. As such, the documentary also surfaced as a function in between those media: documentary value was added in the process of the transposition of one medium to another within that system.

The wind-barbs defined the scenography of a virtual exhibition. The photographs of the flag determined how the sculptures had to be bent. And as for the photographs of these sculptures, they not only documented a gridded surface formed by the wind, but also created new shapes. Like a terrain mesh, they began to resemble a top-down view of strange surfaces – unknown islands on which bursts of chaotic wind seemed to have violently moulded strange, unearthly landscapes. The documentary blew through the structure of photography, flag, sculpture, graph, and text. As it registered one medium by means of another, and began tying them together in a relational and referential field, it also instructed the latter by means of the former.

In its contemporary usage, the word 'document' – as a noun or as a verb – signifies something official, a file with information. It is tied to an event or phenomenon that precedes it, which the document registers or records. But etymologically, it has another meaning. It derives from the Latin *docere* – to teach – and *documentum* – a lesson. In between events and phenomena, the document therefore has an ambiguous temporal and causal place. It functions as a record of what happened, *and* as a guideline for the way in which things must happen. To document: to register, to refer, and to instruct, at the same time. As we documented the wind, the wind documented us.

F#9

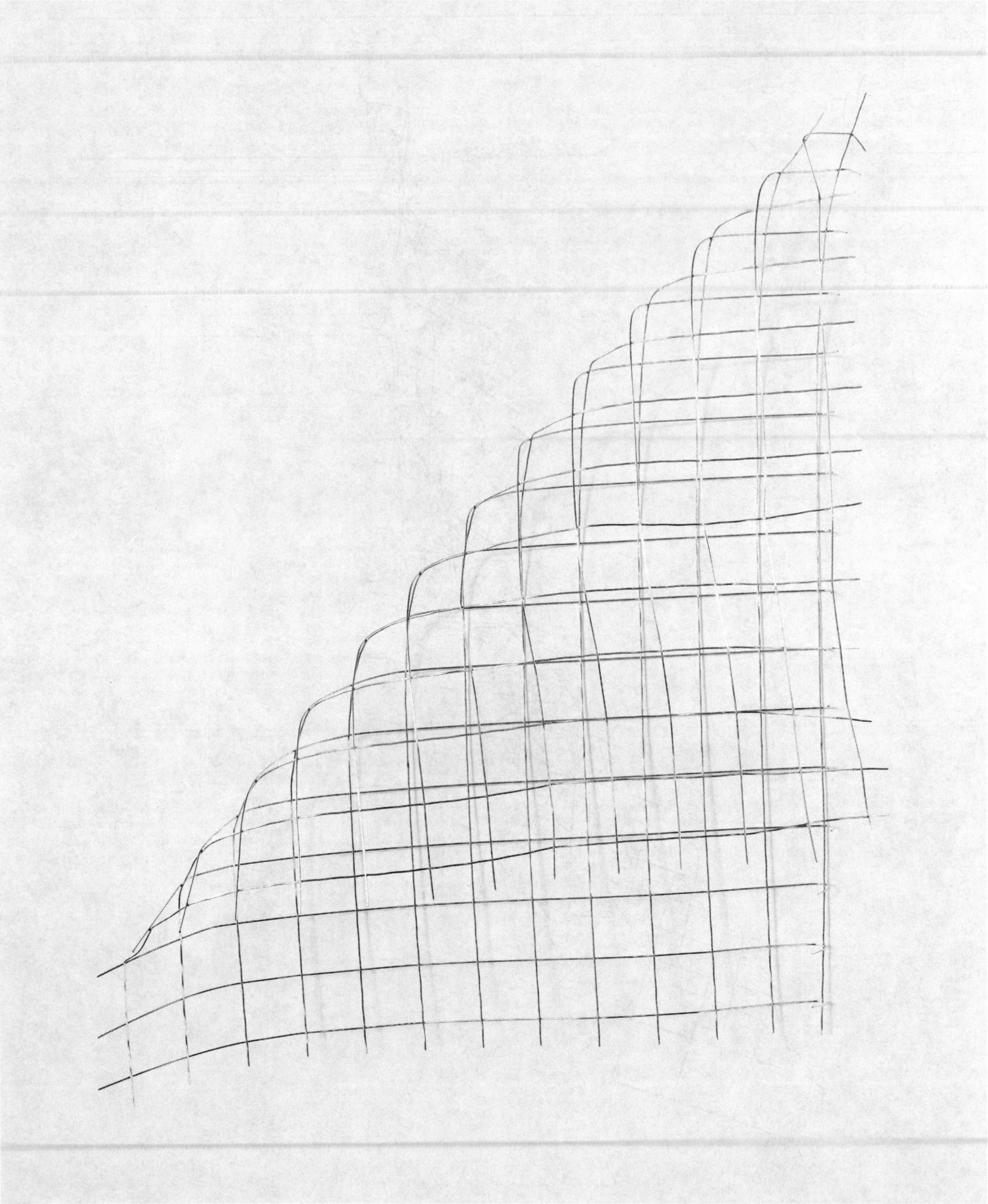

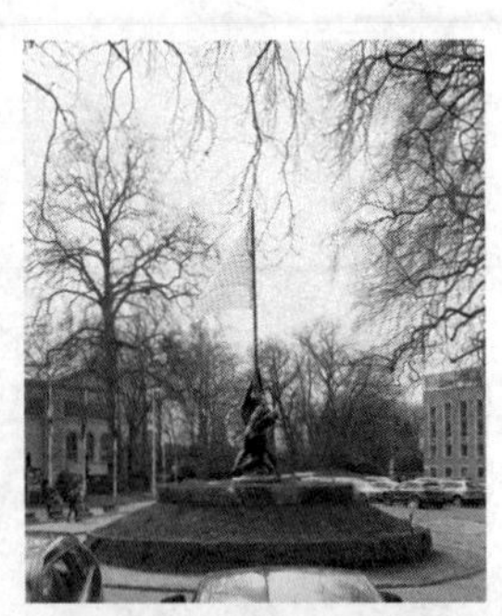

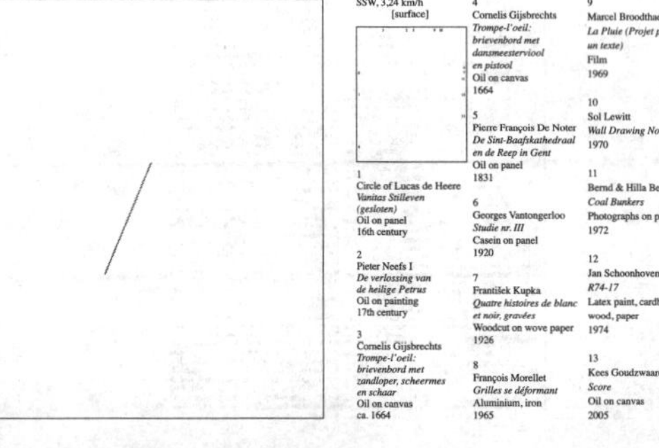

SSW, 3,24 km/h
[surface]

1
Circle of Lucas de Heere
Vanitas Stilleven (gesloten)
Oil on panel
16th century

2
Pieter Neefs I
De verlossing van de heilige Petrus
Oil on painting
17th century

3
Cornelis Gijsbrechts
Trompe-l'oeil: brievenbord met zandloper, scheermes en schaar
Oil on canvas
ca. 1664

4
Cornelis Gijsbrechts
Trompe-l'oeil: brievenbord met dansmeesterviool en pistool
Oil on canvas
1664

5
Pierre François De Noter
De Sint-Baafskathedraal en de Reep in Gent
Oil on panel
1831

6
Georges Vantongerloo
Studie nr. III
Casein on panel
1920

7
František Kupka
Quatre histoires de blanc et noir, gravées
Woodcut on wove paper
1926

8
François Morellet
Grilles se déformant
Aluminium, iron
1965

9
Marcel Broodthaers
La Pluie (Projet pour un texte)
Film
1969

10
Sol Lewitt
Wall Drawing No. 36
1970

11
Bernd & Hilla Becher
Coal Bunkers
Photographs on panel
1972

12
Jan Schoonhoven
R74-17
Latex paint, cardboard, wood, paper
1974

13
Kees Goudzwaard
Score
Oil on canvas
2005

F#10

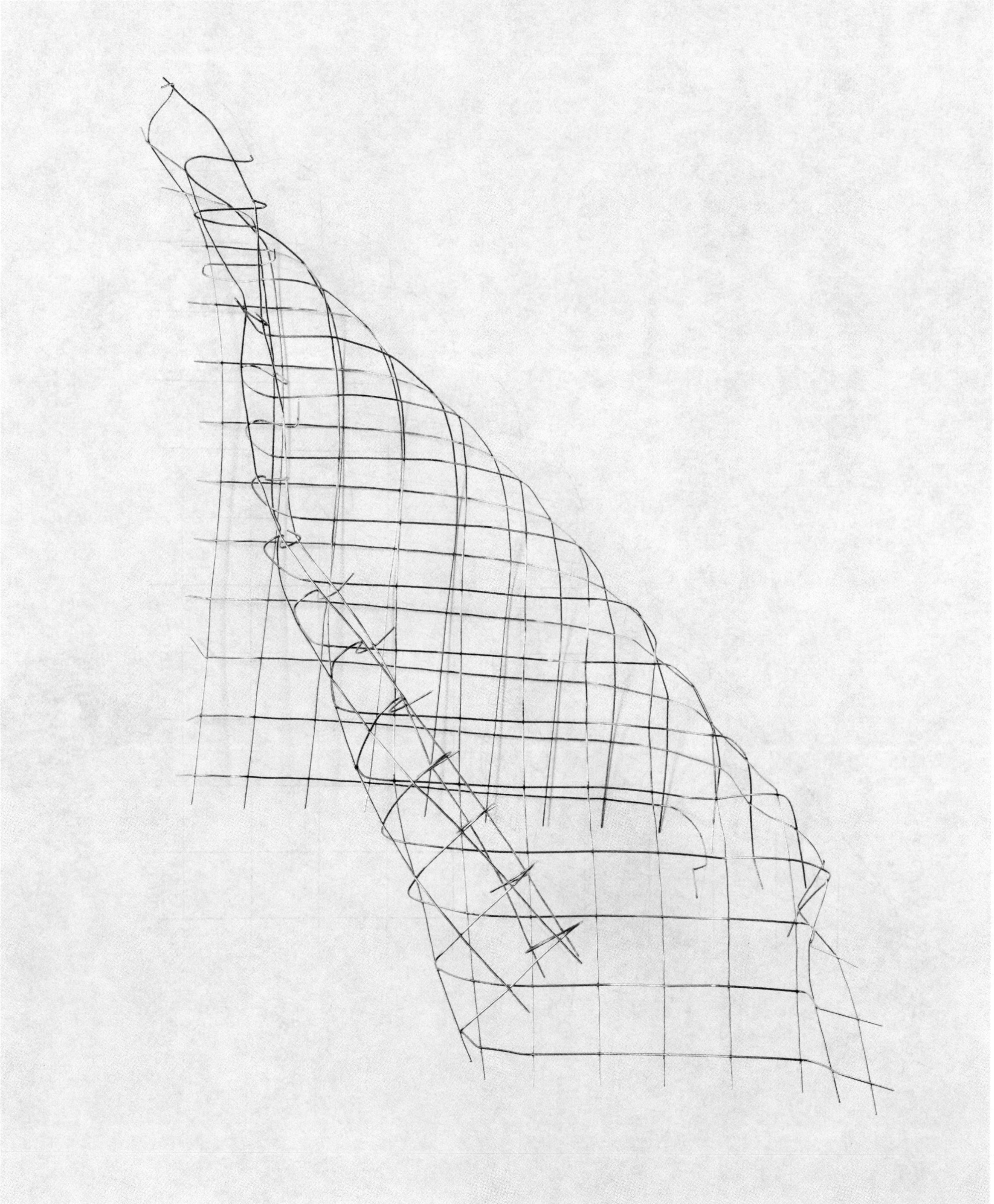

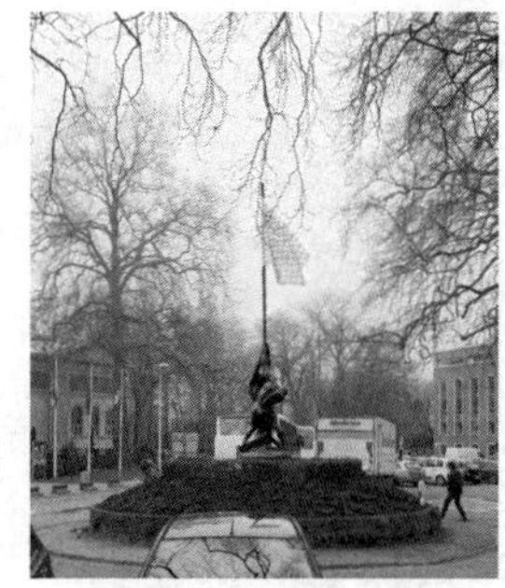

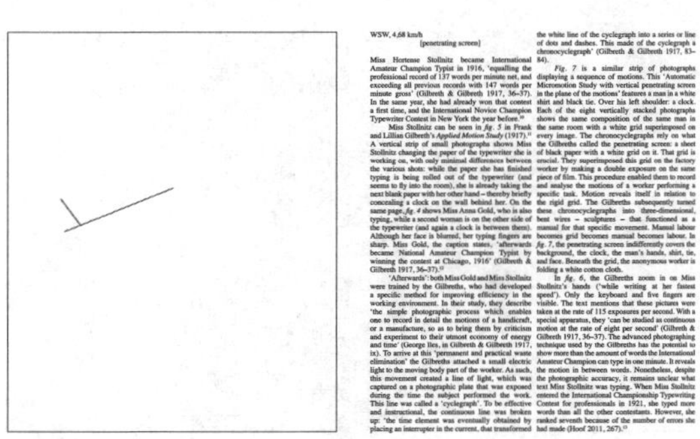

WSW, 4,68 km/h

[penetrating screen]

Miss Hortense Stollnitz became International Amateur Champion Typist in 1916, 'equalling the professional record of 137 words per minute net, and exceeding all previous records with 147 words per minute gross' (Gilbreth & Gilbreth 1917, 36–37). In the same year, she had already won that contest a first time, and the International Novice Champion Typewriter Contest in New York the year before.[10]

Miss Stollnitz can be seen in *fig. 5* in Frank and Lillian Gilbreth's *Applied Motion Study* (1917).[11] A vertical strip of small photographs shows Miss Stollnitz changing the paper of the typewriter she is working on, with only minimal differences between the various shots: while the paper she has finished typing is being rolled out of the typewriter (and seems to fly into the room), she is already taking the next blank paper with her other hand – thereby briefly concealing a clock on the wall behind her. On the same page, *fig. 4* shows Miss Anna Gold, who is also typing, while a second woman is on the other side of the typewriter (and again a clock is between them). Although her face is blurred, her typing fingers are sharp. Miss Gold, the caption states, 'afterwards became National Amateur Champion Typist by winning the contest at Chicago, 1916' (Gilbreth & Gilbreth 1917, 36–37).[12]

'Afterwards': both Miss Gold and Miss Stollnitz were trained by the Gilbreths, who had developed a specific method for improving efficiency in the working environment. In their study, they describe 'the simple photographic process which enables one to record in detail the motions of a handicraft, or a manufacture, so as to bring them by criticism and experiment to their utmost economy of energy and time' (George Iles, in Gilbreth & Gilbreth 1917, ix). To arrive at this 'permanent and practical waste elimination' the Gilbreths attached a small electric light to the moving body part of the worker. As such, this movement created a line of light, which was captured on a photographic plate that was exposed during the time the subject performed the work. This line was called a 'cyclegraph'. To be effective and instructional, the continuous line was broken up: 'the time element was eventually obtained by placing an interrupter in the current, that transformed the white line of the cyclegraph into a series or line of dots and dashes. This made of the cyclegraph a chronocyclegraph' (Gilbreth & Gilbreth 1917, 83–84).

Fig. 7 is a similar strip of photographs displaying a sequence of motions. This 'Automatic Micromotion Study with vertical penetrating screen in the plane of the motions' features a man in a white shirt and black tie. Over his left shoulder: a clock. Each of the eight vertically stacked photographs shows the same composition of the same man in the same room with a white grid superimposed on every image. The chronocyclegraphs rely on what the Gilbreths called the penetrating screen: a sheet of black paper with a white grid on it. That grid is crucial. They superimposed this grid on the factory worker by making a double exposure on the same piece of film. This procedure enabled them to record and analyse the motions of a worker performing a specific task. Motion reveals itself in relation to the rigid grid. The Gilbreths subsequently turned these chronocyclegraphs into three-dimensional, bent wires – sculptures – that functioned as a manual for that specific movement. Manual labour becomes grid becomes manual becomes labour. In *fig. 7*, the penetrating screen indifferently covers the background, the clock, the man's hands, shirt, tie, and face. Beneath the grid, the anonymous worker is folding a white cotton cloth.

In *fig. 6*, the Gilbreths zoom in on Miss Stollnitz's hands ('while writing at her fastest speed'). Only the keyboard and five fingers are visible. The text mentions that these pictures were taken at the rate of 115 exposures per second. With a special apparatus, they 'can be studied as continuous motion at the rate of eight per second' (Gilbreth & Gilbreth 1917, 36–37). The advanced photographing technique used by the Gilbreths has the potential to show more than the amount of words the International Amateur Champion can type in one minute. It reveals the motion in between words. Nonetheless, despite the photographic accuracy, it remains unclear what text Miss Stollnitz was typing. When Miss Stollnitz entered the International Championship Typewriting Contest for professionals in 1921, she typed more words than all the other contestants. However, she ranked seventh because of the number of errors she had made (Hoof 2011, 267).[13]

F#11

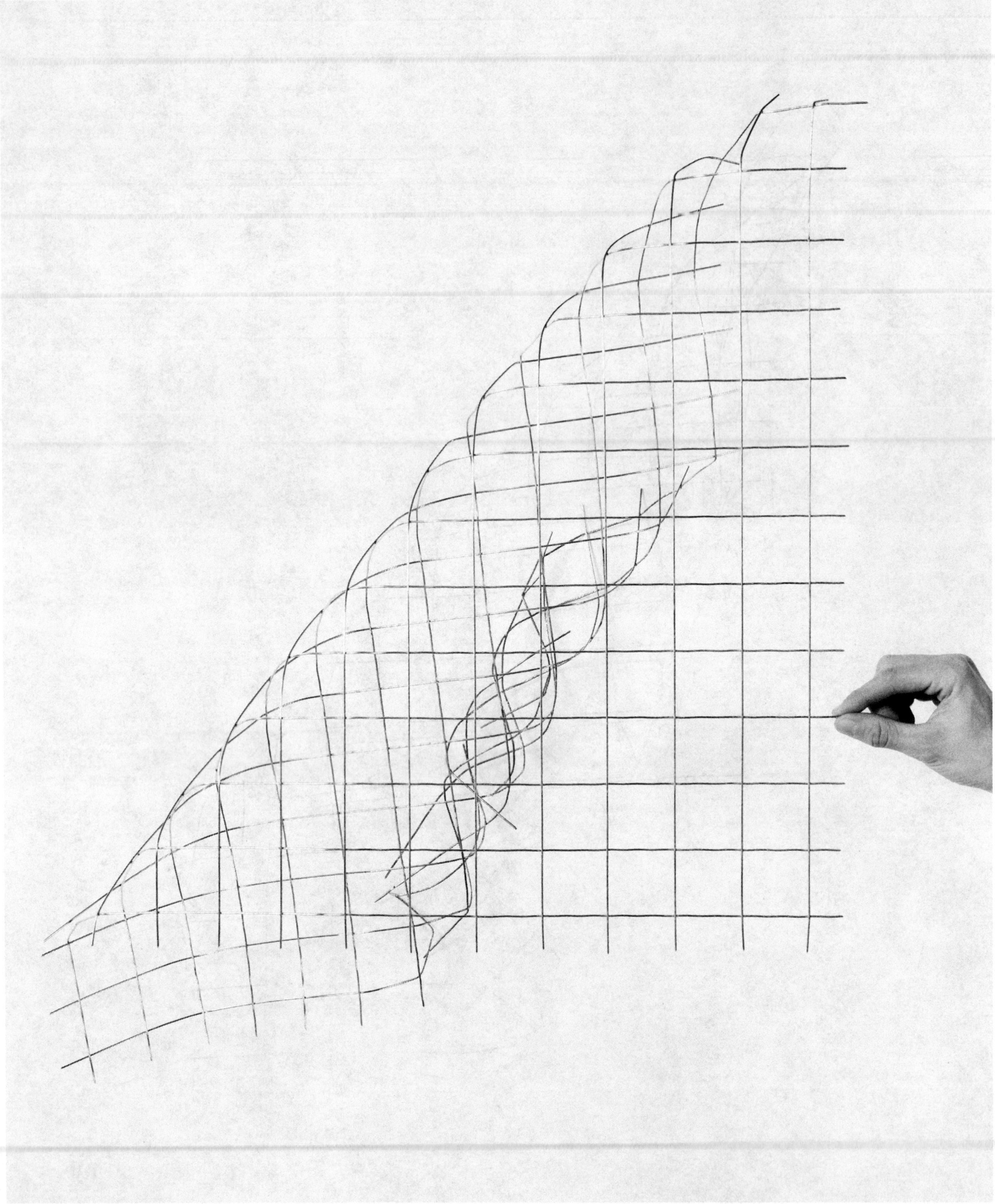

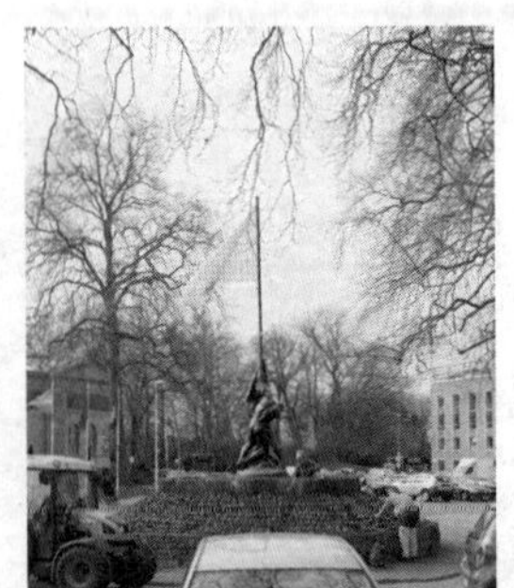

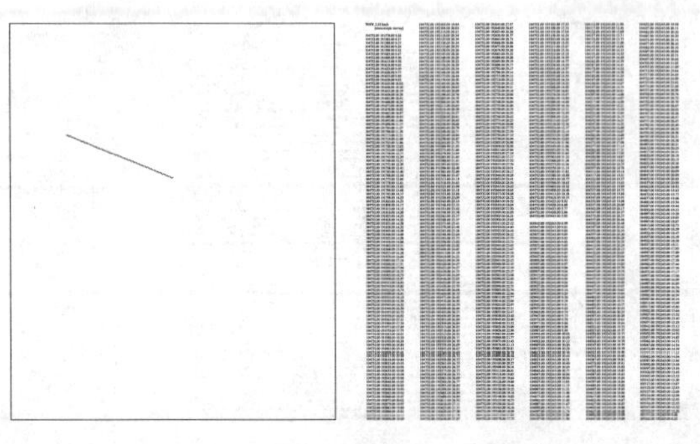

F#12

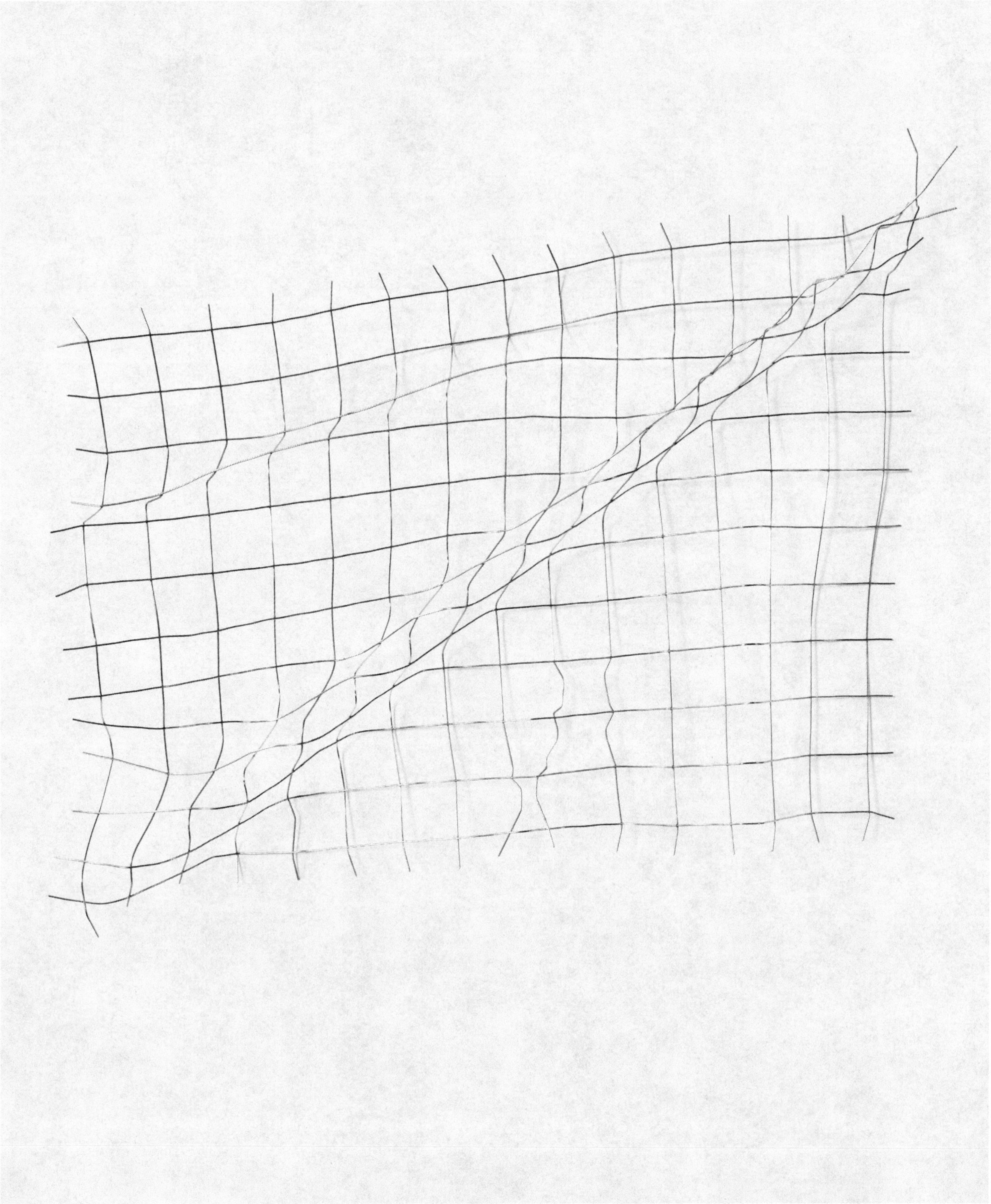

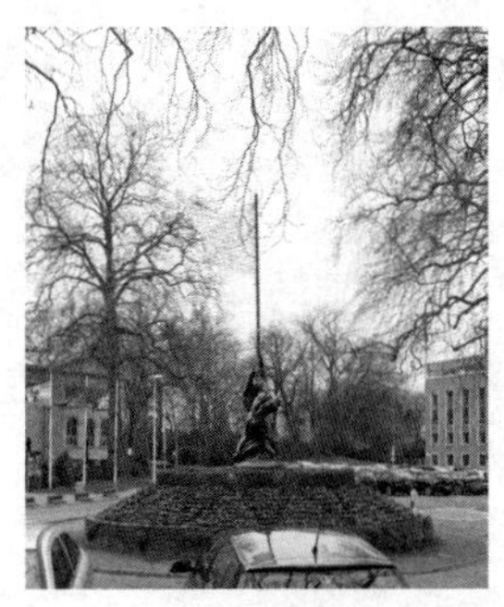

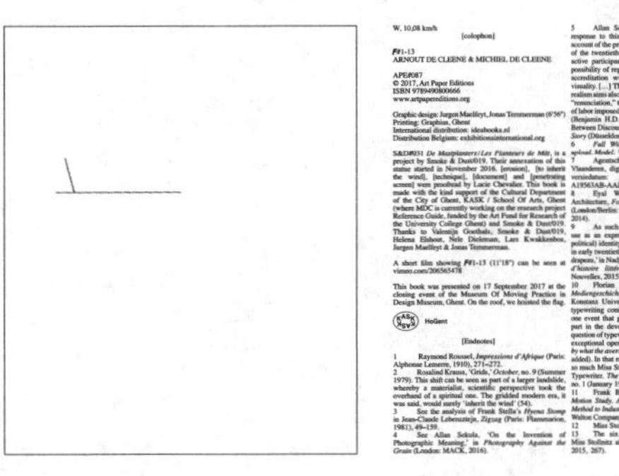

W, 10,08 km/h

[colophon]

***F#*1-13
ARNOUT DE CLEENE & MICHIEL DE CLEENE

APE#087

© 2017, Art Paper Editions

ISBN 9789490800666
www.artpapereditions.org

Graphic design: Jurgen Maelfeyt, Jonas Temmerman (6'56")
Printing: Graphius, Ghent
International distribution: ideabooks.nl
Distribution Belgium: exhibitionsinternational.org

S&D#031 *De Mastplanters / Les Planteurs de Mât*, is a project by Smoke & Dust/019. Their annexation of this statue started in November 2016. [erosion], [to inherit the wind], [technique], [document] and [penetrating screen] were proofread by Lucie Chevalier. This book is made with the kind support of the Cultural Department of the City of Ghent, KASK / School Of Arts, Ghent (where MDC is currently working on the research project Reference Guide, funded by the Art Fund for Research of the University College Ghent) and Smoke & Dust/019. Thanks to Valentijn Goethals, Smoke & Dust/019, Helena Elshout, Nele Dieleman, Lars Kwakkenbos, Jurgen Maelfeyt & Jonas Temmerman.

A short film showing ***F#*1-13 (11'18") can be seen at vimeo.com/206565478

This book was presented on 17 September 2017 at the closing event of the Museum Of Moving Practice in Design Museum, Ghent. On the roof, we hoisted the flag.

KASK HoGent

[Endnotes]

1 Raymond Roussel, *Impressions d'Afrique* (Paris: Alphonse Lemerre, 1910), 271–272.

2 Rosalind Krauss, 'Grids,' *October*, no. 9 (Summer 1979). This shift can be seen as part of a larger landslide, whereby a materialist, scientific perspective took the overhand of a spiritual one. The gridded modern era, it was said, would surely 'inherit the wind' (54).

3 See the analysis of Frank Stella's *Hyena Stomp* in Jean-Claude Lebensztejn, *Zigzag* (Paris: Flammarion, 1981), 49–159.

4 See Allan Sekula, 'On the Invention of Photographic Meaning,' in *Photography Against the Grain* (London: MACK, 2016).

5 Allan Sekula's work can be interpreted as a response to this aesthetic: 'The Bechers' monumental account of the principal work sites of industrial capitalism of the twentieth century apparently had to exclude the active participants from these locations and from the possibility of representation in order to gain its aesthetic accreditation within the larger account of modernist visuality. [...] Thus Sekula's attempt to develop a critical realism aims also to systematically overcome this aspect of "renunciation," to overcome the ban on the representation of labor imposed by an aesthetic of modernist restrictions' (Benjamin H.D. Buchloh, 'Allan Sekula: Photography Between Discourse and Document,' in Allan Sekula, *Fish Story* (Düsseldorf: Richter Verlag, 1995), 194).

6 *Full Wireless Weather Station Kit with USB upload. Model: WMR89/WMR89A. User Manual.*

7 Agentschap voor Geografische Informatie Vlaanderen, digitaal hoogtemodel Vlaanderen, punten, versiedatum: 2006-05-29, dataset identificatie: A19563AB-AAD5-4120-ABFB-2687EA486262.

8 Eyal Weizman, 'Introduction,' in Forensic Architecture, *Forensis. The Architecture of Public Truth* (London/Berlin: Forensic Architecture/Sternberg Press, 2014).

9 As such, the flag differs from its conventional use as an expression of (geographical, communal, or political) identity. For an analysis of the flag as an object in early twentieth-century literature, see Jan Baetens, 'Le drapeau,' in Nadja Cohen & Anne Reverseau, *Petit musée d'histoire littéraire, 1900-1950* (Paris: Impressions Nouvelles, 2015).

10 Florian Hoof, *Engel der Effizienz. Eine Mediengeschichte der Unternehmensberatung* (Konstanz: Konstanz University Press, 2015), 267. On the 1915 typewriting contest *The Rotarian* writes: 'It is [...] the one event that gives a real indication of the machine's part in the development of speed in typewriting. The question of typewriter merit is not determined by what the exceptional operator of exceptional training can do, *but by what the average operator can do*' (1916, 59, emphasis added). In that respect, the winner of the contest was not so much Miss Stollnitz, as it was a Model 10 Remington Typewriter. *The Rotarian. Magazine of Service*, vol. 8, no. 1 (January 1916).

11 Frank B. Gilbreth & L.M. Gilbreth, *Applied Motion Study. A Collection of Papers on the Efficient Method to Industrial Preparedness* (New York: Sturgis & Walton Company, 1917).

12 Miss Stollnitz came second (Hoof 2015, 267).

13 The six contestants who ranked higher than Miss Stollnitz all used an Underwood typewriter (Hoof 2015, 267).

*F#*13

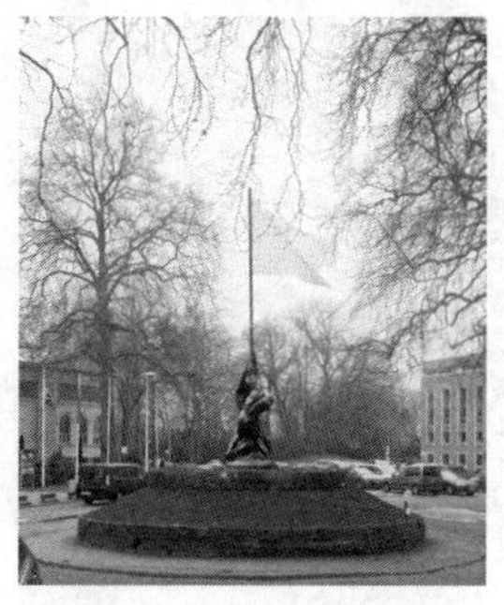

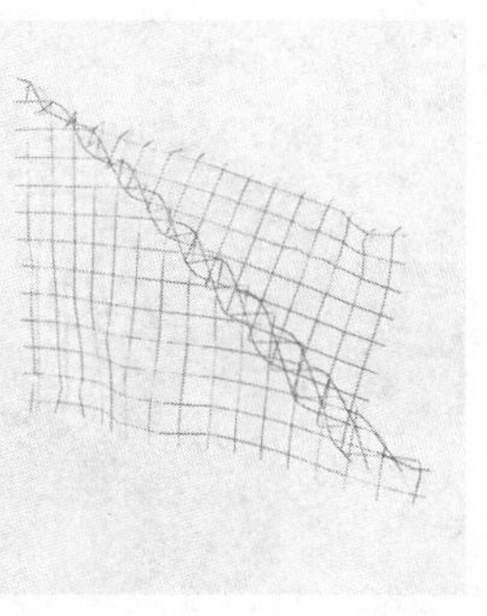

E, 8,64 km/h

[erosion]

Citadel Park lies between the Scheldt and the Lys. It rises from its surroundings. In the park, there are two museums, an animal shelter, a congress hall, man-made caves, ponds, and a velodrome. The wind blows between the trees. Dust is lifted from the soil and flies out of the park.

'Would it be possible to ascribe a kind of prophetic gift or intention to the forces that shaped this landscape?'
'You mean: did the two rivers want to carve out a hill at the edge of what would become the heart of the city?'
'Did they anticipate an elevation on which a park, statues, and museums would be built? As if a physical height might strengthen the symbolic value of the elements that would be displayed on it.'
'Could be, but maybe it's not about the landscape. When depicted in a painting or a photograph, landscapes tend to function as a combination of elements that are outlined against a background. There is a surface – hills, a stormy sea – that supports a composition of trees, buildings, or a battle scene. The surface tends to disappear beneath and behind the landscape. The surface functions as a way to show, make visible, something other than itself. An affect, an event.'
'So it would be futile to ask whether one could find a motivation in this landscape.'
'You would have to take the surface as a forensic surface upon which nothing but the surface itself is being written. You would have to take erosion into consideration. In 1984, the park was officially recognized as a protected landscape for its dendrological, aesthetical, and historical values. To protect a park has many consequences: for example, it implies that erosion – how the land will gradually wear away – is neglected, and human labour will be necessary to maintain it as it is. It is to fix what is mere flux. The question thus becomes: what did nature anticipate before it was designated a protected landscape.'
'OK. So one would have to search the landscape for traces of that anticipation. The question is not only what it wanted to build, but also what it wants to erase. A landscape architect told me that Mount Fuji is slowly crumbling. The authorities are trying to preserve and even reconstruct its famous conical shape. To do so, they are studying old paintings of the mountain. The rock formations they depict become a guideline for the preservation of the mountain. But I wonder if the almost invisible surface structure of those paintings inadvertently moulds Mount Fuji as well, maybe even more so than what they represent. As such, Mount Fuji would not only be shaped by the slopes in Hokusai's drawings, but also inscribed with the texture of the woodblocks used to print them.'
'There are structures, both visible and not, that are an integral part of Citadel Park. In the nineteenth century, a fortress was built. It was conceived as two overlapping grids – two crossed pentagons. This park is not a place of silence and tranquillity, but rather a place where powers are continuously and aggressively trying to reshape it. But those powers themselves have also been altered in the course of history.'
'Winds shape surfaces and surfaces shape winds.'
'Indeed. We should document the surface as an unrelenting chain of events of which the causality cannot be grasped, and strive to reconfigure the narratives that were silenced. We should tell the stories of the surface, circumvent the park it became, and take into account the specks of dust that inconspicuously fly around.'

*F#*1

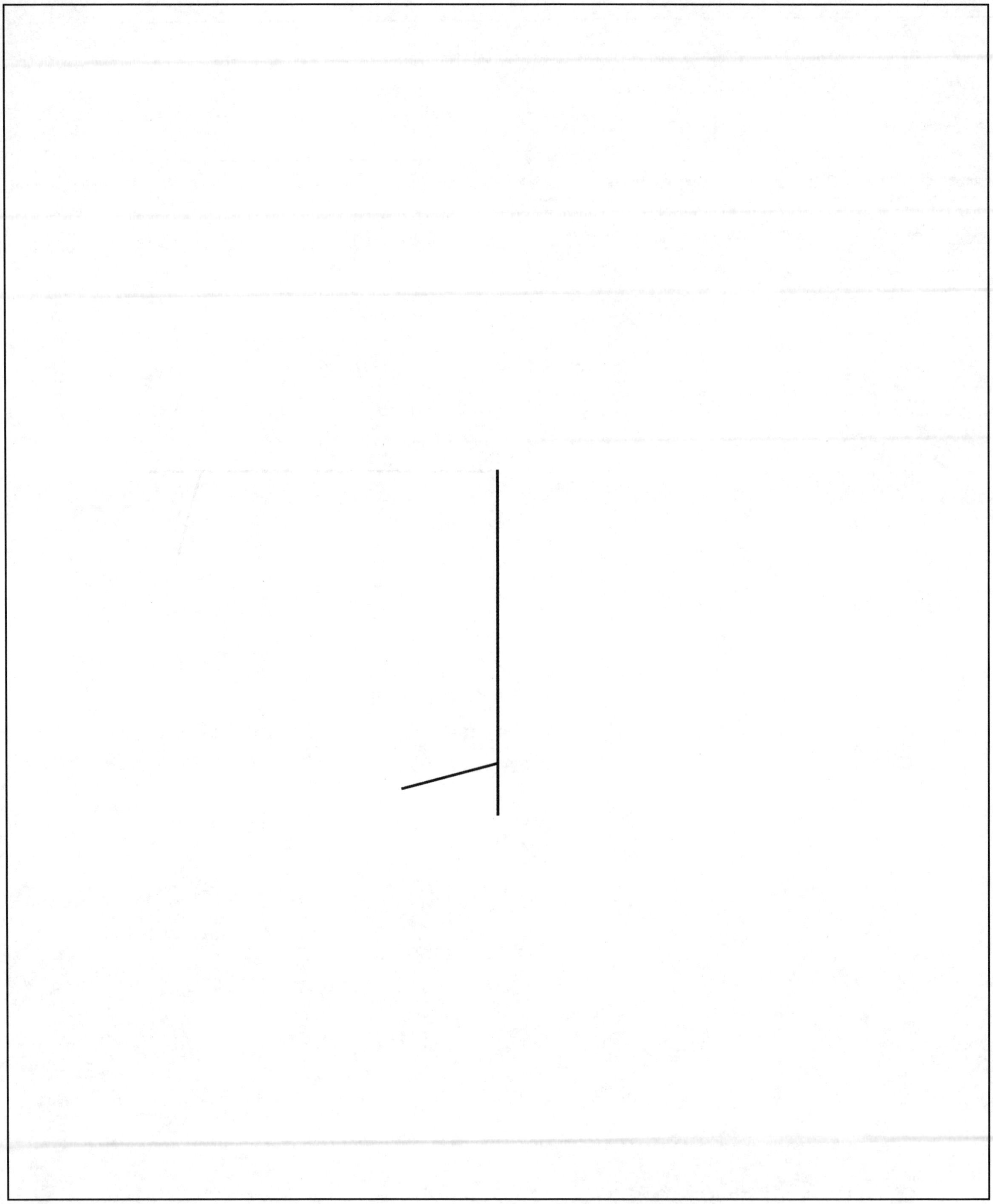

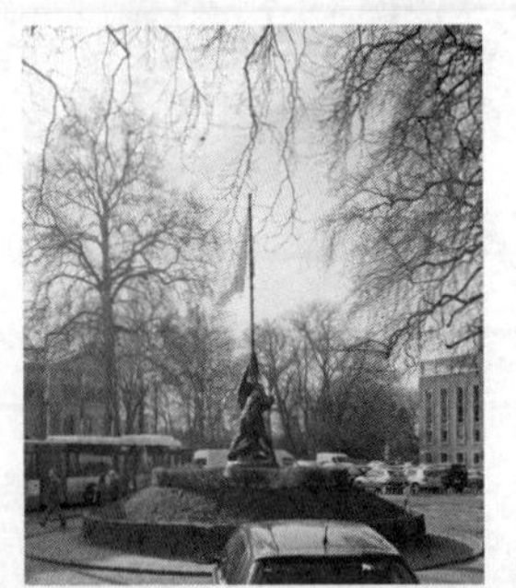

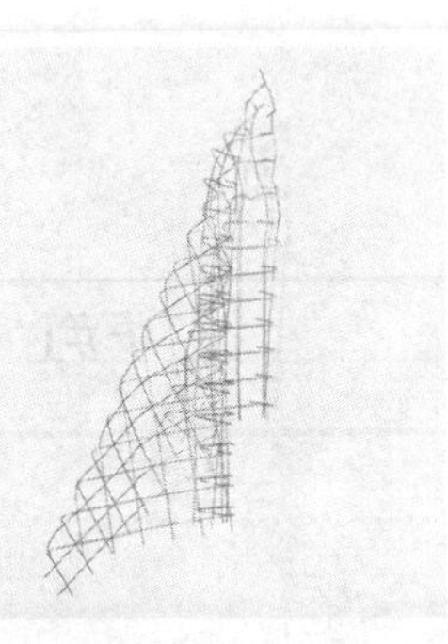

S, 6,48 km/h

[data]

12.02.2017	12:02:50	_44A8205	1/80	8	800	2,4	4,66	E
13.02.2017	#####	#####	#####	#####	#####	#####	#####	#####
14.02.2017	#####	#####	#####	#####	#####	#####	#####	#####
15.02.2017	12:04:09	_44A8280	1/640	8	500	1,8	3,50	S
16.02.2017	#####	#####	#####	#####	#####	#####	#####	#####
17.02.2017	#####	#####	#####	#####	#####	#####	#####	#####
18.02.2017	15:20:13	_44A8446	1/320	8	200	1,7	3,30	SSE
19.02.2017	#####	#####	#####	#####	#####	#####	#####	#####
20.02.2017	#####	#####	#####	#####	#####	#####	#####	#####
21.02.2017	14:05:40	_44A8473	1/250	8	1250	5,1	9,91	WSW
22.02.2017	#####	#####	#####	#####	#####	#####	#####	#####
23.02.2017	#####	#####	#####	#####	#####	#####	#####	#####
24.02.2017	15:52:53	_44A9577	1/200	8	800	1,4	2,72	S
25.02.2017	#####	#####	#####	#####	#####	#####	#####	#####
26.02.2017	#####	#####	#####	#####	#####	#####	#####	#####
27.02.2017	15:23:10	_44A9591	1/125	8	2000	1,4	2,72	NE
28.02.2017	#####	#####	#####	#####	#####	#####	#####	#####
01.03.2017	#####	#####	#####	#####	#####	#####	#####	#####
02.03.2017	11:00:43	_44A0257	1/200	8	640	10,2	19,83	WSW
03.03.2017	#####	#####	#####	#####	#####	#####	#####	#####
04.03.2017	#####	#####	#####	#####	#####	#####	#####	#####
05.03.2017	10:18:47	_44A0320	1/320	8	200	2,5	4,86	ESE
06.03.2017	#####	#####	#####	#####	#####	#####	#####	#####
07.03.2017	#####	#####	#####	#####	#####	#####	#####	#####
08.03.2017	09:27:18	_44A0325	1/200	8	1250	0,6	1,17	SSW
09.03.2017	#####	#####	#####	#####	#####	#####	#####	#####
10.03.2017	#####	#####	#####	#####	#####	#####	#####	#####
11.03.2017	12:12:44	_44A0367	1/250	8	160	0,9	1,75	SSW
12.03.2017	#####	#####	#####	#####	#####	#####	#####	#####
13.03.2017	#####	#####	#####	#####	#####	#####	#####	#####
14.03.2017	11:16:47	_44A0383	1/250	8	400	1,3	2,53	WSW
15.03.2017	#####	#####	#####	#####	#####	#####	#####	#####
16.03.2017	#####	#####	#####	#####	#####	#####	#####	#####
17.03.2017	09:51:38	_44A0427	1/250	8	400	0,7	1,36	WNW
18.03.2017	#####	#####	#####	#####	#####	#####	#####	#####
19.03.2017	#####	#####	#####	#####	#####	#####	#####	#####
20.03.2017	13:07:08	_44A0477	1/200	8	1000	2,8	5,44	W

F#2

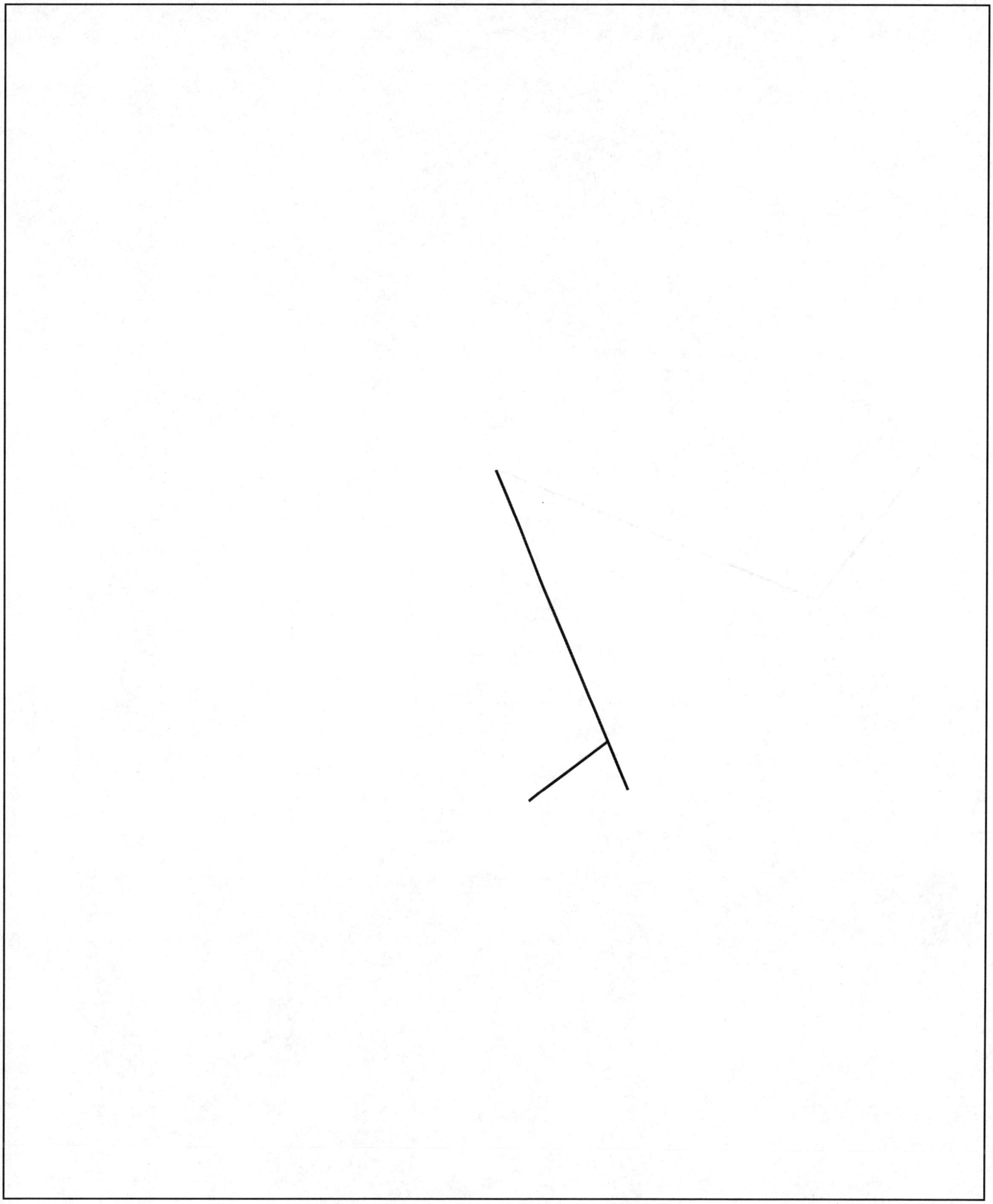

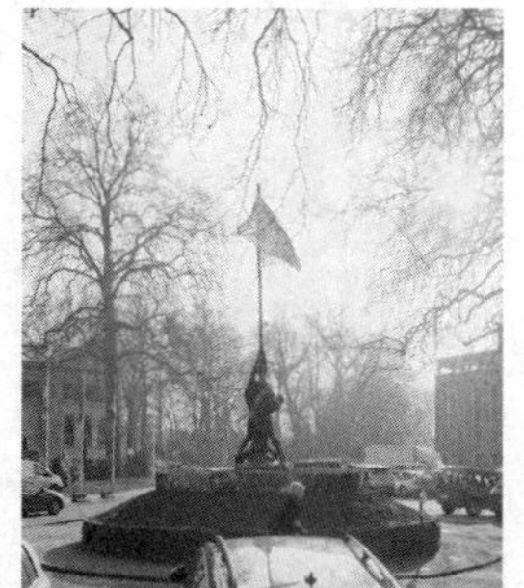

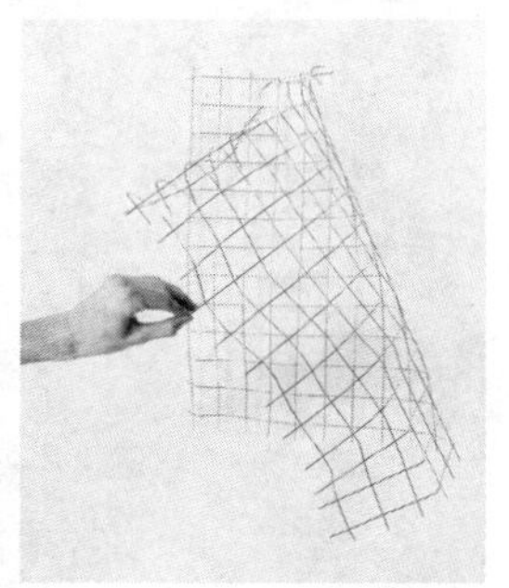

SSE, 6,12 km/h
[a dialogue, every 3d]

The flag is up. We've decided on the point of view from which the photographs will be taken. Both museums are closing and the parking lot empties out.

+3d
A man gets out of a small blue car and walks towards me. He saw me and someone else raising the flag three days ago, asks me what I'm doing.
'We've made a flag. Every third day, someone comes and takes a photograph of it.'
Why every third day?
'Because the flag is up for thirty-nine days, and it had to be divided into equal parts.'
Of course.
He asks me if I have a girlfriend.

+3d
He stays in the car. He waves. Talks to another man who I think was also there the previous session.

+3d
Heavy wind. The sun is setting. The facades of the museums are already lit, and the lights in the park might come on any minute now.
No blue car. But it's late in the evening, everything looks increasingly yellowish, and maybe I was too focused on the flag.

+3d
The parking lot has been sealed off for a bicycle race that finishes in the park. (Two days later, the live broadcast of the race didn't show the flag.) The man says he's from a town, which is thirty minutes from Ghent, that he comes here every day, better than sitting at home alone.

+3d
He says that a French artist (with some kind of Dutch-sounding name) already put up a flag at *De Mastplanters*. He doesn't like contemporary art.
'It's just another flag.'

+3d
Even stronger winds. Bursts of rain. There's a warning telling people to stay out of parks. Branches might fall. The wind's speed is estimated as 8 beaufort. The wind whips the flag. There's a determined jogger in the background.

+3d
He tells me that there's an underground nuclear command bunker in the park. It has supplies, communication channels and can hold up to 50 people. Might be useful one day. Detail: the generator feeding the heating system is outside the safe zone. Maybe they were hoping that the bomb would be dropped during the summer. The Museum of Contemporary Art used it around ten years ago and left lights and moveable walls in there. The fungus eating away at the wood is said to be lethal when inhaled for an extended period of time. If the outside world was radiant and cold, would one think that danger might arise *from within*? As if the park would refuse to tolerate our presence. He says if I got stuck down there, I could still make an exhibition, but the flag would be rather pointless.

+3d
A group of schoolchildren walks from the James Welling exhibition to the one on Francisco Goya. Some of them gaze into the lens, while I read the wind strength from the display, and he watches the flag (I imagine).

+3d
'Can you take the car and move it out of the frame?' I'm not sure if I'm allowed to ask.

+3d
Do both our timings create a system? Like the hands of a clock. A rhythm, perhaps a waltz.

+3d
A breeze.
Not much wind, he says.
Gardeners are planting flowers at the foot of the sculpture.
'No.'

+3d
He asks if it is the last photograph.

[While we were taking down the flag some ten police cars and a tank passed by. There was a speech on immigration given by a politician in a university building nearby. They parked behind the Museum of Fine Arts. Riding backwards, the tank hit a lamppost, which subsequently took on a strange 65° angle. Seven policemen stepped out of their cars and examined the situation. The flag had already been taken down. There was no way for us to document the scene.]

F#3

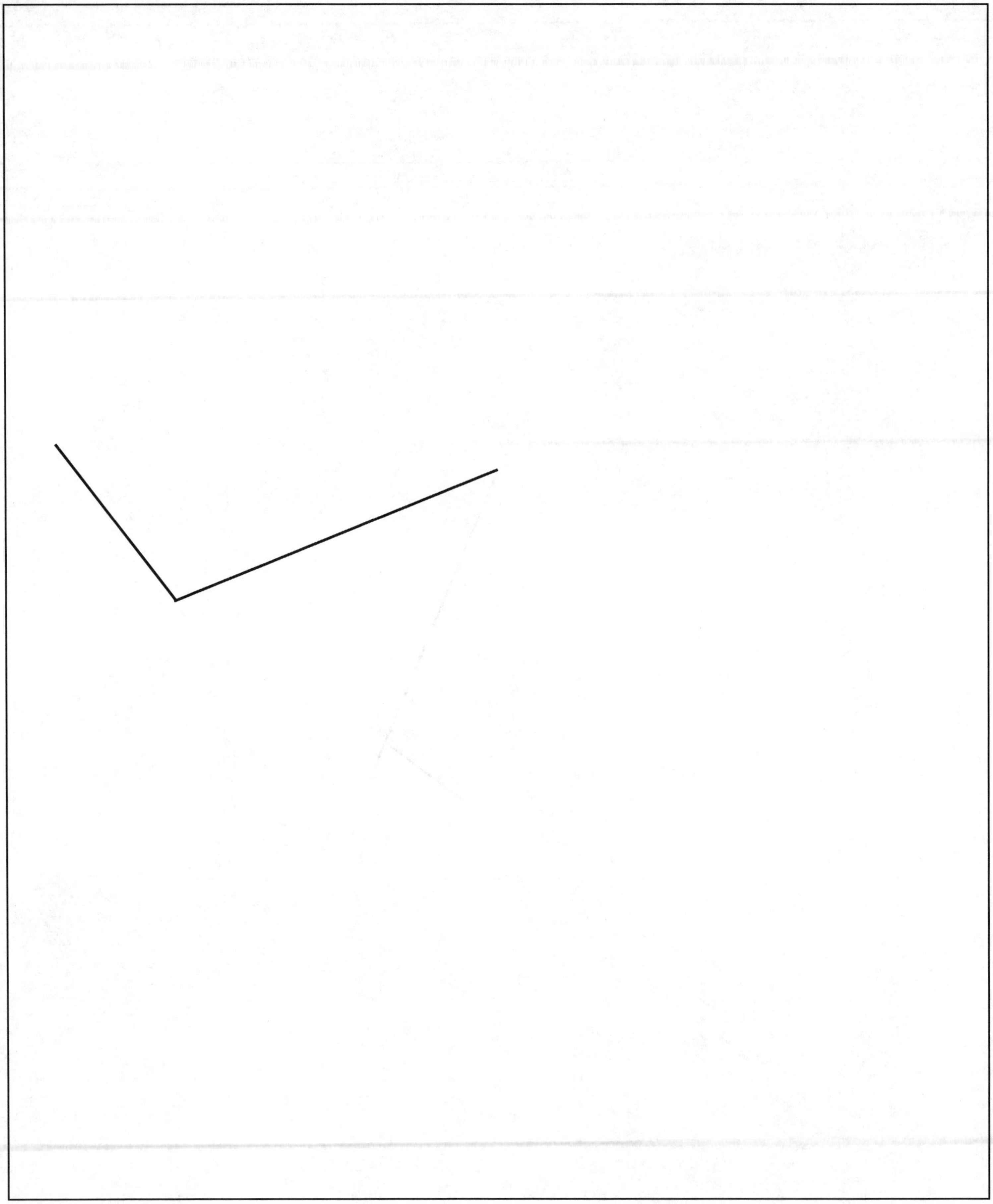

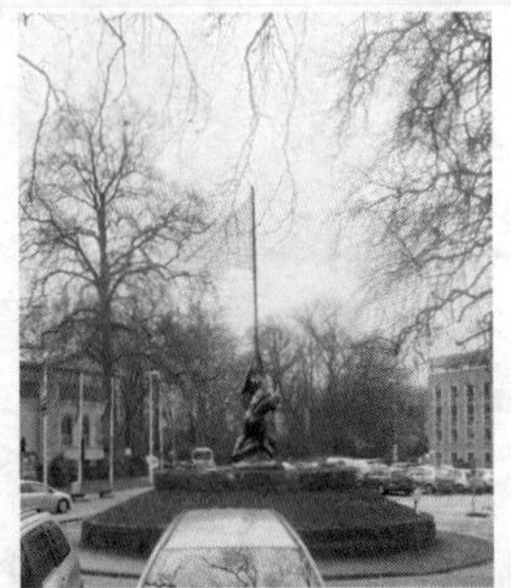

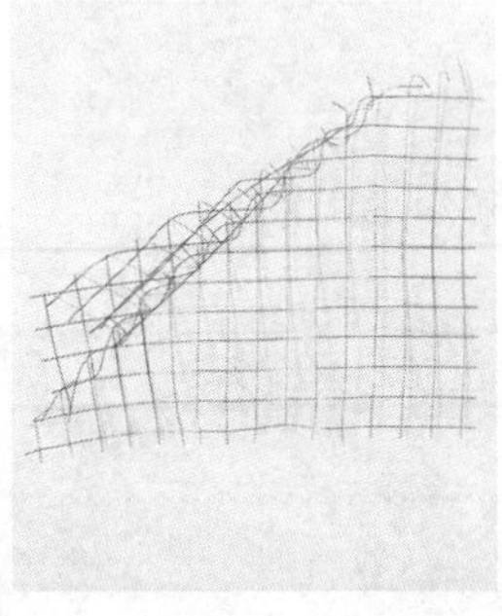

WSW, 18,36 km/h
[grille de lecture]

'Angélique remit le planisphère dans son cabas et sortit des profondeurs du vieux sac une feuille de carton percée d'un certain nombre de trous irrégulièrement disposés. Cet appareil, appelé *grille* en langage cryptographique, devait permettre aux deux amants de correspondre sans danger. Une phrase, écrite au moyen des trous appliqués sur du papier blanc, pouvait être rendue inintelligible par l'adjonction de lettres quelconques, tracées au hasard pour remplir avec ordre les intervalles primitivement ménagés. Seul Velbar saurait retrouver le sens du billet en plaçant sur le texte une grille exactement semblable.'

– Raymond Roussel,
Impressions d'Afrique[1]

F#4

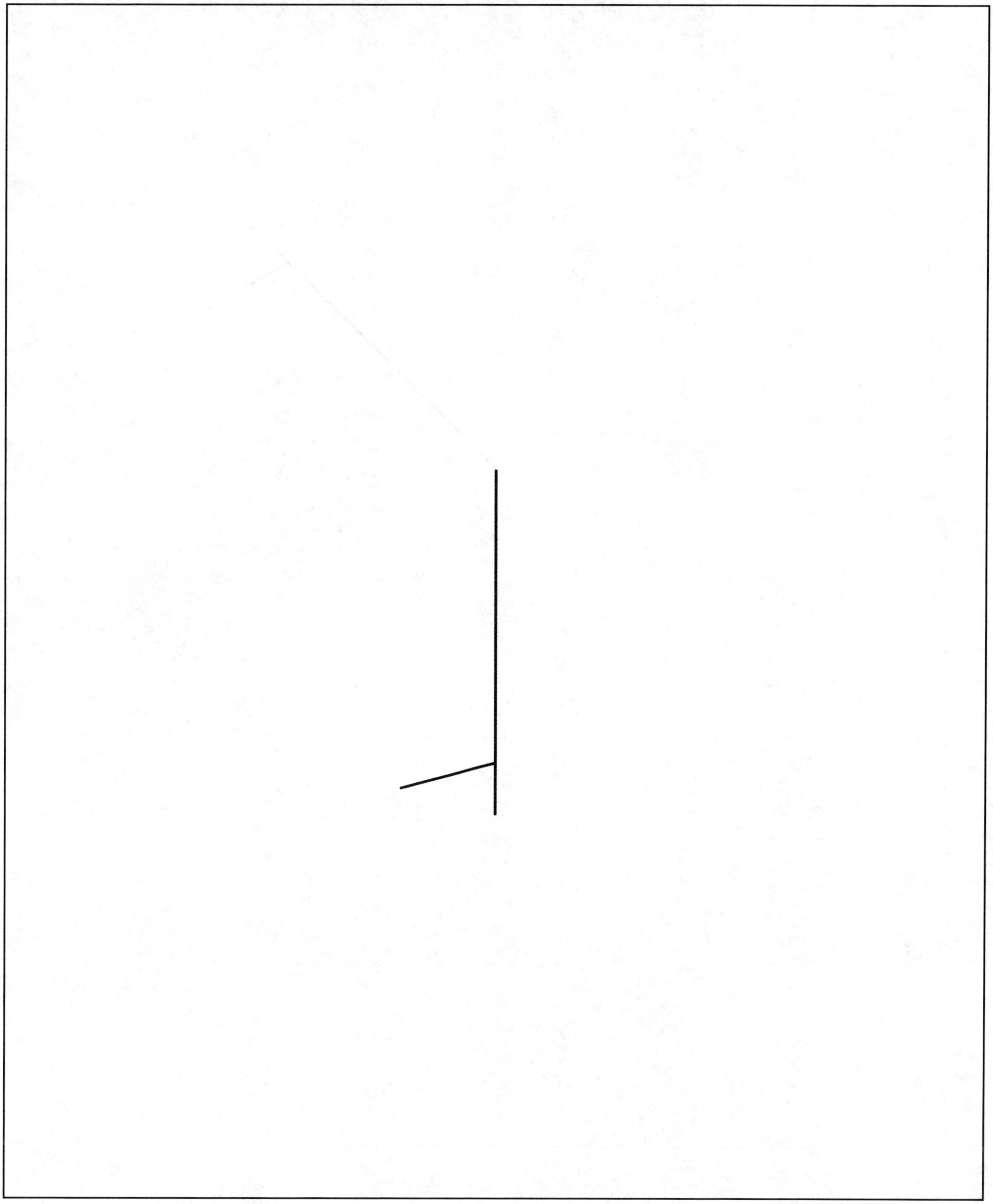

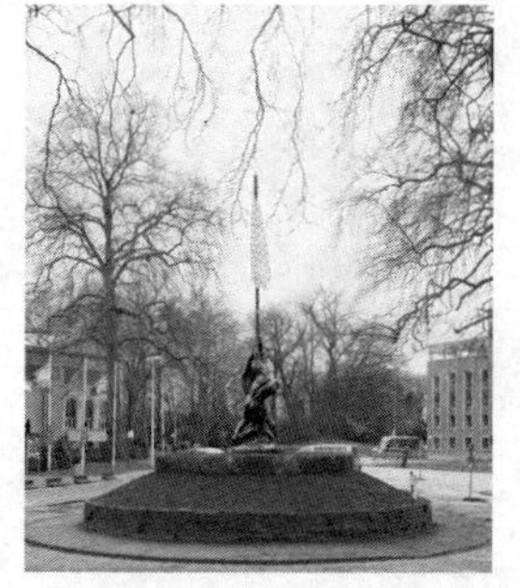

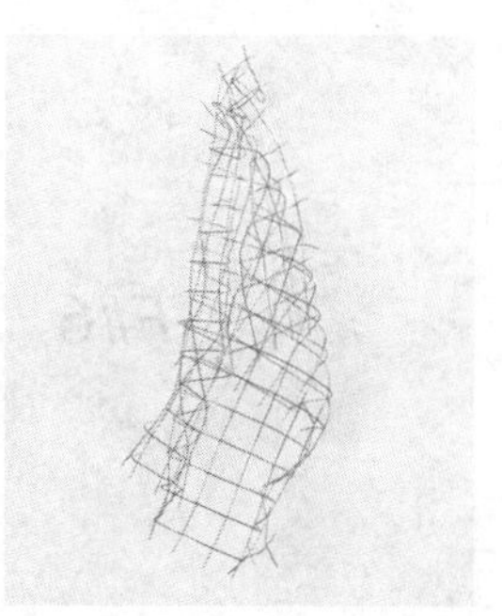

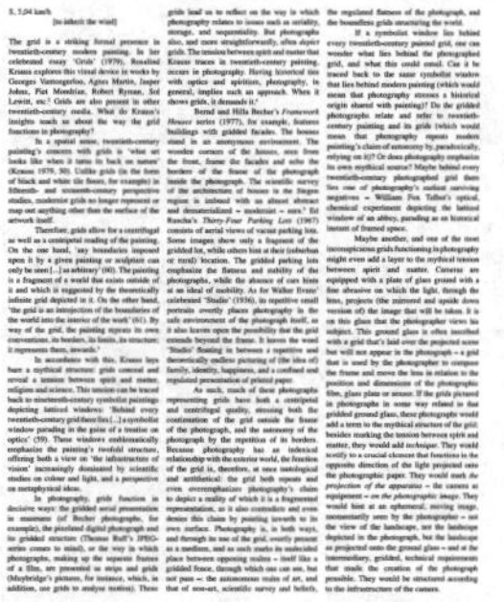

F#5

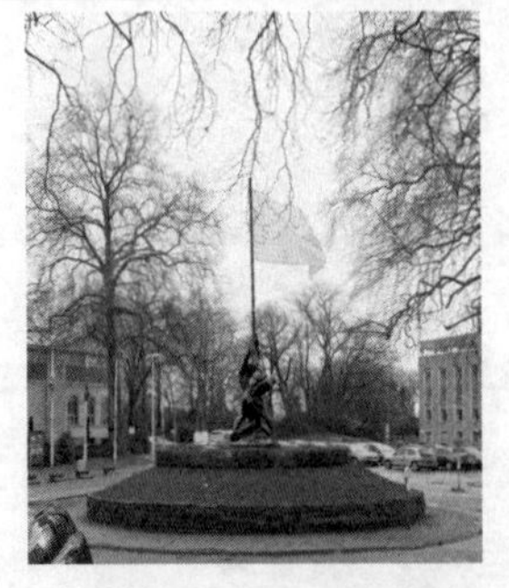

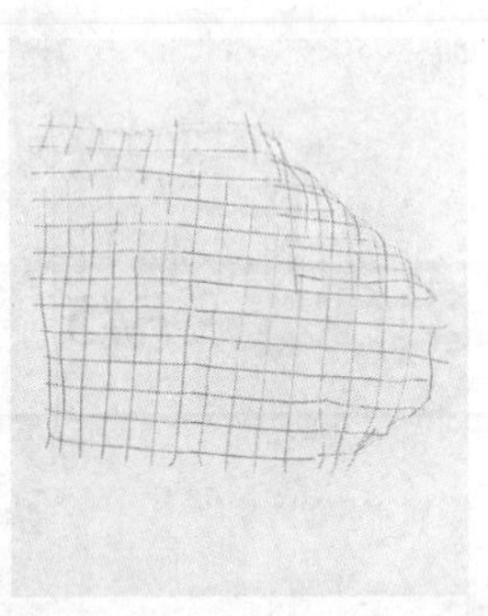

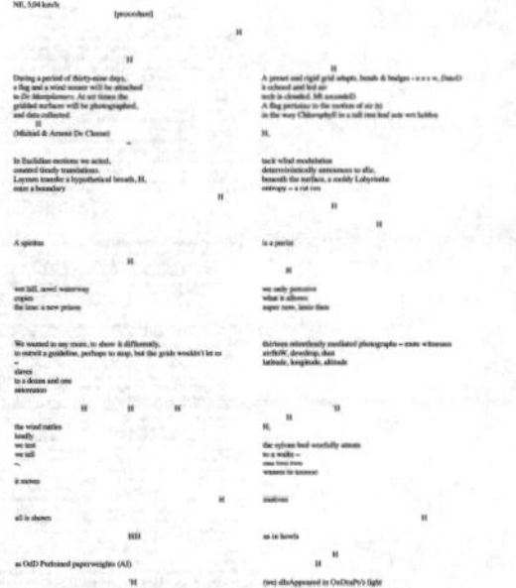

F#6

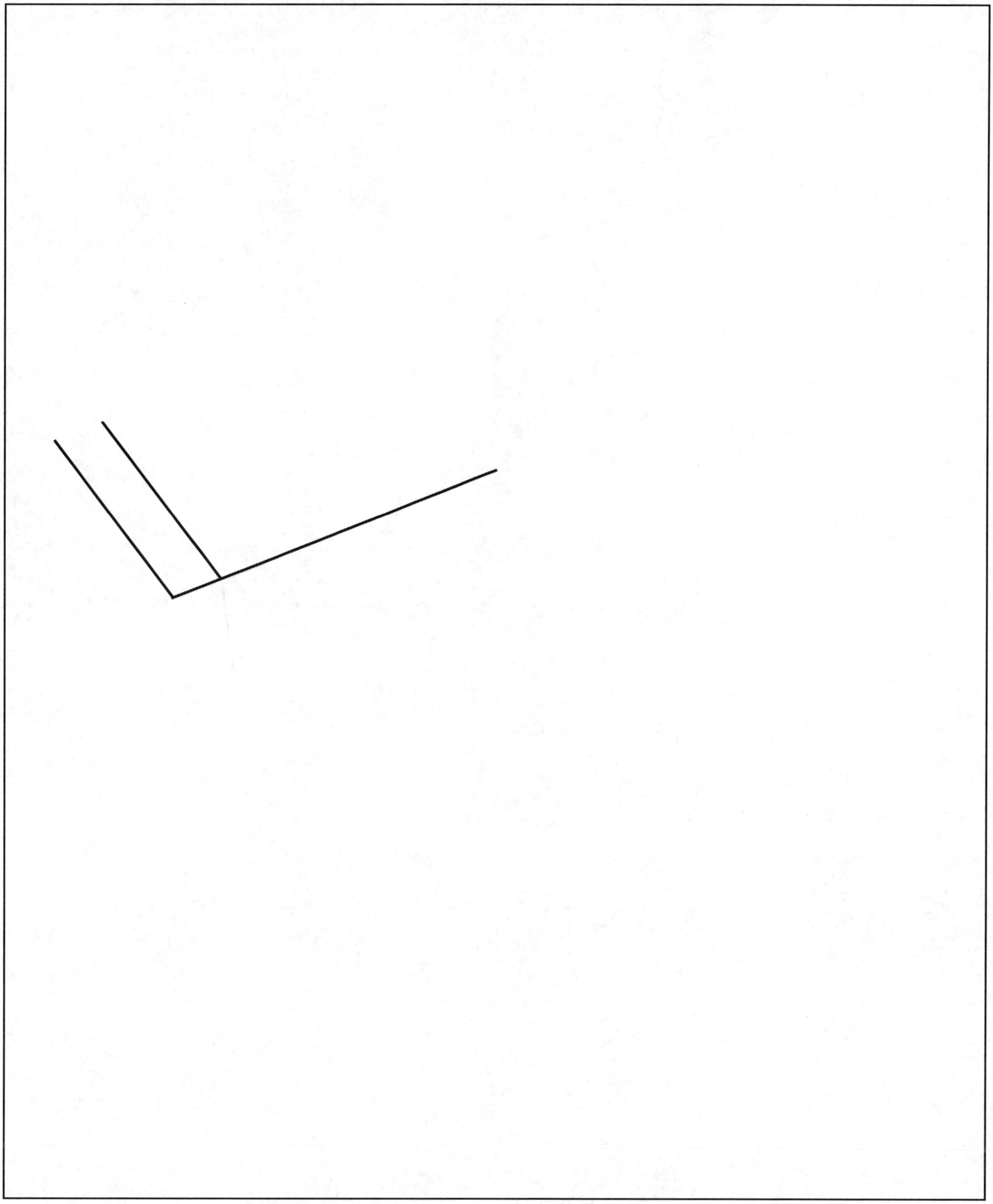

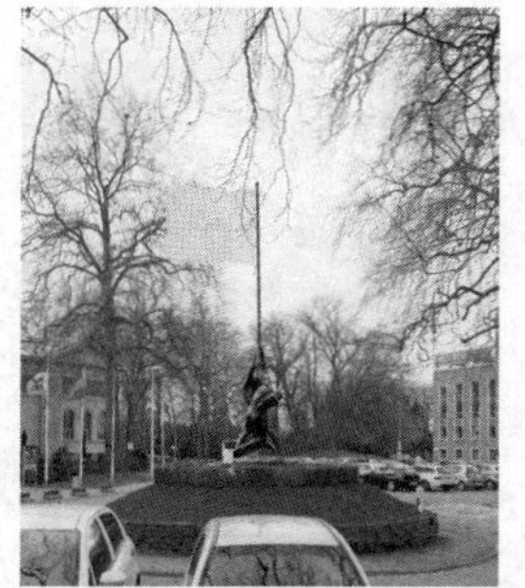

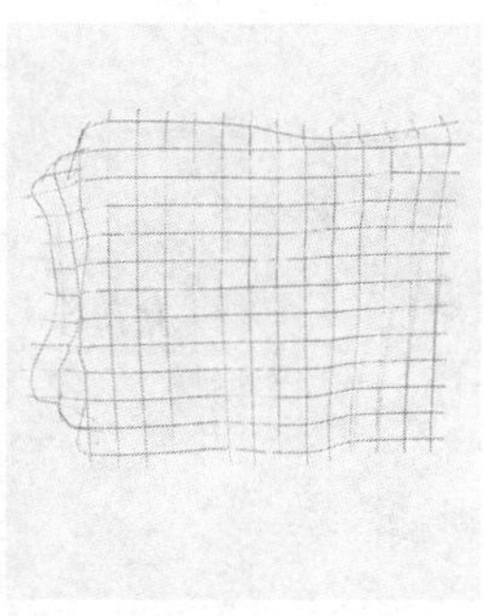

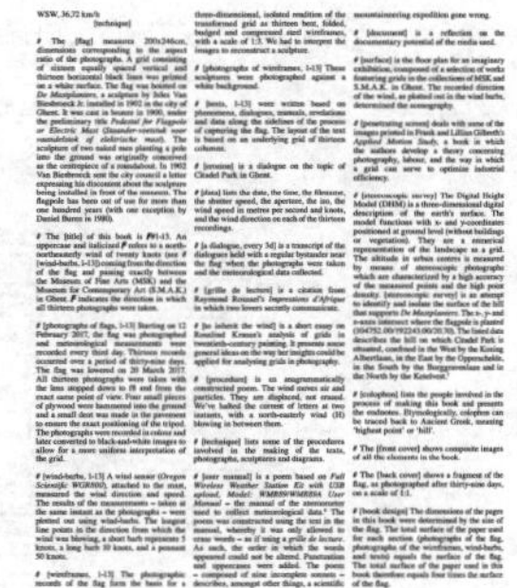

F#7

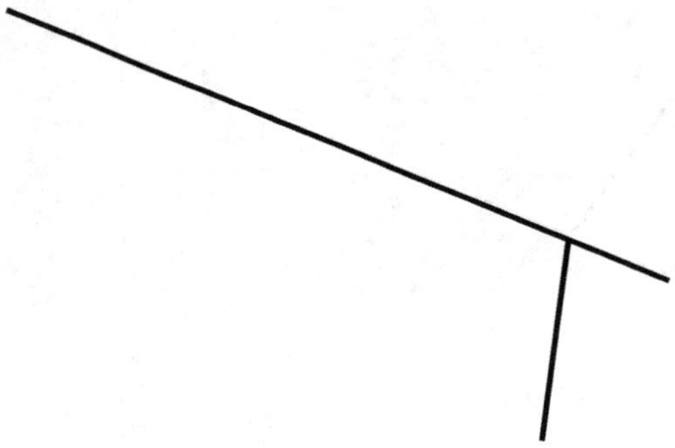

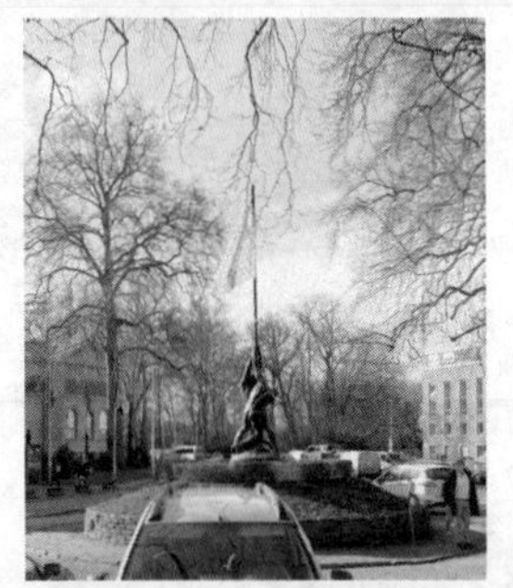

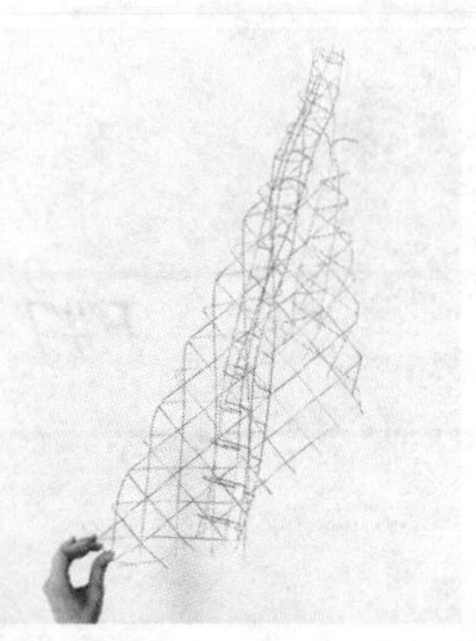

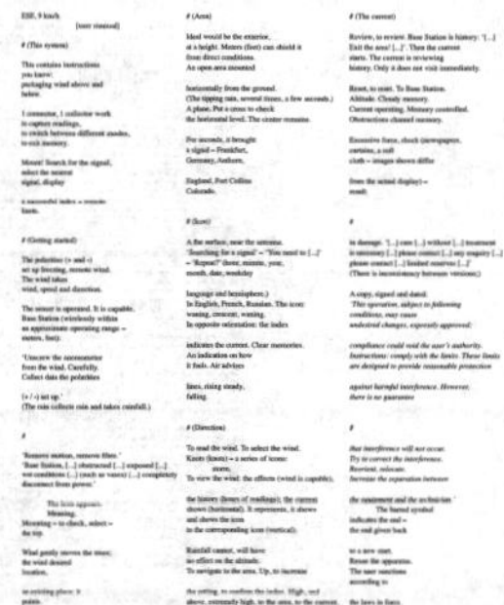

F#8

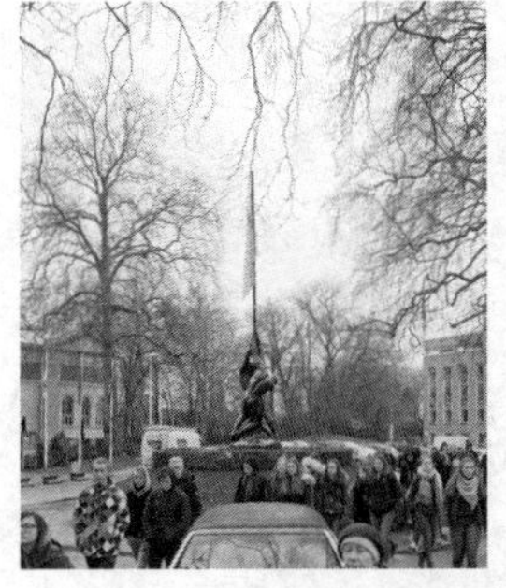

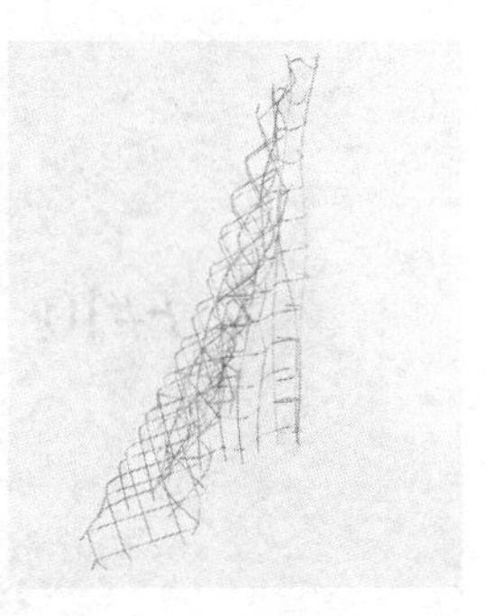

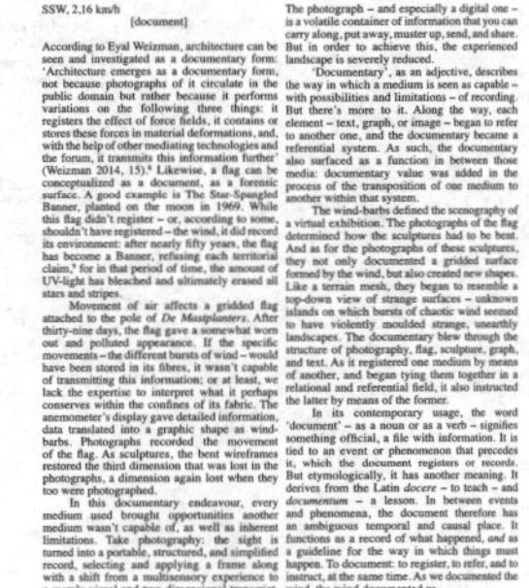

SSW, 2,16 km/h

[document]

According to Eyal Weizman, architecture can be seen and investigated as a documentary form: 'Architecture emerges as a documentary form, not because photographs of it circulate in the public domain but rather because it performs variations on the following three things: it registers the effect of force fields, it contains or stores these forces in material deformations, and, with the help of other mediating technologies and the forum, it transmits this information further' (Weizman 2014, 15).[8] Likewise, a flag can be conceptualized as a document, as a forensic surface. A good example is The Star-Spangled Banner, planted on the moon in 1969. While this flag didn't register – or, according to some, shouldn't have registered – the wind, it did record its environment: after nearly fifty years, the flag has become a Banner, refusing each territorial claim,[9] for in that period of time, the amount of UV-light has bleached and ultimately erased all stars and stripes.

Movement of air affects a gridded flag attached to the pole of *De Mastplanters*. After thirty-nine days, the flag gave a somewhat worn out and polluted appearance. If the specific movements – the different bursts of wind – would have been stored in its fibres, it wasn't capable of transmitting this information; or at least, we lack the expertise to interpret what it perhaps conserves within the confines of its fabric. The anemometer's display gave detailed information, data translated into a graphic shape as wind-barbs. Photographs recorded the movement of the flag. As sculptures, the bent wireframes restored the third dimension that was lost in the photographs, a dimension again lost when they too were photographed.

In this documentary endeavour, every medium used brought opportunities another medium wasn't capable of, as well as inherent limitations. Take photography: the sight is turned into a portable, structured, and simplified record, selecting and applying a frame along with a shift from a multisensory experience to a merely visual and two-dimensional transcript. The photograph – and especially a digital one – is a volatile container of information that you can carry along, put away, muster up, send, and share. But in order to achieve this, the experienced landscape is severely reduced.

'Documentary', as an adjective, describes the way in which a medium is seen as capable – with possibilities and limitations – of recording. But there's more to it. Along the way, each element – text, graph, or image – began to refer to another one, and the documentary became a referential system. As such, the documentary also surfaced as a function in between those media: documentary value was added in the process of the transposition of one medium to another within that system.

The wind-barbs defined the scenography of a virtual exhibition. The photographs of the flag determined how the sculptures had to be bent. And as for the photographs of these sculptures, they not only documented a gridded surface formed by the wind, but also created new shapes. Like a terrain mesh, they began to resemble a top-down view of strange surfaces – unknown islands on which bursts of chaotic wind seemed to have violently moulded strange, unearthly landscapes. The documentary blew through the structure of photography, flag, sculpture, graph, and text. As it registered one medium by means of another, and began tying them together in a relational and referential field, it also instructed the latter by means of the former.

In its contemporary usage, the word 'document' – as a noun or as a verb – signifies something official, a file with information. It is tied to an event or phenomenon that precedes it, which the document registers or records. But etymologically, it has another meaning. It derives from the Latin *docere* – to teach – and *documentum* – a lesson. In between events and phenomena, the document therefore has an ambiguous temporal and causal place. It functions as a record of what happened, *and* as a guideline for the way in which things must happen. To document: to register, to refer, and to instruct, at the same time. As we documented the wind, the wind documented us.

F#9

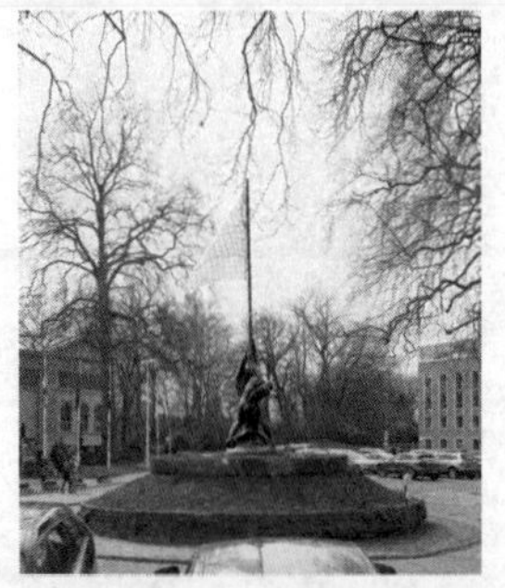

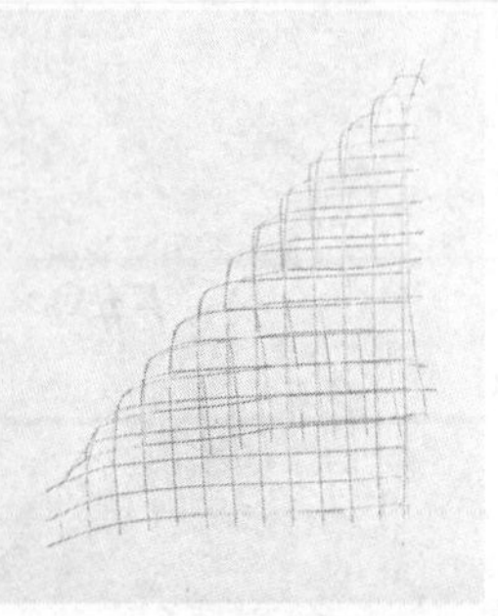

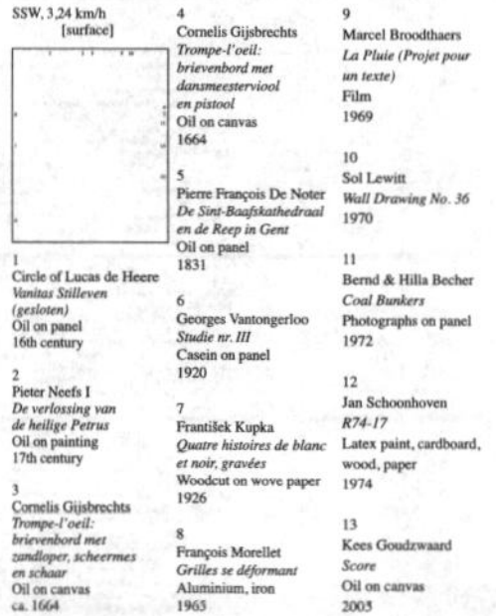

SSW, 3,24 km/h
[surface]

1
Circle of Lucas de Heere
Vanitas Stilleven (gesloten)
Oil on panel
16th century

2
Pieter Neefs I
De verlossing van de heilige Petrus
Oil on painting
17th century

3
Cornelis Gijsbrechts
Trompe-l'oeil: brievenbord met zandloper, scheermes en schaar
Oil on canvas
ca. 1664

4
Cornelis Gijsbrechts
Trompe-l'oeil: brievenbord met dansmeesterviool en pistool
Oil on canvas
1664

5
Pierre François De Noter
De Sint-Baafskathedraal en de Reep in Gent
Oil on panel
1831

6
Georges Vantongerloo
Studie nr. III
Casein on panel
1920

7
František Kupka
Quatre histoires de blanc et noir, gravées
Woodcut on wove paper
1926

8
François Morellet
Grilles se déformant
Aluminium, iron
1965

9
Marcel Broodthaers
La Pluie (Projet pour un texte)
Film
1969

10
Sol Lewitt
Wall Drawing No. 36
1970

11
Bernd & Hilla Becher
Coal Bunkers
Photographs on panel
1972

12
Jan Schoonhoven
R74-17
Latex paint, cardboard, wood, paper
1974

13
Kees Goudzwaard
Score
Oil on canvas
2005

F#10

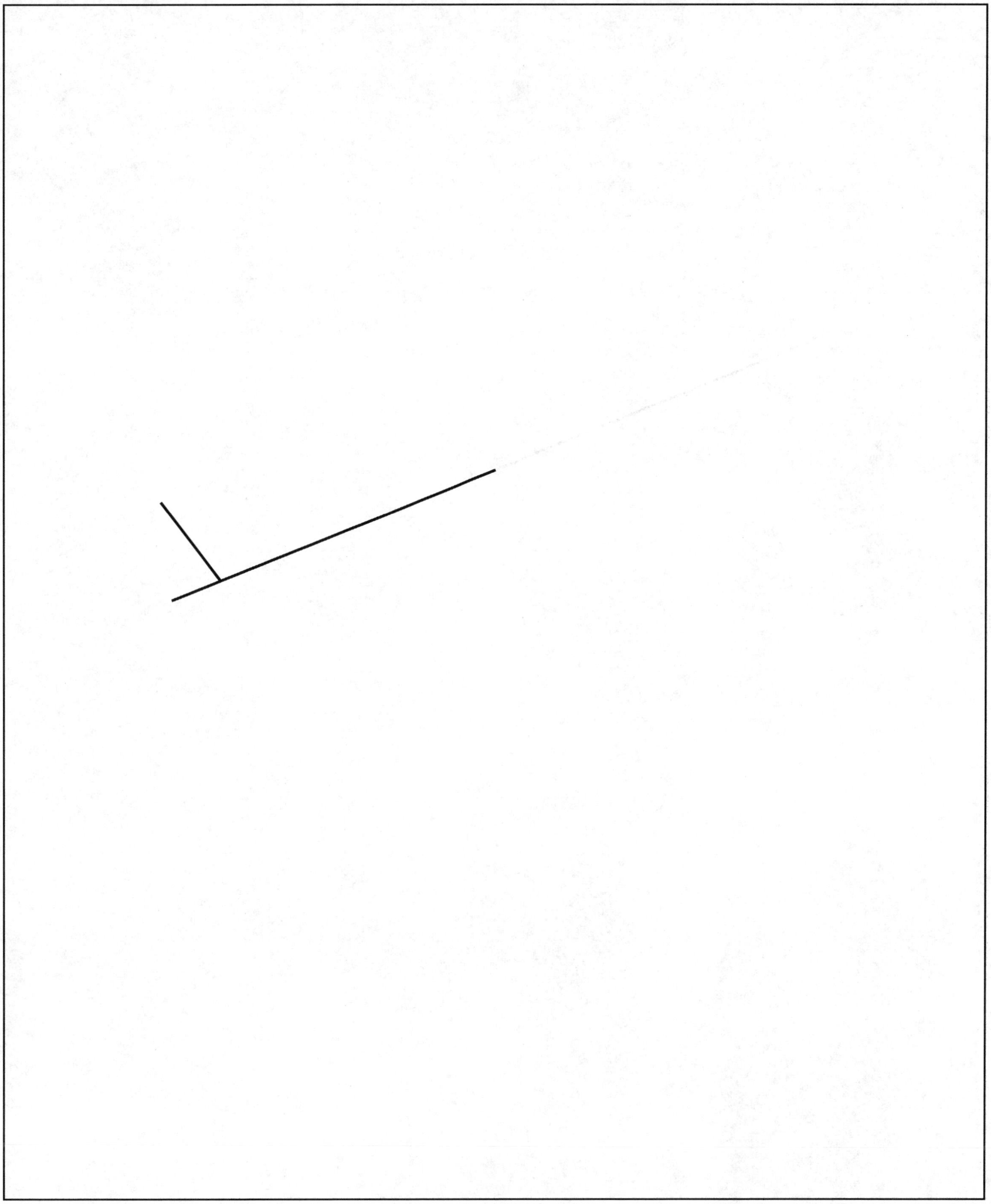

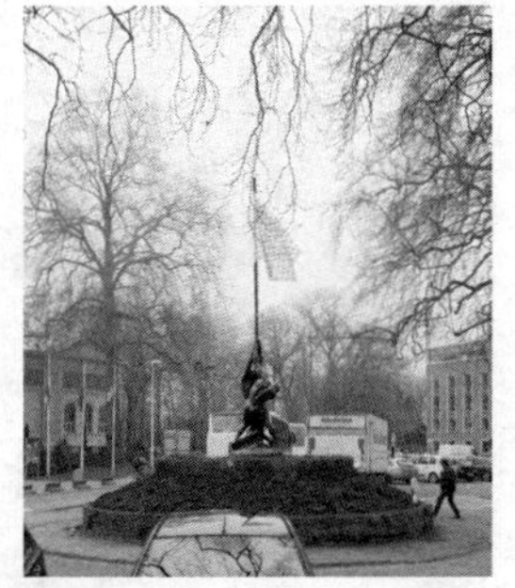

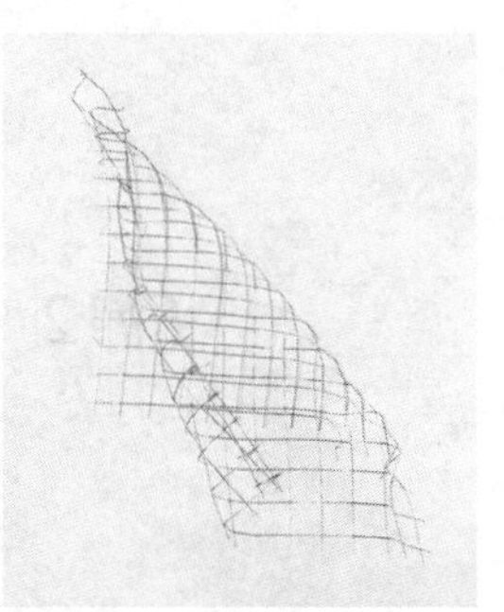

WSW, 4,68 km/h

[penetrating screen]

Miss Hortense Stollnitz became International Amateur Champion Typist in 1916, 'equalling the professional record of 137 words per minute net, and exceeding all previous records with 147 words per minute gross' (Gilbreth & Gilbreth 1917, 36–37). In the same year, she had already won that contest a first time, and the International Novice Champion Typewriter Contest in New York the year before.[10]

Miss Stollnitz can be seen in *fig. 5* in Frank and Lillian Gilbreth's *Applied Motion Study* (1917).[11] A vertical strip of small photographs shows Miss Stollnitz changing the paper of the typewriter she is working on, with only minimal differences between the various shots: while the paper she has finished typing is being rolled out of the typewriter (and seems to fly into the room), she is already taking the next blank paper with her other hand – thereby briefly concealing a clock on the wall behind her. On the same page, *fig. 4* shows Miss Anna Gold, who is also typing, while a second woman is on the other side of the typewriter (and again a clock is between them). Although her face is blurred, her typing fingers are sharp. Miss Gold, the caption states, 'afterwards became National Amateur Champion Typist by winning the contest at Chicago, 1916' (Gilbreth & Gilbreth 1917, 36–37).[12]

'Afterwards': both Miss Gold and Miss Stollnitz were trained by the Gilbreths, who had developed a specific method for improving efficiency in the working environment. In their study, they describe 'the simple photographic process which enables one to record in detail the motions of a handicraft, or a manufacture, so as to bring them by criticism and experiment to their utmost economy of energy and time' (George Iles, in Gilbreth & Gilbreth 1917, ix). To arrive at this 'permanent and practical waste elimination' the Gilbreths attached a small electric light to the moving body part of the worker. As such, this movement created a line of light, which was captured on a photographic plate that was exposed during the time the subject performed the work. This line was called a 'cyclegraph'. To be effective and instructional, the continuous line was broken up: 'the time element was eventually obtained by placing an interrupter in the current, that transformed the white line of the cyclegraph into a series or line of dots and dashes. This made of the cyclegraph a chronocyclegraph' (Gilbreth & Gilbreth 1917, 83–84).

Fig. 7 is a similar strip of photographs displaying a sequence of motions. This 'Automatic Micromotion Study with vertical penetrating screen in the plane of the motions' features a man in a white shirt and black tie. Over his left shoulder: a clock. Each of the eight vertically stacked photographs shows the same composition of the same man in the same room with a white grid superimposed on every image. The chronocyclegraphs rely on what the Gilbreths called the penetrating screen: a sheet of black paper with a white grid on it. That grid is crucial. They superimposed this grid on the factory worker by making a double exposure on the same piece of film. This procedure enabled them to record and analyse the motions of a worker performing a specific task. Motion reveals itself in relation to the rigid grid. The Gilbreths subsequently turned these chronocyclegraphs into three-dimensional, bent wires – sculptures – that functioned as a manual for that specific movement. Manual labour becomes grid becomes manual becomes labour. In *fig. 7*, the penetrating screen indifferently covers the background, the clock, the man's hands, shirt, tie, and face. Beneath the grid, the anonymous worker is folding a white cotton cloth.

In *fig. 6*, the Gilbreths zoom in on Miss Stollnitz's hands ('while writing at her fastest speed'). Only the keyboard and five fingers are visible. The text mentions that these pictures were taken at the rate of 115 exposures per second. With a special apparatus, they 'can be studied as continuous motion at the rate of eight per second' (Gilbreth & Gilbreth 1917, 36–37). The advanced photographing technique used by the Gilbreths has the potential to show more than the amount of words the International Amateur Champion can type in one minute. It reveals the motion in between words. Nonetheless, despite the photographic accuracy, it remains unclear what text Miss Stollnitz was typing. When Miss Stollnitz entered the International Championship Typewriting Contest for professionals in 1921, she typed more words than all the other contestants. However, she ranked seventh because of the number of errors she had made (Hoof 2011, 267).[13]

F#11

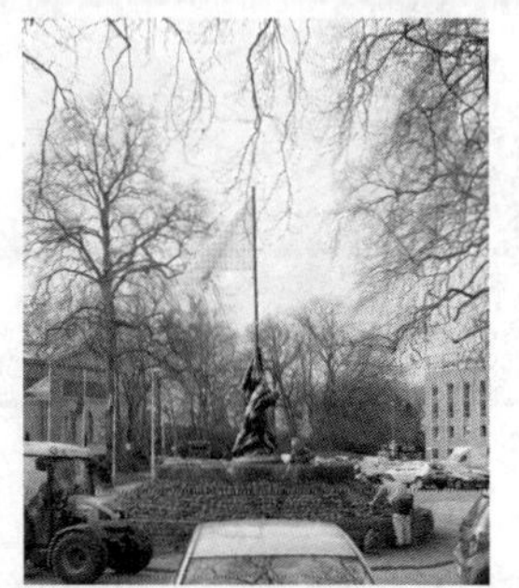

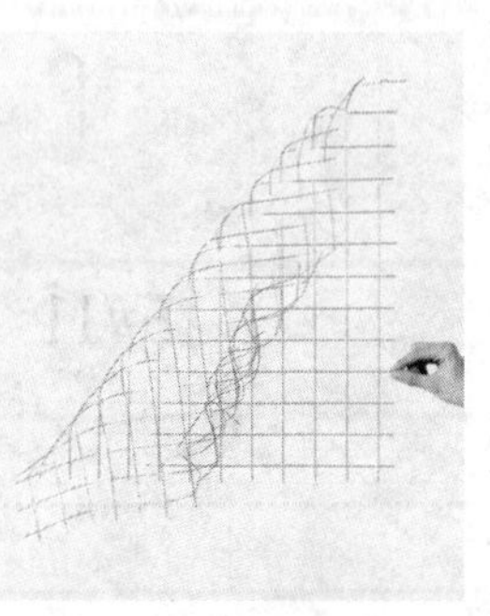

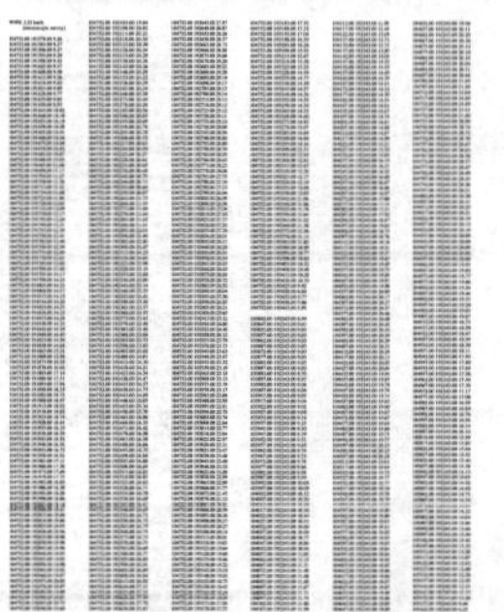

F#12

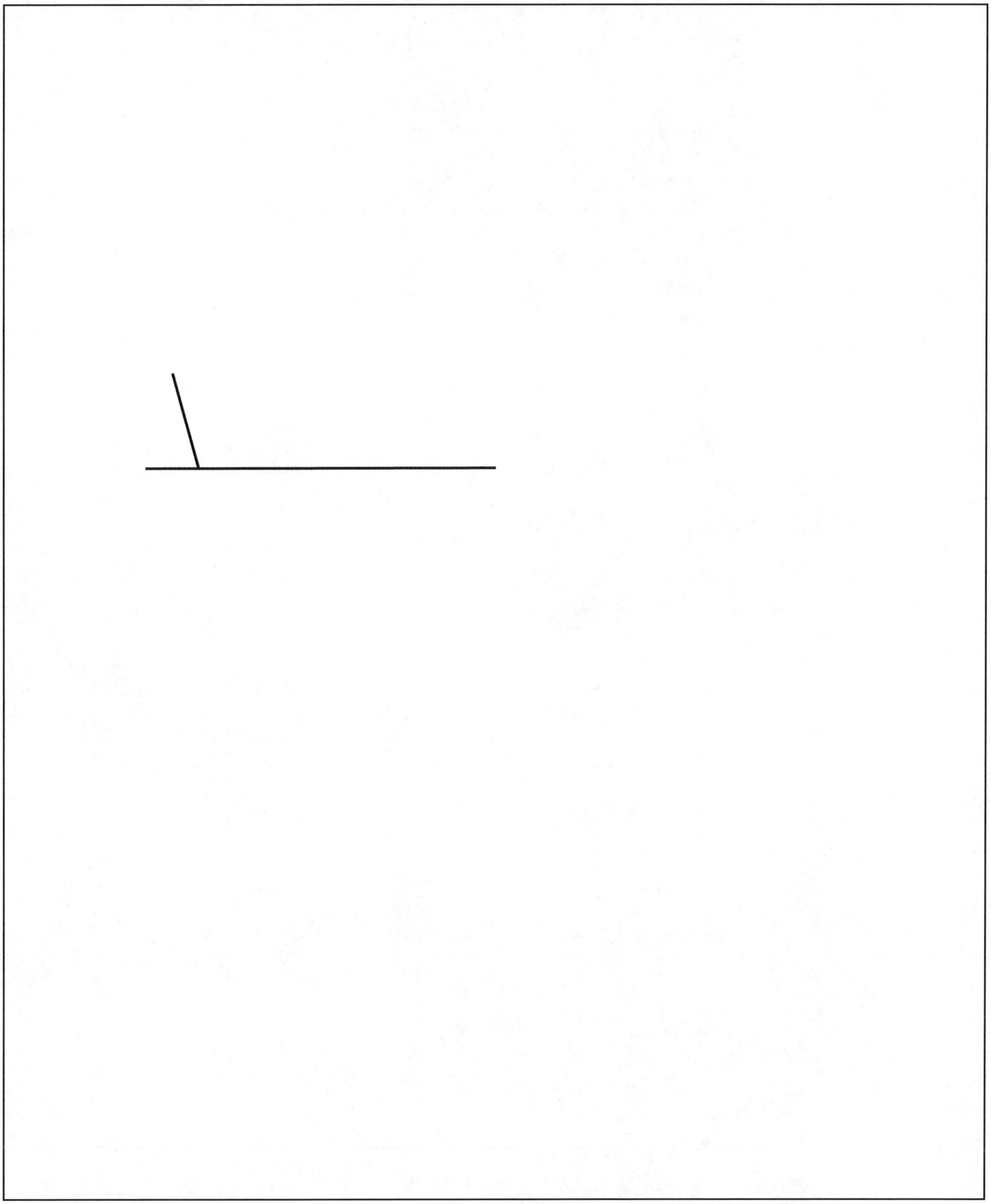

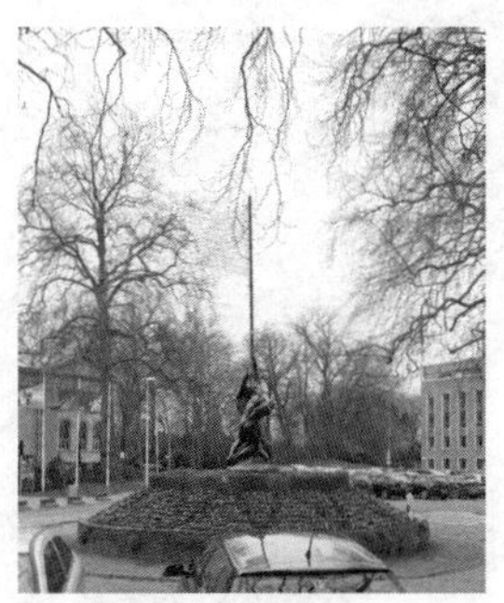

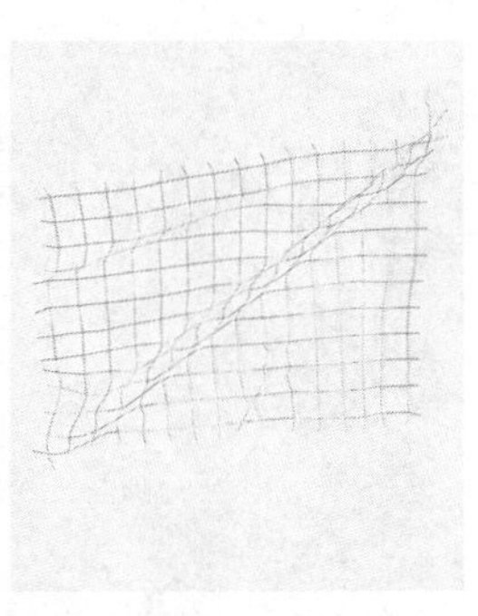

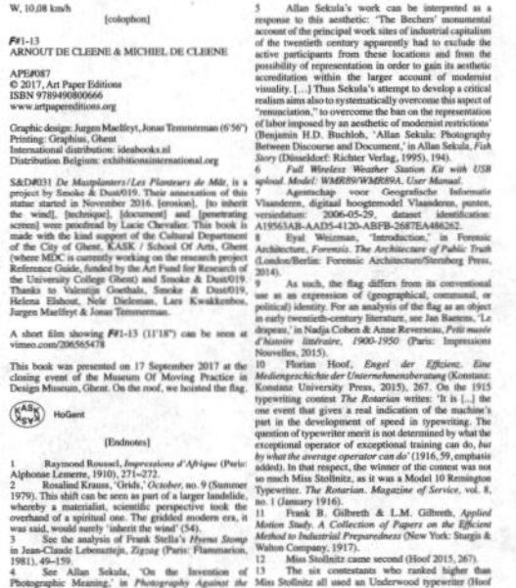

W, 10,08 km/h

[colophon]

F#1-13
ARNOUT DE CLEENE & MICHIEL DE CLEENE

APE#087
© 2017, Art Paper Editions
ISBN 9789490800666
www.artpapereditions.org

Graphic design: Jurgen Maelfeyt, Jonas Temmerman (6'56")
Printing: Graphius, Ghent
International distribution: ideabooks.nl
Distribution Belgium: exhibitionsinternational.org

S&D#031 *De Mastplanters / Les Planteurs de Mât*, is a project by Smoke & Dust/019. Their annexation of this statue started in November 2016. [erosion], [to inherit the wind], [technique], [document] and [penetrating screen] were proofread by Lucie Chevalier. This book is made with the kind support of the Cultural Department of the City of Ghent, KASK / School Of Arts, Ghent (where MDC is currently working on the research project Reference Guide, funded by the Art Fund for Research of the University College Ghent) and Smoke & Dust/019. Thanks to Valentijn Goethals, Smoke & Dust/019, Helena Elshout, Nele Dieleman, Lars Kwakkenbos, Jurgen Maelfeyt & Jonas Temmerman.

A short film showing **F**#1-13 (11'18") can be seen at vimeo.com/206565478

This book was presented on 17 September 2017 at the closing event of the Museum Of Moving Practice in Design Museum, Ghent. On the *roof*, we hoisted the flag.

KASK HoGent

[Endnotes]

1 Raymond Roussel, *Impressions d'Afrique* (Paris: Alphonse Lemerre, 1910), 271–272.

2 Rosalind Krauss, 'Grids,' *October*, no. 9 (Summer 1979). This shift can be seen as part of a larger landslide, whereby a materialist, scientific perspective took the overhand of a spiritual one. The gridded modern era, it was said, would surely 'inherit the wind' (54).

3 See the analysis of Frank Stella's *Hyena Stomp* in Jean-Claude Lebensztejn, *Zigzag* (Paris: Flammarion, 1981), 49–159.

4 See Allan Sekula, 'On the Invention of Photographic Meaning,' in *Photography Against the Grain* (London: MACK, 2016).

5 Allan Sekula's work can be interpreted as a response to this aesthetic: 'The Bechers' monumental account of the principal work sites of industrial capitalism of the twentieth century apparently had to exclude the active participants from these locations and from the possibility of representation in order to gain its aesthetic accreditation within the larger account of modernist visuality. [...] Thus Sekula's attempt to develop a critical realism aims also to systematically overcome this aspect of "renunciation," to overcome the ban on the representation of labor imposed by an aesthetic of modernist restrictions' (Benjamin H.D. Buchloh, 'Allan Sekula: Photography Between Discourse and Document,' in Allan Sekula, *Fish Story* (Düsseldorf: Richter Verlag, 1995), 194).

6 *Full Wireless Weather Station Kit with USB upload. Model: WMR89/WMR89A. User Manual.*

7 Agentschap voor Geografische Informatie Vlaanderen, digitaal hoogtemodel Vlaanderen, punten, versiedatum: 2006-05-29, dataset identification: A19563AB-AAD5-4120-ABFB-2687EA486262.

8 Eyal Weizman, 'Introduction,' in Forensic Architecture, *Forensis. The Architecture of Public Truth* (London/Berlin: Forensic Architecture/Sternberg Press, 2014).

9 As such, the flag differs from its conventional use as an expression of (geographical, communal, or political) identity. For an analysis of the flag as an object in early twentieth-century literature, see Jan Baetens, 'Le drapeau,' in Nadja Cohen & Anne Reverseau, *Petit musée d'histoire littéraire, 1900-1950* (Paris: Impressions Nouvelles, 2015).

10 Florian Hoof, *Engel der Effizienz. Eine Mediengeschichte der Unternehmensberatung* (Konstanz: Konstanz University Press, 2015), 267. On the 1915 typewriting contest *The Rotarian* writes: 'It is [...] the one event that gives a real indication of the machine's part in the development of speed in typewriting. The question of typewriter merit is not determined by what the exceptional operator of exceptional training can do, *but by what the average operator can do*' (1916, 59, emphasis added). In that respect, the winner of the contest was not so much Miss Stollnitz, as it was a Model 10 Remington Typewriter. *The Rotarian. Magazine of Service*, vol. 8, no. 1 (January 1916).

11 Frank B. Gilbreth & L.M. Gilbreth, *Applied Motion Study. A Collection of Papers on the Efficient Method to Industrial Preparedness* (New York: Sturgis & Walton Company, 1917).

12 Miss Stollnitz came second (Hoof 2015, 267).

13 The six contestants who ranked higher than Miss Stollnitz all used an Underwood typewriter (Hoof 2015, 267).

F#13

E, 8,64 km/h

[erosion]

Citadel Park lies between the Scheldt and the Lys. It rises from its surroundings. In the park, there are two museums, an animal shelter, a congress hall, man-made caves, ponds, and a velodrome. The wind blows between the trees. Dust is lifted from the soil and flies out of the park.

'Would it be possible to ascribe a kind of prophetic gift or intention to the forces that shaped this landscape?'
'You mean: did the two rivers want to carve out a hill at the edge of what would become the heart of the city?'
'Did they anticipate an elevation on which a park, statues, and museums would be built? As if a physical height might strengthen the symbolic value of the elements that would be displayed on it.'
'Could be, but maybe it's not about the landscape. When depicted in a painting or a photograph, landscapes tend to function as a combination of elements that are outlined against a background. There is a surface – hills, a stormy sea – that supports a composition of trees, buildings, or a battle scene. The surface tends to disappear beneath and behind the landscape. The surface functions as a way to show, make visible, something other than itself. An affect, an event.'
'So it would be futile to ask whether one could find a motivation in this landscape.'
'You would have to take the surface as a forensic surface upon which nothing but the surface itself is being written. You would have to take erosion into consideration. In 1984, the park was officially recognized as a protected landscape for its dendrological, aesthetical, and historical values. To protect a park has many consequences: for example, it implies that erosion – how the land will gradually wear away – is neglected, and human labour will be necessary to maintain it as it is. It is to fix what is mere flux. The question thus becomes: what did nature anticipate before it was designated a protected landscape.'
'OK. So one would have to search the landscape for traces of that anticipation. The question is not only what it wanted to build, but also what it wants to erase. A landscape architect told me that Mount Fuji is slowly crumbling. The authorities are trying to preserve and even reconstruct its famous conical shape. To do so, they are studying old paintings of the mountain. The rock formations they depict become a guideline for the preservation of the mountain. But I wonder if the almost invisible surface structure of those paintings inadvertently moulds Mount Fuji as well, maybe even more so than what they represent. As such, Mount Fuji would not only be shaped by the slopes in Hokusai's drawings, but also inscribed with the texture of the woodblocks used to print them.'
'There are structures, both visible and not, that are an integral part of Citadel Park. In the nineteenth century, a fortress was built. It was conceived as two overlapping grids – two crossed pentagons. This park is not a place of silence and tranquillity, but rather a place where powers are continuously and aggressively trying to reshape it. But those powers themselves have also been altered in the course of history.'
'Winds shape surfaces and surfaces shape winds.'
'Indeed. We should document the surface as an unrelenting chain of events of which the causality cannot be grasped, and strive to reconfigure the narratives that were silenced. We should tell the stories of the surface, circumvent the park it became, and take into account the specks of dust that inconspicuously fly around.'

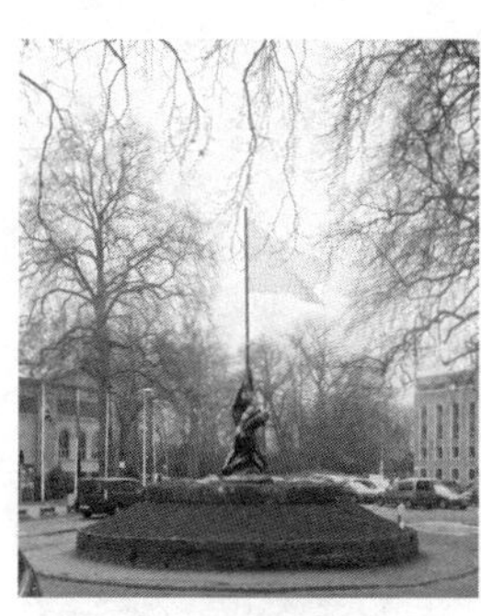

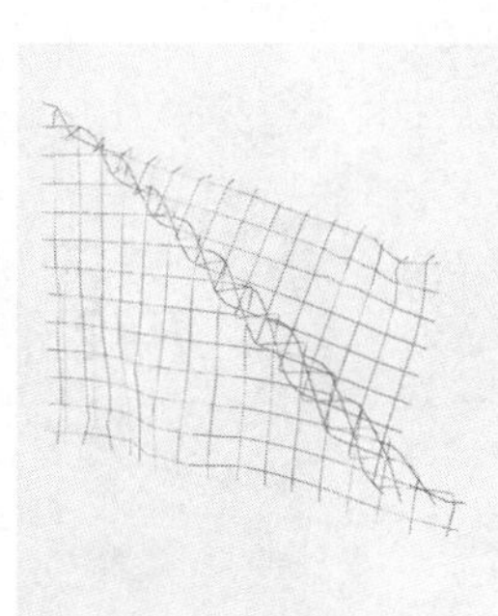

F#1

S, 6,48 km/h

[data]

12.02.2017	12:02:50	_44A8205	1/80	8	800	2,4	4,66	E
13.02.2017	#####	#####	#####	#####	#####	#####	#####	#####
14.02.2017	#####	#####	#####	#####	#####	#####	#####	#####
15.02.2017	12:04:09	_44A8280	1/640	8	500	1,8	3,50	S
16.02.2017	#####	#####	#####	#####	#####	#####	#####	#####
17.02.2017	#####	#####	#####	#####	#####	#####	#####	#####
18.02.2017	15:20:13	_44A8446	1/320	8	200	1,7	3,30	SSE
19.02.2017	#####	#####	#####	#####	#####	#####	#####	#####
20.02.2017	#####	#####	#####	#####	#####	#####	#####	#####
21.02.2017	14:05:40	_44A8473	1/250	8	1250	5,1	9,91	WSW
22.02.2017	#####	#####	#####	#####	#####	#####	#####	#####
23.02.2017	#####	#####	#####	#####	#####	#####	#####	#####
24.02.2017	15:52:53	_44A9577	1/200	8	800	1,4	2,72	S
25.02.2017	#####	#####	#####	#####	#####	#####	#####	#####
26.02.2017	#####	#####	#####	#####	#####	#####	#####	#####
27.02.2017	15:23:10	_44A9591	1/125	8	2000	1,4	2,72	NE
28.02.2017	#####	#####	#####	#####	#####	#####	#####	#####
01.03.2017	#####	#####	#####	#####	#####	#####	#####	#####
02.03.2017	11:00:43	_44A0257	1/200	8	640	10,2	19,83	WSW
03.03.2017	#####	#####	#####	#####	#####	#####	#####	#####
04.03.2017	#####	#####	#####	#####	#####	#####	#####	#####
05.03.2017	10:18:47	_44A0320	1/320	8	200	2,5	4,86	ESE
06.03.2017	#####	#####	#####	#####	#####	#####	#####	#####
07.03.2017	#####	#####	#####	#####	#####	#####	#####	#####
08.03.2017	09:27:18	_44A0325	1/200	8	1250	0,6	1,17	SSW
09.03.2017	#####	#####	#####	#####	#####	#####	#####	#####
10.03.2017	#####	#####	#####	#####	#####	#####	#####	#####
11.03.2017	12:12:44	_44A0367	1/250	8	160	0,9	1,75	SSW
12.03.2017	#####	#####	#####	#####	#####	#####	#####	#####
13.03.2017	#####	#####	#####	#####	#####	#####	#####	#####
14.03.2017	11:16:47	_44A0383	1/250	8	400	1,3	2,53	WSW
15.03.2017	#####	#####	#####	#####	#####	#####	#####	#####
16.03.2017	#####	#####	#####	#####	#####	#####	#####	#####
17.03.2017	09:51:38	_44A0427	1/250	8	400	0,7	1,36	WNW
18.03.2017	#####	#####	#####	#####	#####	#####	#####	#####
19.03.2017	#####	#####	#####	#####	#####	#####	#####	#####
20.03.2017	13:07:08	_44A0477	1/200	8	1000	2,8	5,44	W

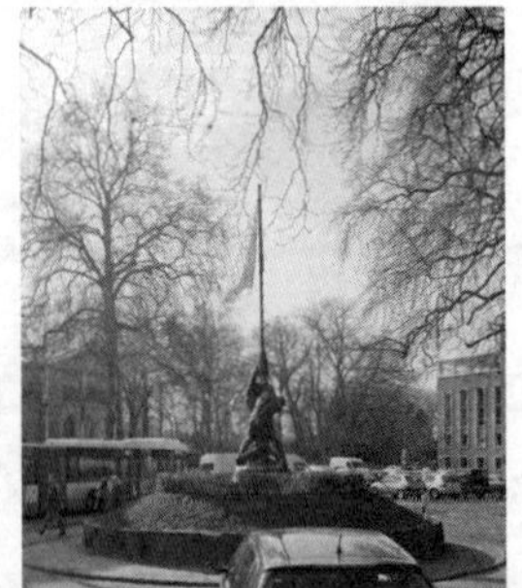

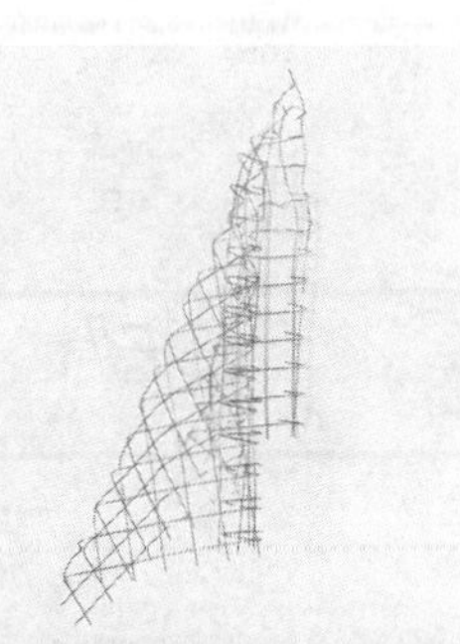

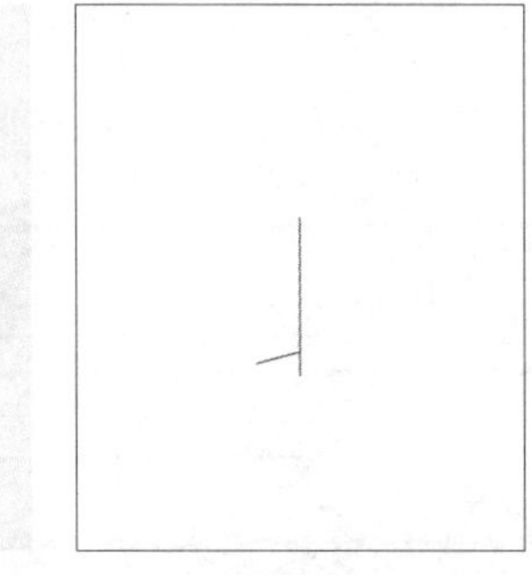

F#2

SSE, 6,12 km/h
[a dialogue, every 3d]

The flag is up. We've decided on the point of view from which the photographs will be taken. Both museums are closing and the parking lot empties out.

+3d
A man gets out of a small blue car and walks towards me. He saw me and someone else raising the flag three days ago, asks me what I'm doing.
'We've made a flag. Every third day, someone comes and takes a photograph of it.'
Why every third day?
'Because the flag is up for thirty-nine days, and it had to be divided into equal parts.'
Of course.
He asks me if I have a girlfriend.

+3d
He stays in the car. He waves. Talks to another man who I think was also there the previous session.

+3d
Heavy wind. The sun is setting. The facades of the museums are already lit, and the lights in the park might come on any minute now.
No blue car. But it's late in the evening, everything looks increasingly yellowish, and maybe I was too focused on the flag.

+3d
The parking lot has been sealed off for a bicycle race that finishes in the park. (Two days later, the live broadcast of the race didn't show the flag.) The man says he's from a town, which is thirty minutes from Ghent, that he comes here every day, better than sitting at home alone.

+3d
He says that a French artist (with some kind of Dutch-sounding name) already put up a flag at *De Mastplanters*. He doesn't like contemporary art.
'It's just another flag.'

+3d
Even stronger winds. Bursts of rain. There's a warning telling people to stay out of parks. Branches might fall. The wind's speed is estimated as 8 beaufort. The wind whips the flag. There's a determined jogger in the background.

+3d
He tells me that there's an underground nuclear command bunker in the park. It has supplies, communication channels and can hold up to 50 people. Might be useful one day. Detail: the generator feeding the heating system is outside the safe zone. Maybe they were hoping that the bomb would be dropped during the summer. The Museum of Contemporary Art used it around ten years ago and left lights and moveable walls in there. The fungus eating away at the wood is said to be lethal when inhaled for an extended period of time. If the outside world was radiant and cold, would one think that danger might arise *from within*? As if the park would refuse to tolerate our presence. He says if I got stuck down there, I could still make an exhibition, but the flag would be rather pointless.

+3d
A group of schoolchildren walks from the James Welling exhibition to the one on Francisco Goya. Some of them gaze into the lens, while I read the wind strength from the display, and he watches the flag (I imagine).

+3d
'Can you take the car and move it out of the frame?' I'm not sure if I'm allowed to ask.

+3d
Do both our timings create a system? Like the hands of a clock. A rhythm, perhaps a waltz.

+3d
A breeze.
Not much wind, he says.
Gardeners are planting flowers at the foot of the sculpture.
'No.'

+3d
He asks if it is the last photograph.

[While we were taking down the flag some ten police cars and a tank passed by. There was a speech on immigration given by a politician in a university building nearby. They parked behind the Museum of Fine Arts. Riding backwards, the tank hit a lamppost, which subsequently took on a strange 65° angle. Seven policemen stepped out of their cars and examined the situation. The flag had already been taken down. There was no way for us to document the scene.]

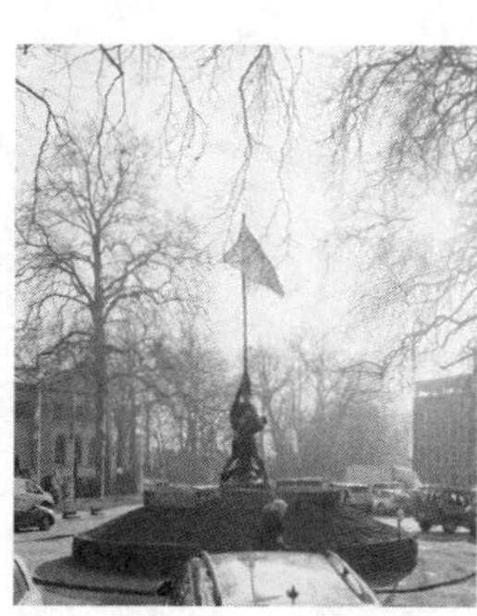
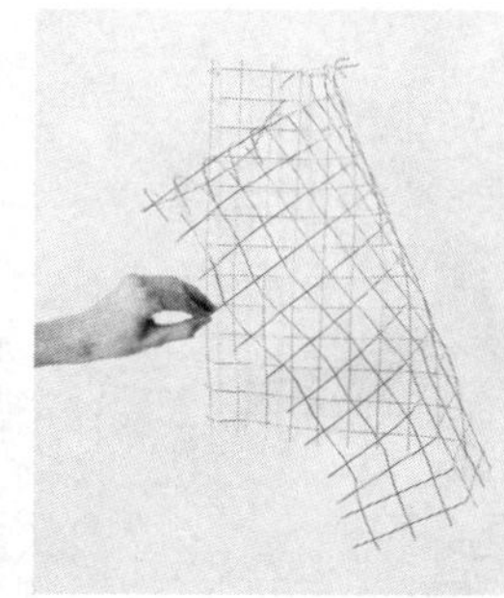
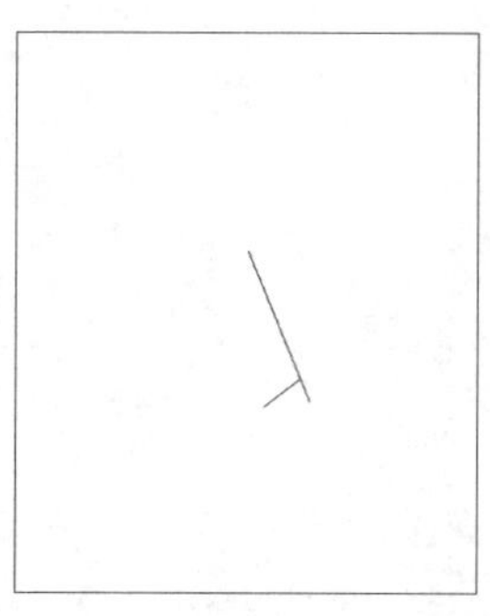

F#3

WSW, 18,36 km/h
[grille de lecture]

‘Angélique remit le planisphère dans son cabas et sortit des profondeurs du vieux sac une feuille de carton percée d’un certain nombre de trous irrégulièrement disposés. Cet appareil, appelé *grille* en langage cryptographique, devait permettre aux deux amants de correspondre sans danger. Une phrase, écrite au moyen des trous appliqués sur du papier blanc, pouvait être rendue inintelligible par l’adjonction de lettres quelconques, tracées au hasard pour remplir avec ordre les intervalles primitivement ménagés. Seul Velbar saurait retrouver le sens du billet en plaçant sur le texte une grille exactement semblable.’

– Raymond Roussel,
Impressions d’Afrique[1]

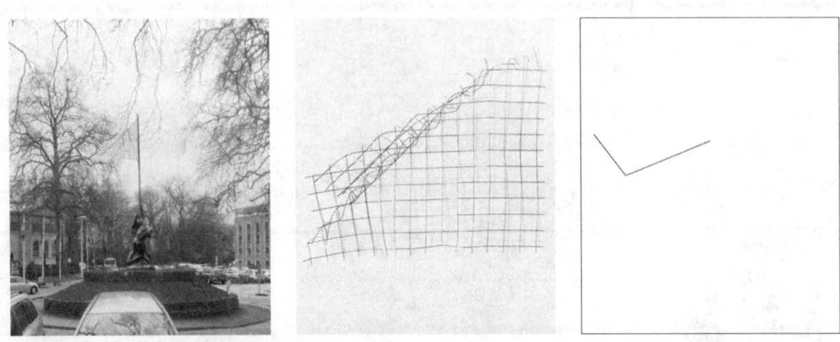

S, 5,04 km/h

[to inherit the wind]

The grid is a striking formal presence in twentieth-century modern painting. In her celebrated essay 'Grids' (1979), Rosalind Krauss explores this visual device in works by Georges Vantongerloo, Agnes Martin, Jasper Johns, Piet Mondrian, Robert Ryman, Sol Lewitt, etc.[2] Grids are also present in other twentieth-century media. What do Krauss's insights teach us about the way the grid functions in photography?

In a spatial sense, twentieth-century painting's concern with grids is 'what art looks like when it turns its back on nature' (Krauss 1979, 50). Unlike grids (in the form of black and white tile floors, for example) in fifteenth- and sixteenth-century perspective studies, modernist grids no longer represent or map out anything other than the surface of the artwork itself.

Therefore, grids allow for a centrifugal as well as a centripetal reading of the painting. On the one hand, 'any boundaries imposed upon it by a given painting or sculpture can only be seen [...] as arbitrary' (60). The painting is a fragment of a world that exists outside of it and which is suggested by the theoretically infinite grid depicted in it. On the other hand, 'the grid is an introjection of the boundaries of the world into the interior of the work' (61). By way of the grid, the painting repeats its own conventions, its borders, its limits, its structure; it represents them, inwards.[3]

In accordance with this, Krauss lays bare a mythical structure: grids conceal and reveal a tension between spirit and matter, religion and science. This tension can be traced back to nineteenth-century symbolist paintings depicting latticed windows: 'Behind every twentieth-century grid there lies [...] a symbolist window parading in the guise of a treatise on optics' (59). These windows emblematically emphasize the painting's twofold structure, offering both a view on 'the infrastructure of vision' increasingly dominated by scientific studies on colour and light, and a perspective on metaphysical ideas.

In photography, grids function in decisive ways: the gridded serial presentation in museums (of Becher photographs, for example), the pixelated digital photograph and its gridded structure (Thomas Ruff's JPEG-series comes to mind), or the way in which photographs, making up the separate frames of a film, are presented as strips and grids (Muybridge's pictures, for instance, which, in addition, use grids to analyse motion). These grids lead us to reflect on the way in which photography relates to issues such as seriality, storage, and sequentiality. But photographs also, and more straightforwardly, often *depict* grids. The tension between spirit and matter that Krauss traces in twentieth-century painting, occurs in photography. Having historical ties with optics and spiritism, photography, in general, implies such an approach. When it shows grids, it demands it.[4]

Bernd and Hilla Becher's *Framework Houses* series (1977), for example, features buildings with gridded facades. The houses stand in an anonymous environment. The wooden corners of the houses, seen from the front, frame the facades and echo the borders of the frame of the photograph inside the photograph. The scientific survey of the architecture of houses in the Siegen region is imbued with an almost abstract and dematerialized – modernist – aura.[5] Ed Ruscha's *Thirty-Four Parking Lots* (1967) consists of aerial views of vacant parking lots. Some images show only a fragment of the gridded lot, while others hint at their (suburban or rural) location. The gridded parking lots emphasize the flatness and stability of the photographs, while the absence of cars hints at an ideal of mobility. As for Walker Evans' celebrated 'Studio' (1936), its repetitive small portraits overtly places photography in the safe environment of the photograph itself, as it also leaves open the possibility that the grid extends beyond the frame. It leaves the word 'Studio' floating in between a repetitive and theoretically endless picturing of (the idea of) family, identity, happiness, and a confined and regulated presentation of printed paper.

As such, much of these photographs representing grids have both a centripetal and centrifugal quality, stressing both the continuation of the grid outside the frame of the photograph, and the autonomy of the photograph by the repetition of its borders. Because photography has an indexical relationship with the exterior world, the function of the grid is, therefore, at once tautological and antithetical: the grid both repeats and even overemphasizes photography's claim to depict a reality of which it is a fragmented representation, as it also contradicts and even denies this claim by pointing inwards to its own surface. Photography is, in both ways, and through its use of the grid, overtly present as a medium, and as such marks its undecided place between opposing realms – itself like a gridded fence, through which one can see, but not pass –: the autonomous realm of art, and that of non-art, scientific survey and beliefs, the regulated flatness of the photograph, and the boundless grids structuring the world.

If a symbolist window lies behind every twentieth-century painted grid, one can wonder what lies behind the photographed grid, and what this could entail. Can it be traced back to the same symbolist window that lies behind modern painting (which would mean that photography stresses a historical origin shared with painting)? Do the gridded photographs relate and refer to twentieth-century painting and its grids (which would mean that photography repeats modern painting's claim of autonomy by, paradoxically, relying on it)? Or does photography emphasize its own mythical source? Maybe behind every twentieth-century photographed grid there lies one of photography's earliest surviving negatives – William Fox Talbot's optical, chemical experiment depicting the latticed window of an abbey, parading as an historical instant of framed space.

Maybe another, and one of the most inconspicuous grids functioning in photography might even add a layer to the mythical tension between spirit and matter. Cameras are equipped with a plate of glass ground with a fine abrasive on which the light, through the lens, projects (the mirrored and upside down version of) the image that will be taken. It is on this glass that the photographer views his subject. This ground glass is often inscribed with a grid that's laid over the projected scene but will not appear in the photograph – a grid that is used by the photographer to compose the frame and move the lens in relation to the position and dimensions of the photographic film, glass plate or sensor. If the grids pictured in photographs in some way related to that gridded ground glass, these photographs would add a term to the mythical structure of the grid: besides marking the tension between spirit and matter, they would add *technique*. They would testify to a crucial element that functions in the opposite direction of the light projected onto the photographic paper. They would mark *the projection of the apparatus* – the camera as equipment – *on the photographic image*. They would hint at an ephemeral, moving image, momentarily seen by the photographer – not the view of the landscape, not the landscape depicted in the photograph, but the landscape as projected onto the ground glass – and at the intermediary, gridded, technical requirements that made the creation of the photograph possible. They would be structured according to the infrastructure of the camera.

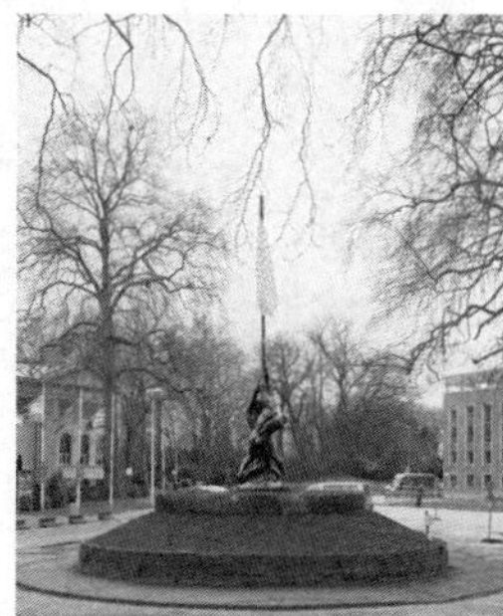

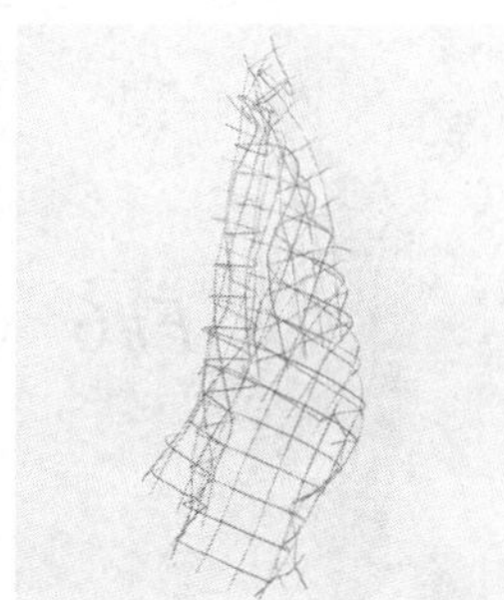

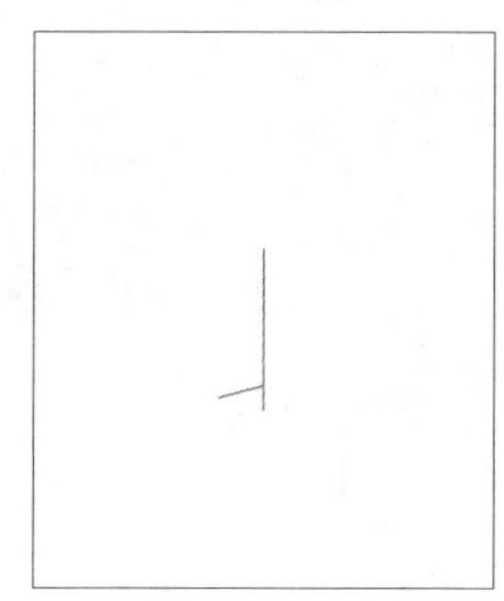

F#5

NE, 5,04 km/h

[procedure]

H

H

During a period of thirty-nine days,
a flag and a wind sensor will be attached
to *De Mastplanters*. At set times the
gridded surfaces will be photographed,
and data collected.

H

(Michiel & Arnout De Cleene)

–

In Euclidian motions we acted,
counted timely translations.
Laymen transfer a hypothetical breath, H,
enter a boundary

H

A spiritus

H

wet hill, novel waterway
copies
the lens: a new prison

We wanted to say more, to show it differently,
to outwit a guideline, perhaps to stop, but the grids wouldn't let us
–
slaves
to a dozen and one
automaton

H H H

the wind rattles
loudly
we test
we tell
–,

it moves

H

all is shown

HH

as OdD Purloined paperweights (AI)

'H

H

A preset and rigid grid adapts, bends & budges - n e s w, *Date*D
it echoed and led air
tech is clouded. Mt ascendeD.
A flag pertains to the motion of air (e)
in the way Chlorophyll in a tall tree leaf acts wrt luMen

H,

tacit wInd modulation
deterministically announces to sEe,
beneath the surface, a moldy Labyrinthe.
entropy – a rat ran

H

H

is a purist

H

we only perceive
what it allows:
asper now, lenis then

thirteen relentlessly mediated photographs – mute witnesses
airfloW, dewdrop, dust
latitude, longitude, altitude

'H

H

H,

the sylvan bed woefully attests
to a waltz –
one two two
wannn tu tooooo

motives

H

as in howls

H

H

(we) dIsAppeared in OuDraPo's light

H

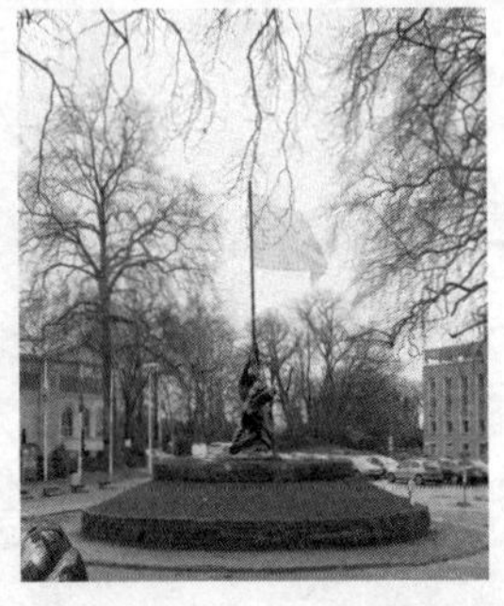

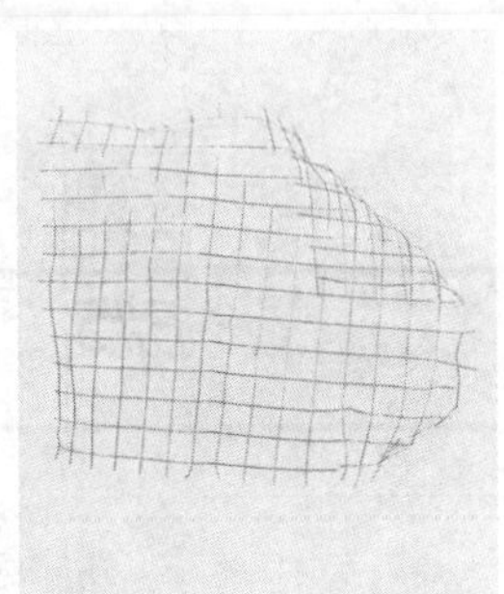

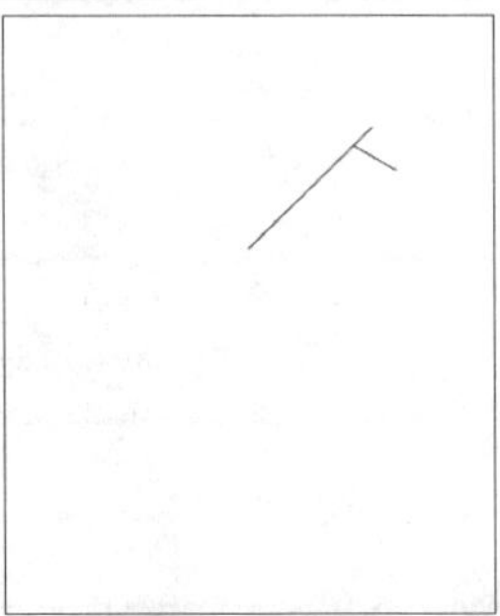

F#6

WSW, 36,72 km/h

[technique]

The [flag] measures 200x246cm, dimensions corresponding to the aspect ratio of the photographs. A grid consisting of sixteen equally spaced vertical and thirteen horizontal black lines was printed on a white surface. The flag was hoisted on *De Mastplanters,* a sculpture by Jules Van Biesbroeck Jr. installed in 1902 in the city of Ghent. It was cast in bronze in 1900, under the preliminary title *Pedestal for Flagpole or Electric Mast* (*Staander-voetstuk voor vaandelstok of elektrische mast*). The sculpture of two naked men planting a pole into the ground was originally conceived as the centrepiece of a roundabout. In 1902 Van Biesbroeck sent the city council a letter expressing his discontent about the sculpture being installed in front of the museum. The flagpole has been out of use for more than one hundred years (with one exception by Daniel Buren in 1980).

The [title] of this book is *F*#1-13. An uppercase and italicized *F* refers to a north-northeasterly wind of twenty knots (see # [wind-barbs, 1-13]) coming from the direction of the flag and passing exactly between the Museum of Fine Arts (MSK) and the Museum for Contemporary Art (S.M.A.K.) in Ghent. *F* indicates the direction in which all thirteen photographs were taken.

[photographs of flags, 1-13] Starting on 12 February 2017, the flag was photographed and meteorological measurements were recorded every third day. Thirteen records occurred over a period of thirty-nine days. The flag was lowered on 20 March 2017. All thirteen photographs were taken with the lens stopped down to f8 and from the exact same point of view. Four small pieces of plywood were hammered into the ground and a small dent was made in the pavement to ensure the exact positioning of the tripod. The photographs were recorded in colour and later converted to black-and-white images to allow for a more uniform interpretation of the grid.

[wind-barbs, 1-13] A wind sensor (*Oregon Scientific WGR800*), attached to the mast, measured the wind direction and speed. The results of the measurements – taken at the same instant as the photographs – were plotted out using wind-barbs. The longest line points in the direction from which the wind was blowing, a short barb represents 5 knots, a long barb 10 knots, and a pennant 50 knots.

[wireframes, 1-13] The photographic records of the flag form the basis for a three-dimensional, isolated rendition of the transformed grid as thirteen bent, folded, budged and compressed steel wireframes, with a scale of 1:3. We had to interpret the images to reconstruct a sculpture.

[photographs of wireframes, 1-13] These sculptures were photographed against a white background.

[texts, 1-13] were written based on phenomena, dialogues, manuals, revelations and data along the sidelines of the process of capturing the flag. The layout of the text is based on an underlying grid of thirteen columns.

[erosion] is a dialogue on the topic of Citadel Park in Ghent.

[data] lists the date, the time, the filename, the shutter speed, the aperture, the iso, the wind speed in metres per second and knots, and the wind direction on each of the thirteen recordings.

[a dialogue, every 3d] is a transcript of the dialogues held with a regular bystander near the flag when the photographs were taken and the meteorological data collected.

[grille de lecture] is a citation from Raymond Roussel's *Impressions d'Afrique* in which two lovers secretly communicate.

[to inherit the wind] is a short essay on Rosalind Krauss's analysis of grids in twentieth-century painting. It presents some general ideas on the way her insights could be applied for analysing grids in photography.

[procedure] is an anagrammatically constructed poem. The wind moves air and particles. They are displaced, not erased. We've halted the current of letters at two instants, with a north-easterly wind (H) blowing in between them.

[technique] lists some of the procedures involved in the making of the texts, photographs, sculptures and diagrams.

[user manual] is a poem based on *Full Wireless Weather Station Kit with USB upload, Model: WMR89/WMR89A User Manual* – the manual of the anemometer used to collect meteorological data.[6] The poem was constructed using the text in the manual, whereby it was only allowed to erase words – as if using a *grille de lecture*. As such, the order in which the words appeared could not be altered. Punctuation and uppercases were added. The poem – composed of nine incomplete sonnets – describes, amongst other things, a scientific mountaineering expedition gone wrong.

[document] is a reflection on the documentary potential of the media used.

[surface] is the floor plan for an imaginary exhibition, composed of a selection of works featuring grids in the collections of MSK and S.M.A.K. in Ghent. The recorded direction of the wind, as plotted out in the wind barbs, determined the scenography.

[penetrating screen] deals with some of the images printed in Frank and Lillian Gilbreth's *Applied Motion Study,* a book in which the authors develop a theory concerning photography, labour, and the way in which a grid can serve to optimize industrial efficiency.

[stereoscopic survey] The Digital Height Model (DHM) is a three-dimensional digital description of the earth's surface. The model functions with x- and y-coordinates positioned at ground level (without buildings or vegetation). They are a numerical representation of the landscape as a grid. The altitude in urban centres is measured by means of stereoscopic photographs which are characterized by a high accuracy of the measured points and the high point density. [stereoscopic survey] is an attempt to identify and isolate the surface of the hill that supports *De Mastplanters*. The x-, y- and z-axes intersect where the flagpole is planted (104752.00/192243.00/20.70). The listed data describes the hill on which Citadel Park is situated, confined in the West by the Koning Albertlaan, in the East by the Opperschelde, in the South by the Burggravenlaan and in the North by the Ketelvest.[7]

[colophon] lists the people involved in the process of making this book and presents the endnotes. Etymologically, colophon can be traced back to Ancient Greek, meaning 'highest point' or 'hill'.

The [front cover] shows composite images of all the elements in the book.

The [back cover] shows a fragment of the flag, as photographed after thirty-nine days, on a scale of 1:1.

[book design] The dimensions of the pages in this book were determined by the size of the flag. The total surface of the paper used for each section (photographs of the flag, photographs of the wireframes, wind-barbs, and texts) equals the surface of the flag. The total surface of the paper used in this book therefore equals four times the surface of the flag.

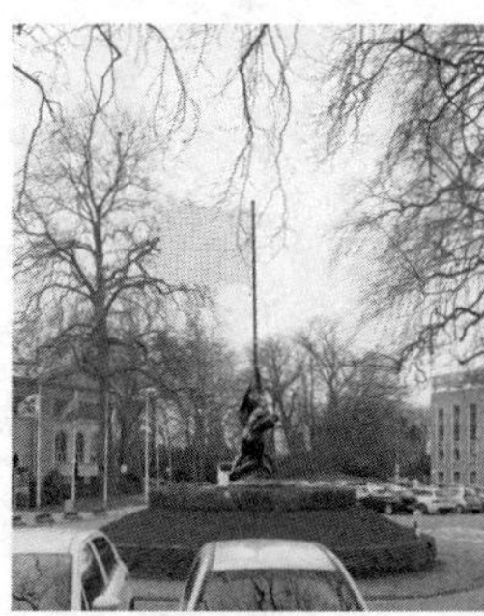

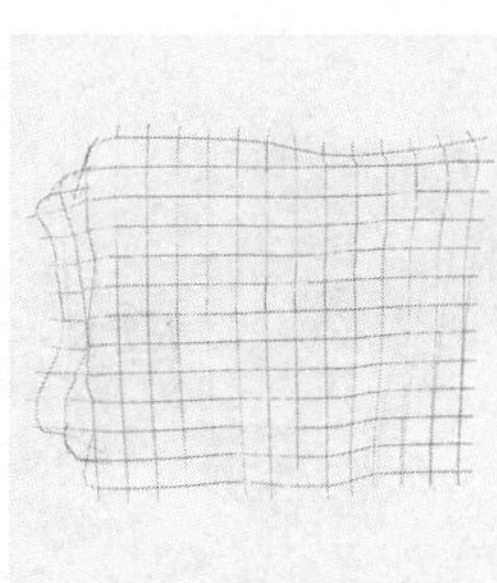

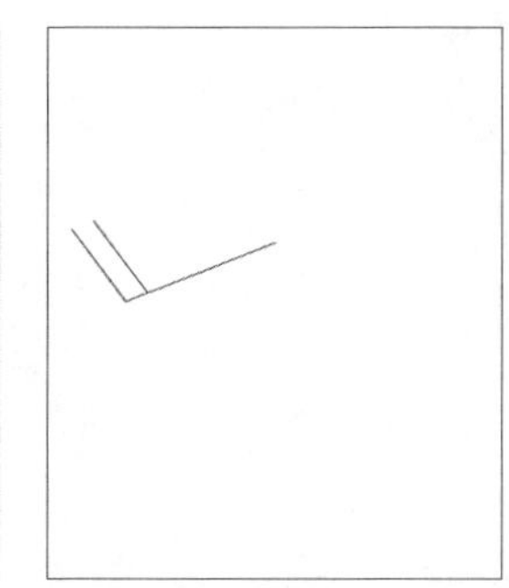

F#7

ESE, 9 km/h

[user manual]

(This system)

This contains instructions
you know:
packaging wind above and
below.

1 connector, 1 collector work
to capture readings,
to switch between different modes,
to exit memory.

Mount! Search for the signal,
select the nearest
signal, display

a successful index – remote
knots.

(Getting started)

The polarities (+ and -)
set up freezing, remote wind.
The wind takes
wind, speed and direction.

The sensor is operated. It is capable.
Base Station (wirelessly within
an approximate operating range –
meters, feet):

'Unscrew the anemometer
from the wind. Carefully.
Collect data the polarities

(+ / -) set up.'
(The rain collects rain and takes rainfall.)

#

'Remove motion, remove fibre.'
'Base Station, [...] obstructed [...] exposed [...]
wet conditions [...] (such as vases) [...] completely
disconnect from power.'

The icon appears.
Meaning.
Mounting – to check, select –
the top.

Wind gently moves the trees;
the wind desired
location,

an existing place; it
points.

(Area)

Ideal would be the exterior,
at a height. Meters (feet) can shield it
from direct conditions.
An open area mounted

horizontally from the ground.
(The tipping rain, several times, a few seconds.)
A plane. Put a cross to check
the horizontal level. The center remains.

For seconds, it brought
a signal – Frankfurt,
Germany, Anthorn,

England, Fort Collins
Colorado.

(Icon)

A flat surface, near the antenna.
'Searching for a signal' – 'You need to [...]'
– 'Repeat?' (hour, minute, year,
month, date, weekday

language and hemisphere.)
In English, French, Russian. The icon:
waning, crescent, waning.
In opposite orientation: the index

indicates the current. Clear memories.
An indication on how
it feels. Air advises

lines, rising steady,
falling.

(Direction)

To read the wind. To select the wind.
Knots (knots) – a series of icons:
storm.
To view the wind: the effects (wind is capable),

the history (hours of readings); the current
shown (horizontal). It represents, it shows
and shows the icon
to the corresponding icon (vertical).

Rainfall cannot, will have
no effect on the altitude.
To navigate to the area. Up, to increase

the setting, to confirm the index. High, and
above, extremely high, to the area, to the current.

(The current)

Review, to review. Base Station is history: '[...]
Exit the area! [...]'. Then the current
starts. The current is reviewing
history. Only it does not visit immediately.

Reset, to reset. To Base Station.
Altitude. Cloudy memory.
Current operating. Memory controlled.
Obstructions channel memory.

Excessive force, shock (newspapers,
curtains, a soft
cloth – images shown differ

from the actual display) –
result

#

in damage. '[...] care [...] without [...] treatment
is necessary [...] please contact [...] any enquiry [...]
please contact [...] limited reserves [...]'
(There is inconsistency between versions;)

A copy, signed and dated:
*'This operation, subject to following
conditions, may cause
undesired changes, expressly approved;*

*compliance could void the user's authority.
Instructions: comply with the limits. These limits
are designed to provide reasonable protection*

*against harmful interference. However,
there is no guarantee*

#

*that interference will not occur.
Try to correct the interference.
Reorient, relocate.
Increase the separation between*

the equipment and the technician.'
The barred symbol
indicates the end –
the end given back

to a new start.
Reuse the apparatus.
The user sanctions
according to

the laws in force.

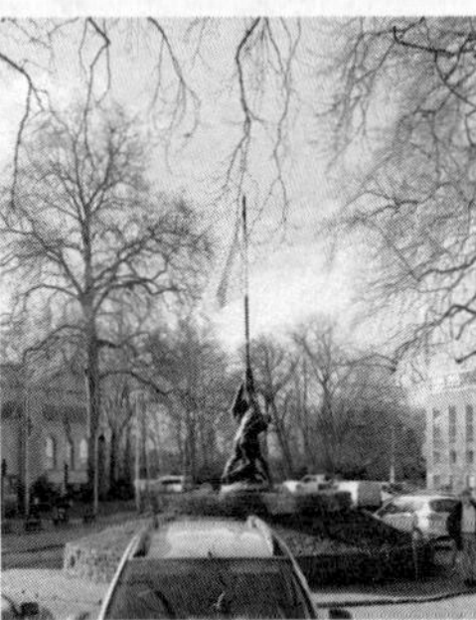

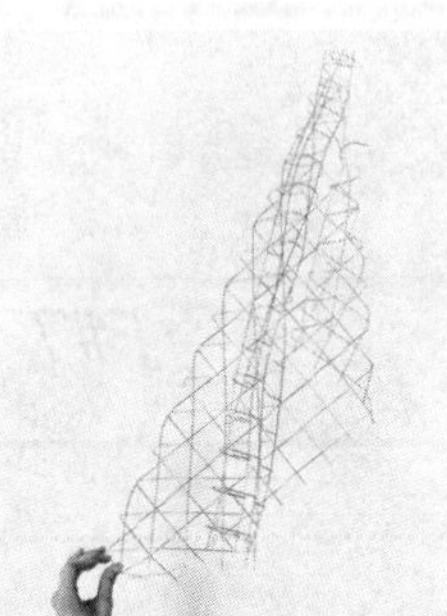

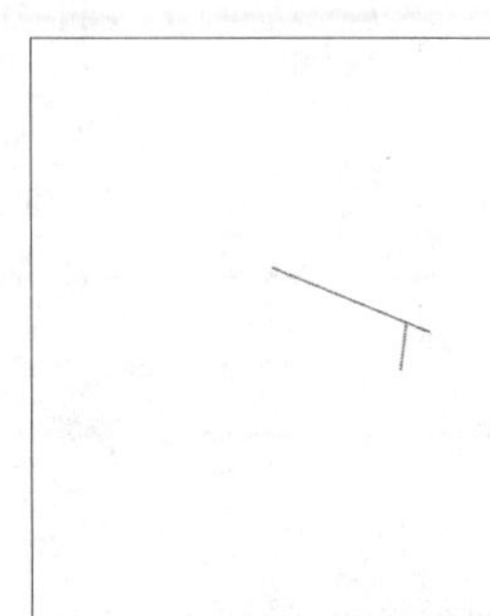

F#8

SSW, 2,16 km/h

[document]

According to Eyal Weizman, architecture can be seen and investigated as a documentary form: 'Architecture emerges as a documentary form, not because photographs of it circulate in the public domain but rather because it performs variations on the following three things: it registers the effect of force fields, it contains or stores these forces in material deformations, and, with the help of other mediating technologies and the forum, it transmits this information further' (Weizman 2014, 15).[8] Likewise, a flag can be conceptualized as a document, as a forensic surface. A good example is The Star-Spangled Banner, planted on the moon in 1969. While this flag didn't register – or, according to some, shouldn't have registered – the wind, it did record its environment: after nearly fifty years, the flag has become a Banner, refusing each territorial claim,[9] for in that period of time, the amount of UV-light has bleached and ultimately erased all stars and stripes.

Movement of air affects a gridded flag attached to the pole of *De Mastplanters*. After thirty-nine days, the flag gave a somewhat worn out and polluted appearance. If the specific movements – the different bursts of wind – would have been stored in its fibres, it wasn't capable of transmitting this information; or at least, we lack the expertise to interpret what it perhaps conserves within the confines of its fabric. The anemometer's display gave detailed information, data translated into a graphic shape as wind-barbs. Photographs recorded the movement of the flag. As sculptures, the bent wireframes restored the third dimension that was lost in the photographs, a dimension again lost when they too were photographed.

In this documentary endeavour, every medium used brought opportunities another medium wasn't capable of, as well as inherent limitations. Take photography: the sight is turned into a portable, structured, and simplified record, selecting and applying a frame along with a shift from a multisensory experience to a merely visual and two-dimensional transcript. The photograph – and especially a digital one – is a volatile container of information that you can carry along, put away, muster up, send, and share. But in order to achieve this, the experienced landscape is severely reduced.

'Documentary', as an adjective, describes the way in which a medium is seen as capable – with possibilities and limitations – of recording. But there's more to it. Along the way, each element – text, graph, or image – began to refer to another one, and the documentary became a referential system. As such, the documentary also surfaced as a function in between those media: documentary value was added in the process of the transposition of one medium to another within that system.

The wind-barbs defined the scenography of a virtual exhibition. The photographs of the flag determined how the sculptures had to be bent. And as for the photographs of these sculptures, they not only documented a gridded surface formed by the wind, but also created new shapes. Like a terrain mesh, they began to resemble a top-down view of strange surfaces – unknown islands on which bursts of chaotic wind seemed to have violently moulded strange, unearthly landscapes. The documentary blew through the structure of photography, flag, sculpture, graph, and text. As it registered one medium by means of another, and began tying them together in a relational and referential field, it also instructed the latter by means of the former.

In its contemporary usage, the word 'document' – as a noun or as a verb – signifies something official, a file with information. It is tied to an event or phenomenon that precedes it, which the document registers or records. But etymologically, it has another meaning. It derives from the Latin *docere* – to teach – and *documentum* – a lesson. In between events and phenomena, the document therefore has an ambiguous temporal and causal place. It functions as a record of what happened, *and* as a guideline for the way in which things must happen. To document: to register, to refer, and to instruct, at the same time. As we documented the wind, the wind documented us.

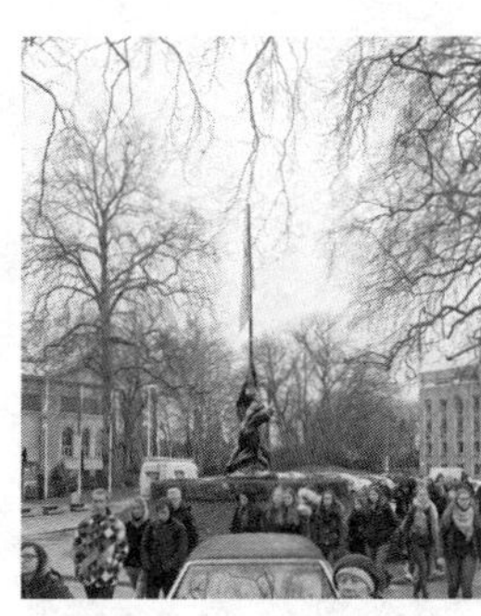

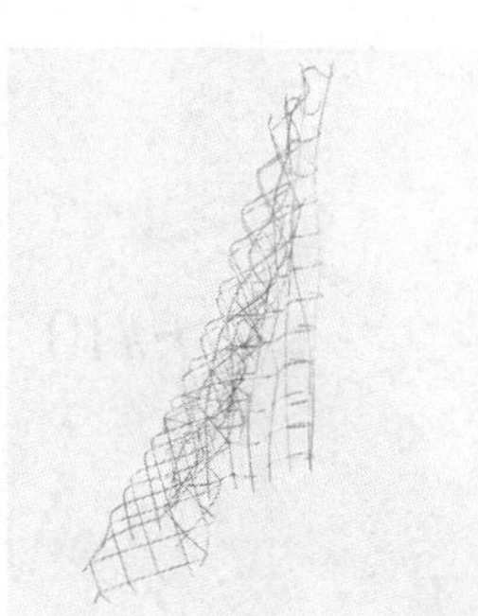

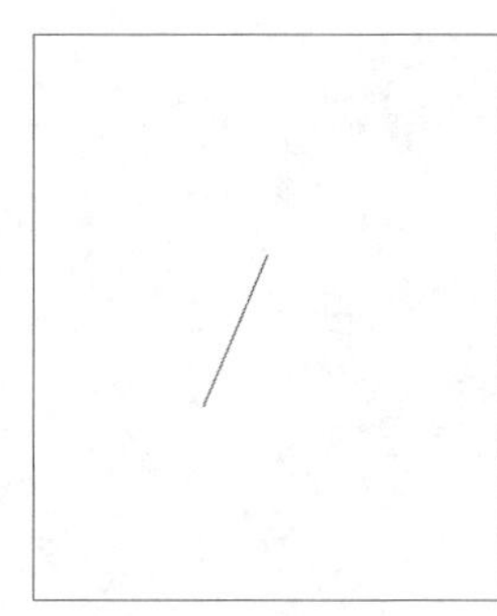

F#9

SSW, 3,24 km/h
[surface]

1
Circle of Lucas de Heere
Vanitas Stilleven (gesloten)
Oil on panel
16th century

2
Pieter Neefs I
De verlossing van de heilige Petrus
Oil on painting
17th century

3
Cornelis Gijsbrechts
Trompe-l'oeil: brievenbord met zandloper, scheermes en schaar
Oil on canvas
ca. 1664

4
Cornelis Gijsbrechts
Trompe-l'oeil: brievenbord met dansmeesterviool en pistool
Oil on canvas
1664

5
Pierre François De Noter
De Sint-Baafskathedraal en de Reep in Gent
Oil on panel
1831

6
Georges Vantongerloo
Studie nr. III
Casein on panel
1920

7
František Kupka
Quatre histoires de blanc et noir, gravées
Woodcut on wove paper
1926

8
François Morellet
Grilles se déformant
Aluminium, iron
1965

9
Marcel Broodthaers
La Pluie (Projet pour un texte)
Film
1969

10
Sol Lewitt
Wall Drawing No. 36
1970

11
Bernd & Hilla Becher
Coal Bunkers
Photographs on panel
1972

12
Jan Schoonhoven
R74-17
Latex paint, cardboard, wood, paper
1974

13
Kees Goudzwaard
Score
Oil on canvas
2005

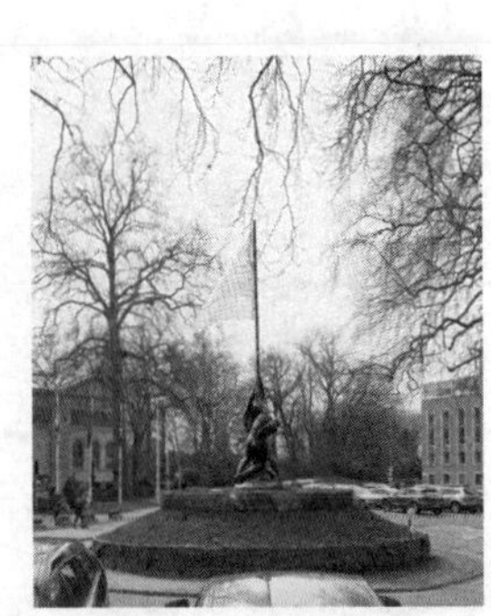

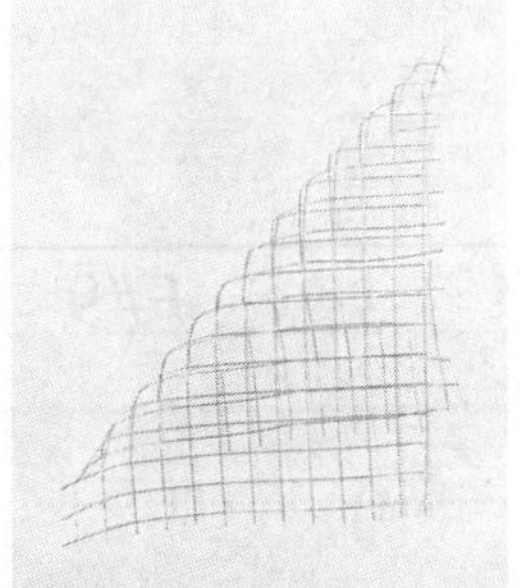

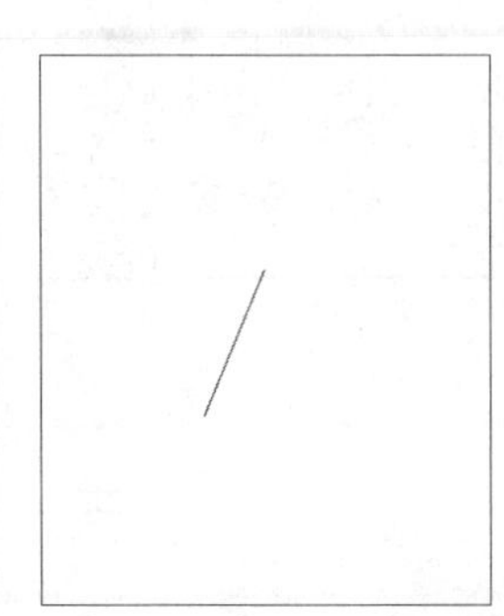

WSW, 4,68 km/h

[penetrating screen]

Miss Hortense Stollnitz became International Amateur Champion Typist in 1916, 'equalling the professional record of 137 words per minute net, and exceeding all previous records with 147 words per minute gross' (Gilbreth & Gilbreth 1917, 36–37). In the same year, she had already won that contest a first time, and the International Novice Champion Typewriter Contest in New York the year before.[10]

Miss Stollnitz can be seen in *fig. 5* in Frank and Lillian Gilbreth's *Applied Motion Study* (1917).[11] A vertical strip of small photographs shows Miss Stollnitz changing the paper of the typewriter she is working on, with only minimal differences between the various shots: while the paper she has finished typing is being rolled out of the typewriter (and seems to fly into the room), she is already taking the next blank paper with her other hand – thereby briefly concealing a clock on the wall behind her. On the same page, *fig. 4* shows Miss Anna Gold, who is also typing, while a second woman is on the other side of the typewriter (and again a clock is between them). Although her face is blurred, her typing fingers are sharp. Miss Gold, the caption states, 'afterwards became National Amateur Champion Typist by winning the contest at Chicago, 1916' (Gilbreth & Gilbreth 1917, 36–37).[12]

'Afterwards': both Miss Gold and Miss Stollnitz were trained by the Gilbreths, who had developed a specific method for improving efficiency in the working environment. In their study, they describe 'the simple photographic process which enables one to record in detail the motions of a handicraft, or a manufacture, so as to bring them by criticism and experiment to their utmost economy of energy and time' (George Iles, in Gilbreth & Gilbreth 1917, ix). To arrive at this 'permanent and practical waste elimination' the Gilbreths attached a small electric light to the moving body part of the worker. As such, this movement created a line of light, which was captured on a photographic plate that was exposed during the time the subject performed the work. This line was called a 'cyclegraph'. To be effective and instructional, the continuous line was broken up: 'the time element was eventually obtained by placing an interrupter in the current, that transformed the white line of the cyclegraph into a series or line of dots and dashes. This made of the cyclegraph a chronocyclegraph' (Gilbreth & Gilbreth 1917, 83–84).

Fig. 7 is a similar strip of photographs displaying a sequence of motions. This 'Automatic Micromotion Study with vertical penetrating screen in the plane of the motions' features a man in a white shirt and black tie. Over his left shoulder: a clock. Each of the eight vertically stacked photographs shows the same composition of the same man in the same room with a white grid superimposed on every image. The chronocyclegraphs rely on what the Gilbreths called the penetrating screen: a sheet of black paper with a white grid on it. That grid is crucial. They superimposed this grid on the factory worker by making a double exposure on the same piece of film. This procedure enabled them to record and analyse the motions of a worker performing a specific task. Motion reveals itself in relation to the rigid grid. The Gilbreths subsequently turned these chronocyclegraphs into three-dimensional, bent wires – sculptures – that functioned as a manual for that specific movement. Manual labour becomes grid becomes manual becomes labour. In *fig. 7*, the penetrating screen indifferently covers the background, the clock, the man's hands, shirt, tie, and face. Beneath the grid, the anonymous worker is folding a white cotton cloth.

In *fig. 6*, the Gilbreths zoom in on Miss Stollnitz's hands ('while writing at her fastest speed'). Only the keyboard and five fingers are visible. The text mentions that these pictures were taken at the rate of 115 exposures per second. With a special apparatus, they 'can be studied as continuous motion at the rate of eight per second' (Gilbreth & Gilbreth 1917, 36–37). The advanced photographing technique used by the Gilbreths has the potential to show more than the amount of words the International Amateur Champion can type in one minute. It reveals the motion in between words. Nonetheless, despite the photographic accuracy, it remains unclear what text Miss Stollnitz was typing. When Miss Stollnitz entered the International Championship Typewriting Contest for professionals in 1921, she typed more words than all the other contestants. However, she ranked seventh because of the number of errors she had made (Hoof 2011, 267).[13]

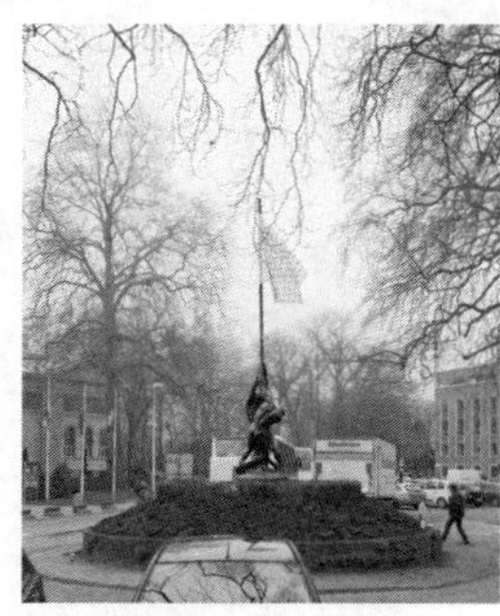

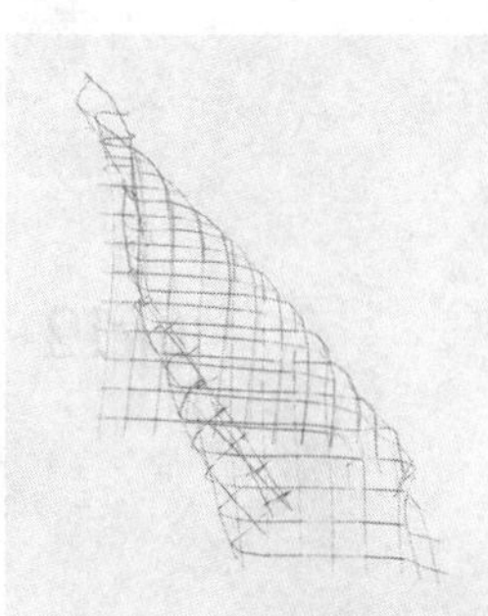

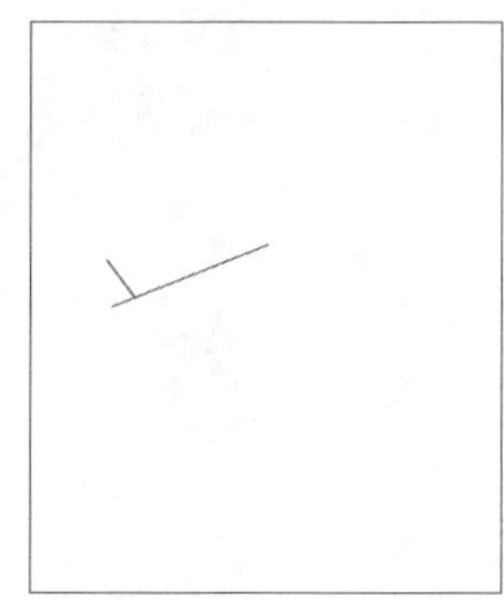

F#11

WNW, 2,52 km/h
[stereoscopic survey]

104752.00 191578.00 9.26
104752.00 191583.00 9.27
104752.00 191588.00 9.27
104752.00 191593.00 9.29
104752.00 191598.00 9.42
104752.00 191603.00 9.47
104752.00 191608.00 9.50
104752.00 191613.00 9.56
104752.00 191618.00 9.62
104752.00 191623.00 9.69
104752.00 191628.00 9.77
104752.00 191633.00 9.85
104752.00 191638.00 9.93
104752.00 191643.00 10.02
104752.00 191648.00 10.10
104752.00 191653.00 10.19
104752.00 191658.00 10.28
104752.00 191663.00 10.41
104752.00 191668.00 10.54
104752.00 191673.00 10.68
104752.00 191678.00 10.82
104752.00 191683.00 10.87
104752.00 191688.00 10.93
104752.00 191693.00 11.06
104752.00 191698.00 11.17
104752.00 191703.00 11.27
104752.00 191708.00 11.38
104752.00 191713.00 11.51
104752.00 191718.00 11.68
104752.00 191723.00 11.86
104752.00 191728.00 12.02
104752.00 191733.00 12.09
104752.00 191738.00 12.17
104752.00 191743.00 12.24
104752.00 191748.00 12.31
104752.00 191753.00 12.39
104752.00 191758.00 12.41
104752.00 191763.00 12.46
104752.00 191768.00 12.54
104752.00 191773.00 12.60
104752.00 191778.00 12.61
104752.00 191783.00 13.02
104752.00 191788.00 13.60
104752.00 191793.00 14.17
104752.00 191798.00 14.23
104752.00 191803.00 14.23
104752.00 191808.00 14.17
104752.00 191813.00 14.15
104752.00 191818.00 14.20
104752.00 191823.00 14.23
104752.00 191828.00 14.25
104752.00 191833.00 14.28
104752.00 191838.00 14.32
104752.00 191843.00 14.39
104752.00 191848.00 14.49
104752.00 191853.00 14.58
104752.00 191858.00 14.68
104752.00 191863.00 15.31
104752.00 191868.00 15.96
104752.00 191873.00 16.28
104752.00 191878.00 16.66
104752.00 191883.00 17.16
104752.00 191888.00 17.51
104752.00 191893.00 17.94
104752.00 191898.00 18.35
104752.00 191903.00 18.73
104752.00 191908.00 18.97
104752.00 191913.00 18.93
104752.00 191918.00 18.82
104752.00 191923.00 18.74
104752.00 191928.00 18.41
104752.00 191933.00 18.19
104752.00 191938.00 18.39
104752.00 191943.00 18.52
104752.00 191948.00 16.56
104752.00 191953.00 16.72
104752.00 191958.00 16.92
104752.00 191963.00 17.11
104752.00 191968.00 17.30
104752.00 191973.00 17.49
104752.00 191978.00 17.75
104752.00 191983.00 18.03
104752.00 191988.00 18.30
104752.00 191993.00 18.58
104752.00 191998.00 18.86
104752.00 192003.00 19.14
104752.00 192008.00 19.41
104752.00 192013.00 19.69
104752.00 192018.00 19.86
104752.00 192023.00 19.93
104752.00 192028.00 19.96
104752.00 192033.00 19.98
104752.00 192038.00 19.98
104752.00 192043.00 19.96
104752.00 192048.00 19.95
104752.00 192053.00 19.93
104752.00 192058.00 19.90
104752.00 192063.00 19.92
104752.00 192068.00 19.97
104752.00 192073.00 20.02
104752.00 192078.00 19.97
104752.00 192083.00 19.89
104752.00 192088.00 19.81
104752.00 192093.00 19.73
104752.00 192098.00 19.69
104752.00 192103.00 19.84
104752.00 192108.00 20.02
104752.00 192113.00 20.21
104752.00 192118.00 20.34
104752.00 192123.00 20.36
104752.00 192128.00 20.34
104752.00 192133.00 20.29
104752.00 192138.00 20.26
104752.00 192143.00 20.26
104752.00 192148.00 20.20
104752.00 192153.00 20.22
104752.00 192158.00 20.29
104752.00 192163.00 20.34
104752.00 192168.00 20.38
104752.00 192173.00 20.44
104752.00 192178.00 20.50
104752.00 192183.00 20.56
104752.00 192188.00 20.63
104752.00 192193.00 20.69
104752.00 192198.00 20.76
104752.00 192203.00 20.78
104752.00 192208.00 20.70
104752.00 192213.00 20.63
104752.00 192218.00 20.59
104752.00 192223.00 20.57
104752.00 192228.00 20.61
104752.00 192233.00 20.65
104752.00 192238.00 20.68
104752.00 192243.00 20.70
104752.00 192248.00 20.71
104752.00 192253.00 20.84
104752.00 192258.00 20.87
104752.00 192263.00 21.73
104752.00 192268.00 21.93
104752.00 192273.00 21.66
104752.00 192278.00 21.64
104752.00 192283.00 21.63
104752.00 192288.00 21.61
104752.00 192293.00 22.01
104752.00 192298.00 22.40
104752.00 192303.00 22.80
104752.00 192308.00 23.47
104752.00 192313.00 24.19
104752.00 192318.00 24.63
104752.00 192323.00 23.98
104752.00 192328.00 23.18
104752.00 192333.00 22.88
104752.00 192338.00 23.00
104752.00 192343.00 23.14
104752.00 192348.00 23.35
104752.00 192353.00 23.42
104752.00 192358.00 23.38
104752.00 192363.00 23.37
104752.00 192368.00 23.37
104752.00 192373.00 23.41
104752.00 192378.00 23.48
104752.00 192383.00 23.56
104752.00 192388.00 23.64
104752.00 192393.00 23.73
104752.00 192398.00 23.82
104752.00 192403.00 23.92
104752.00 192408.00 24.01
104752.00 192413.00 24.10
104752.00 192418.00 24.21
104752.00 192423.00 24.34
104752.00 192428.00 24.47
104752.00 192433.00 24.57
104752.00 192438.00 24.73
104752.00 192443.00 24.89
104752.00 192448.00 25.05
104752.00 192453.00 25.34
104752.00 192458.00 25.70
104752.00 192463.00 26.06
104752.00 192468.00 26.35
104752.00 192473.00 26.42
104752.00 192478.00 26.50
104752.00 192483.00 26.58
104752.00 192488.00 26.66
104752.00 192493.00 26.75
104752.00 192498.00 26.84
104752.00 192503.00 26.88
104752.00 192508.00 26.84
104752.00 192513.00 26.83
104752.00 192518.00 26.83
104752.00 192523.00 26.82
104752.00 192528.00 26.71
104752.00 192533.00 26.70
104752.00 192538.00 26.69
104752.00 192543.00 26.67
104752.00 192548.00 26.69
104752.00 192553.00 26.72
104752.00 192558.00 26.73
104752.00 192563.00 26.75
104752.00 192568.00 26.75
104752.00 192573.00 26.73
104752.00 192578.00 26.73
104752.00 192583.00 26.69
104752.00 192588.00 26.77
104752.00 192593.00 26.85
104752.00 192598.00 26.91
104752.00 192603.00 26.89
104752.00 192608.00 26.84
104752.00 192613.00 26.92
104752.00 192618.00 27.11
104752.00 192623.00 27.31
104752.00 192628.00 27.50
104752.00 192633.00 27.70
104752.00 192638.00 27.87
104752.00 192643.00 27.97
104752.00 192648.00 28.07
104752.00 192653.00 28.26
104752.00 192658.00 28.57
104752.00 192663.00 28.73
104752.00 192668.00 28.88
104752.00 192673.00 29.08
104752.00 192678.00 29.20
104752.00 192683.00 29.22
104752.00 192688.00 29.20
104752.00 192693.00 29.19
104752.00 192698.00 29.17
104752.00 192703.00 29.17
104752.00 192708.00 29.14
104752.00 192713.00 29.13
104752.00 192718.00 29.12
104752.00 192723.00 29.12
104752.00 192728.00 29.11
104752.00 192733.00 29.10
104752.00 192738.00 29.08
104752.00 192743.00 28.96
104752.00 192748.00 28.80
104752.00 192753.00 28.80
104752.00 192758.00 28.70
104752.00 192763.00 28.55
104752.00 192768.00 28.43
104752.00 192773.00 28.23
104752.00 192778.00 28.08
104752.00 192783.00 27.75
104752.00 192788.00 27.39
104752.00 192793.00 27.13
104752.00 192798.00 26.94
104752.00 192803.00 26.98
104752.00 192808.00 26.98
104752.00 192813.00 27.04
104752.00 192818.00 27.18
104752.00 192823.00 27.17
104752.00 192828.00 27.52
104752.00 192833.00 27.76
104752.00 192838.00 28.01
104752.00 192843.00 28.17
104752.00 192848.00 28.28
104752.00 192853.00 28.41
104752.00 192858.00 28.54
104752.00 192863.00 28.65
104752.00 192868.00 28.65
104752.00 192873.00 28.68
104752.00 192878.00 28.72
104752.00 192883.00 28.52
104752.00 192888.00 28.04
104752.00 192893.00 27.50
104752.00 192898.00 26.85
104752.00 192903.00 26.21
104752.00 192908.00 25.65
104752.00 192913.00 25.12
104752.00 192918.00 24.80
104752.00 192923.00 24.46
104752.00 192928.00 24.12
104752.00 192933.00 23.79
104752.00 192938.00 23.73
104752.00 192943.00 23.63
104752.00 192948.00 23.47
104752.00 192953.00 23.32
104752.00 192958.00 23.19
104752.00 192963.00 23.15
104752.00 192968.00 23.13
104752.00 192973.00 23.19
104752.00 192978.00 23.17
104752.00 192983.00 23.08
104752.00 192988.00 22.95
104752.00 192993.00 22.81
104752.00 192998.00 22.75
104752.00 193003.00 22.74
104752.00 193008.00 22.64
104752.00 193013.00 22.77
104752.00 193018.00 23.04
104752.00 193023.00 22.97
104752.00 193028.00 23.31
104752.00 193033.00 23.47
104752.00 193038.00 23.48
104752.00 193043.00 23.40
104752.00 193048.00 23.32
104752.00 193053.00 23.09
104752.00 193058.00 22.99
104752.00 193063.00 22.09
104752.00 193068.00 21.77
104752.00 193073.00 21.45
104752.00 193078.00 21.13
104752.00 193083.00 20.81
104752.00 193088.00 20.59
104752.00 193093.00 20.48
104752.00 193098.00 20.37
104752.00 193103.00 20.27
104752.00 193108.00 20.16
104752.00 193113.00 20.01
104752.00 193118.00 19.83
104752.00 193123.00 19.64
104752.00 193128.00 19.60
104752.00 193133.00 19.46
104752.00 193138.00 19.22
104752.00 193143.00 19.10
104752.00 193148.00 19.03
104752.00 193153.00 18.73
104752.00 193158.00 18.43
104752.00 193163.00 18.16
104752.00 193168.00 18.09
104752.00 193173.00 17.93
104752.00 193178.00 17.73
104752.00 193183.00 17.53
104752.00 193188.00 17.32
104752.00 193193.00 17.04
104752.00 193198.00 16.59
104752.00 193203.00 16.26
104752.00 193208.00 15.93
104752.00 193213.00 15.67
104752.00 193218.00 15.50
104752.00 193223.00 15.25
104752.00 193228.00 14.99
104752.00 193233.00 14.77
104752.00 193238.00 14.59
104752.00 193243.00 14.57
104752.00 193248.00 14.56
104752.00 193253.00 14.55
104752.00 193258.00 14.54
104752.00 193263.00 14.52
104752.00 193268.00 14.60
104752.00 193273.00 14.83
104752.00 193278.00 15.07
104752.00 193283.00 14.89
104752.00 193288.00 14.68
104752.00 193293.00 14.16
104752.00 193298.00 13.31
104752.00 193303.00 12.95
104752.00 193308.00 12.81
104752.00 193313.00 12.67
104752.00 193318.00 12.36
104752.00 193323.00 12.17
104752.00 193328.00 12.14
104752.00 193333.00 12.09
104752.00 193338.00 12.05
104752.00 193343.00 11.96
104752.00 193348.00 11.86
104752.00 193353.00 11.76
104752.00 193358.00 11.64
104752.00 193363.00 11.52
104752.00 193368.00 11.38
104752.00 193373.00 11.26
104752.00 193378.00 11.14
104752.00 193383.00 11.02
104752.00 193388.00 10.89
104752.00 193393.00 10.77
104752.00 193398.00 10.65
104752.00 193403.00 10.52
104752.00 193408.00 10.40
104752.00 193413.00 10.28
104752.00 193418.00 10.33
104752.00 193423.00 9.92
104752.00 193428.00 6.60
104752.00 193433.00 5.77
104752.00 193438.00 5.86
104752.00 193443.00 5.95

103842.00 192243.00 8.99
103847.00 192243.00 9.01
103852.00 192243.00 9.03
103857.00 192243.00 9.03
103862.00 192243.00 9.03
103867.00 192243.00 9.03
103872.00 192243.00 9.03
103877.00 192243.00 9.03
103882.00 192243.00 9.03
103887.00 192243.00 9.03
103892.00 192243.00 8.93
103897.00 192243.00 8.97
103902.00 192243.00 9.06
103907.00 192243.00 9.04
103912.00 192243.00 9.03
103917.00 192243.00 9.04
103922.00 192243.00 9.02
103927.00 192243.00 9.09
103932.00 192243.00 9.16
103937.00 192243.00 9.23
103942.00 192243.00 9.30
103947.00 192243.00 9.39
103952.00 192243.00 9.51
103957.00 192243.00 9.65
103962.00 192243.00 9.74
103967.00 192243.00 9.75
103972.00 192243.00 9.78
103977.00 192243.00 9.86
103982.00 192243.00 9.98
103987.00 192243.00 9.99
103992.00 192243.00 10.05
103997.00 192243.00 10.09
104002.00 192243.00 10.12
104007.00 192243.00 10.20
104012.00 192243.00 10.28
104017.00 192243.00 10.36
104022.00 192243.00 10.44
104027.00 192243.00 10.51
104032.00 192243.00 10.60
104037.00 192243.00 10.69
104042.00 192243.00 10.77
104047.00 192243.00 10.86
104052.00 192243.00 10.96
104057.00 192243.00 11.05
104062.00 192243.00 11.15
104067.00 192243.00 11.31
104072.00 192243.00 11.40
104077.00 192243.00 11.48
104082.00 192243.00 11.60
104087.00 192243.00 11.67
104092.00 192243.00 11.71
104097.00 192243.00 11.74
104102.00 192243.00 11.80
104107.00 192243.00 11.90
104112.00 192243.00 11.90
104117.00 192243.00 12.46
104122.00 192243.00 13.08
104127.00 192243.00 13.71
104132.00 192243.00 13.75
104137.00 192243.00 13.80
104142.00 192243.00 14.06
104147.00 192243.00 14.33
104152.00 192243.00 14.55
104157.00 192243.00 14.49
104162.00 192243.00 14.39
104167.00 192243.00 14.41
104172.00 192243.00 14.52
104177.00 192243.00 14.50
104182.00 192243.00 14.54
104187.00 192243.00 14.61
104192.00 192243.00 14.67
104197.00 192243.00 14.74
104202.00 192243.00 14.81
104207.00 192243.00 14.88
104212.00 192243.00 14.87
104217.00 192243.00 14.90
104222.00 192243.00 15.21
104227.00 192243.00 15.52
104232.00 192243.00 15.84
104237.00 192243.00 16.15
104242.00 192243.00 16.21
104247.00 192243.00 16.52
104252.00 192243.00 16.60
104257.00 192243.00 16.67
104262.00 192243.00 16.88
104267.00 192243.00 16.97
104272.00 192243.00 17.08
104277.00 192243.00 17.14
104282.00 192243.00 17.31
104287.00 192243.00 17.92
104292.00 192243.00 18.87
104297.00 192243.00 19.82
104302.00 192243.00 18.73
104307.00 192243.00 18.76
104312.00 192243.00 19.16
104317.00 192243.00 19.51
104322.00 192243.00 19.57
104327.00 192243.00 19.63
104332.00 192243.00 19.69
104337.00 192243.00 19.75
104342.00 192243.00 19.88
104347.00 192243.00 19.91
104352.00 192243.00 19.98
104357.00 192243.00 20.09
104362.00 192243.00 20.17
104367.00 192243.00 20.27
104372.00 192243.00 20.37
104377.00 192243.00 20.46
104382.00 192243.00 20.48
104387.00 192243.00 20.42
104392.00 192243.00 20.34
104397.00 192243.00 20.30
104402.00 192243.00 20.29
104407.00 192243.00 20.32
104412.00 192243.00 20.29
104417.00 192243.00 20.13
104422.00 192243.00 20.03
104427.00 192243.00 20.04
104432.00 192243.00 19.94
104437.00 192243.00 19.83
104442.00 192243.00 19.76
104447.00 192243.00 19.76
104452.00 192243.00 19.74
104457.00 192243.00 19.63
104462.00 192243.00 19.60
104467.00 192243.00 19.67
104472.00 192243.00 19.67
104477.00 192243.00 19.64
104482.00 192243.00 19.66
104487.00 192243.00 19.71
104492.00 192243.00 19.77
104497.00 192243.00 20.23
104502.00 192243.00 20.25
104507.00 192243.00 20.28
104512.00 192243.00 19.61
104517.00 192243.00 19.64
104522.00 192243.00 19.72
104527.00 192243.00 19.77
104532.00 192243.00 19.77
104537.00 192243.00 19.78
104542.00 192243.00 19.78
104547.00 192243.00 19.79
104552.00 192243.00 19.79
104557.00 192243.00 19.80
104562.00 192243.00 19.80
104567.00 192243.00 19.81
104572.00 192243.00 19.81
104577.00 192243.00 19.82
104582.00 192243.00 19.83
104587.00 192243.00 19.83
104592.00 192243.00 19.84
104597.00 192243.00 19.84
104602.00 192243.00 19.85
104607.00 192243.00 19.85
104612.00 192243.00 19.86
104617.00 192243.00 19.86
104622.00 192243.00 19.87
104627.00 192243.00 19.87
104632.00 192243.00 19.88
104637.00 192243.00 19.88
104642.00 192243.00 19.89
104647.00 192243.00 19.89
104652.00 192243.00 19.96
104657.00 192243.00 20.11
104662.00 192243.00 20.20
104667.00 192243.00 20.20
104672.00 192243.00 20.14
104677.00 192243.00 20.10
104682.00 192243.00 20.10
104687.00 192243.00 20.06
104692.00 192243.00 20.31
104697.00 192243.00 20.66
104702.00 192243.00 21.05
104707.00 192243.00 21.89
104712.00 192243.00 23.04
104717.00 192243.00 24.69
104722.00 192243.00 24.89
104727.00 192243.00 23.61
104732.00 192243.00 21.60
104737.00 192243.00 20.90
104742.00 192243.00 20.74
104747.00 192243.00 20.72
104752.00 192243.00 20.70
104757.00 192243.00 20.67
104762.00 192243.00 20.63
104767.00 192243.00 20.58
104772.00 192243.00 20.57
104777.00 192243.00 20.47
104782.00 192243.00 20.49
104787.00 192243.00 20.35
104792.00 192243.00 20.30
104797.00 192243.00 20.31
104802.00 192243.00 20.38
104807.00 192243.00 20.31
104812.00 192243.00 20.25
104817.00 192243.00 20.21
104822.00 192243.00 20.19
104827.00 192243.00 20.15
104832.00 192243.00 20.10
104837.00 192243.00 20.09
104842.00 192243.00 20.09
104847.00 192243.00 20.09
104852.00 192243.00 20.05
104857.00 192243.00 20.00
104862.00 192243.00 19.93
104867.00 192243.00 19.85
104872.00 192243.00 19.77
104877.00 192243.00 19.66
104882.00 192243.00 19.54
104887.00 192243.00 19.44
104892.00 192243.00 19.33
104897.00 192243.00 19.20
104902.00 192243.00 19.03
104907.00 192243.00 18.87
104912.00 192243.00 18.73
104917.00 192243.00 18.59
104922.00 192243.00 18.47
104927.00 192243.00 18.39
104932.00 192243.00 18.30
104937.00 192243.00 18.11
104942.00 192243.00 17.93
104947.00 192243.00 17.80
104952.00 192243.00 17.69
104957.00 192243.00 17.58
104962.00 192243.00 17.44
104967.00 192243.00 17.30
104972.00 192243.00 17.17
104977.00 192243.00 17.08
104982.00 192243.00 16.99
104987.00 192243.00 16.89
104992.00 192243.00 16.76
104997.00 192243.00 16.56
105002.00 192243.00 16.34
105007.00 192243.00 16.16
105012.00 192243.00 15.99
105017.00 192243.00 15.80
105022.00 192243.00 15.64
105027.00 192243.00 15.52
105032.00 192243.00 15.40
105037.00 192243.00 15.28
105042.00 192243.00 15.12
105047.00 192243.00 15.03
105052.00 192243.00 14.92
105057.00 192243.00 14.82
105062.00 192243.00 14.71
105067.00 192243.00 14.54
105072.00 192243.00 14.39
105077.00 192243.00 14.25
105082.00 192243.00 14.04
105087.00 192243.00 13.86
105092.00 192243.00 13.68
105097.00 192243.00 13.56
105102.00 192243.00 13.45
105107.00 192243.00 13.33
105112.00 192243.00 13.20
105117.00 192243.00 13.07
105122.00 192243.00 12.83
105127.00 192243.00 12.68
105132.00 192243.00 12.58
105137.00 192243.00 12.45
105142.00 192243.00 12.33
105147.00 192243.00 12.22
105152.00 192243.00 12.26
105157.00 192243.00 9.46
105162.00 192243.00 6.25

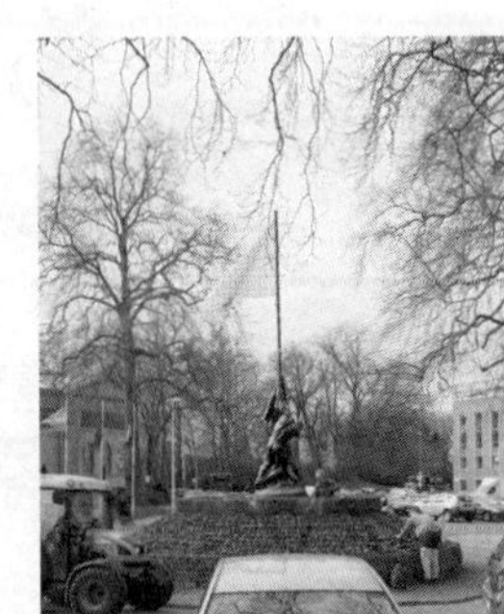

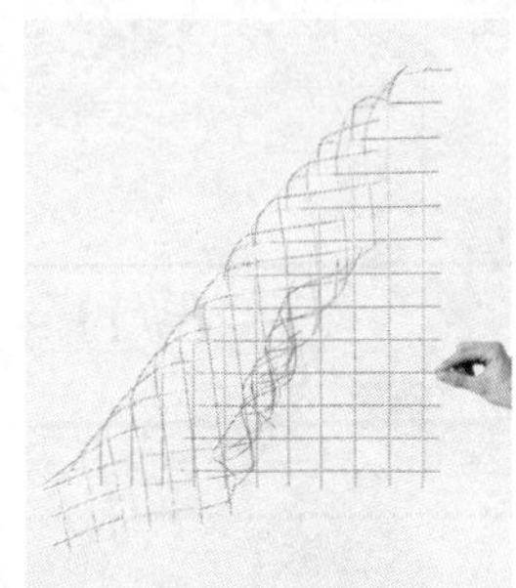

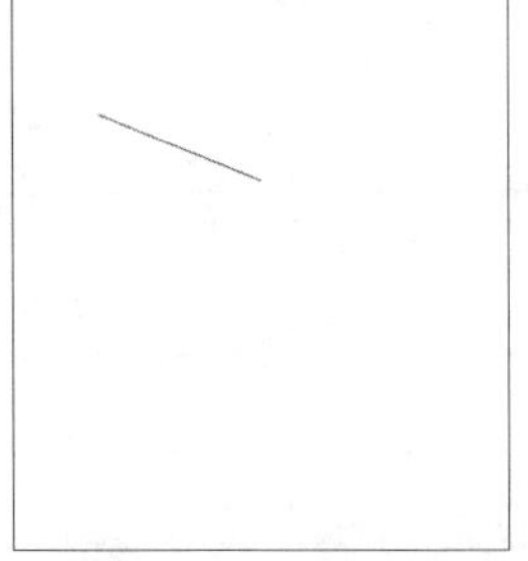

F#12

W, 10,08 km/h

[colophon]

F#1-13
ARNOUT DE CLEENE & MICHIEL DE CLEENE

APE#087
© 2017, Art Paper Editions
ISBN 9789490800666
www.artpapereditions.org

Graphic design: Jurgen Maelfeyt, Jonas Temmerman (6'56")
Printing: Graphius, Ghent
International distribution: ideabooks.nl
Distribution Belgium: exhibitionsinternational.org

S&D#031 *De Mastplanters / Les Planteurs de Mât*, is a project by Smoke & Dust/019. Their annexation of this statue started in November 2016. [erosion], [to inherit the wind], [technique], [document] and [penetrating screen] were proofread by Lucie Chevalier. This book is made with the kind support of the Cultural Department of the City of Ghent, KASK / School Of Arts, Ghent (where MDC is currently working on the research project Reference Guide, funded by the Art Fund for Research of the University College Ghent) and Smoke & Dust/019. Thanks to Valentijn Goethals, Smoke & Dust/019, Helena Elshout, Nele Dieleman, Lars Kwakkenbos, Jurgen Maelfeyt & Jonas Temmerman.

A short film showing *F*#1-13 (11'18") can be seen at vimeo.com/206565478

This book was presented on 17 September 2017 at the closing event of the Museum Of Moving Practice in Design Museum, Ghent. On the roof, we hoisted the flag.

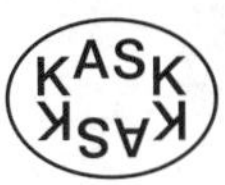
HoGent

[Endnotes]

1 Raymond Roussel, *Impressions d'Afrique* (Paris: Alphonse Lemerre, 1910), 271–272.
2 Rosalind Krauss, 'Grids,' *October*, no. 9 (Summer 1979). This shift can be seen as part of a larger landslide, whereby a materialist, scientific perspective took the overhand of a spiritual one. The gridded modern era, it was said, would surely 'inherit the wind' (54).
3 See the analysis of Frank Stella's *Hyena Stomp* in Jean-Claude Lebensztejn, *Zigzag* (Paris: Flammarion, 1981), 49–159.
4 See Allan Sekula, 'On the Invention of Photographic Meaning,' in *Photography Against the Grain* (London: MACK, 2016).
5 Allan Sekula's work can be interpreted as a response to this aesthetic: 'The Bechers' monumental account of the principal work sites of industrial capitalism of the twentieth century apparently had to exclude the active participants from these locations and from the possibility of representation in order to gain its aesthetic accreditation within the larger account of modernist visuality. [...] Thus Sekula's attempt to develop a critical realism aims also to systematically overcome this aspect of "renunciation," to overcome the ban on the representation of labor imposed by an aesthetic of modernist restrictions' (Benjamin H.D. Buchloh, 'Allan Sekula: Photography Between Discourse and Document,' in Allan Sekula, *Fish Story* (Düsseldorf: Richter Verlag, 1995), 194).
6 *Full Wireless Weather Station Kit with USB upload. Model: WMR89/WMR89A. User Manual.*
7 Agentschap voor Geografische Informatie Vlaanderen, digitaal hoogtemodel Vlaanderen, punten, versiedatum: 2006-05-29, dataset identification: A19563AB-AAD5-4120-ABFB-2687EA486262.
8 Eyal Weizman, 'Introduction,' in Forensic Architecture, *Forensis. The Architecture of Public Truth* (London/Berlin: Forensic Architecture/Sternberg Press, 2014).
9 As such, the flag differs from its conventional use as an expression of (geographical, communal, or political) identity. For an analysis of the flag as an object in early twentieth-century literature, see Jan Baetens, 'Le drapeau,' in Nadja Cohen & Anne Reverseau, *Petit musée d'histoire littéraire, 1900-1950* (Paris: Impressions Nouvelles, 2015).
10 Florian Hoof, *Engel der Effizienz. Eine Mediengeschichte der Unternehmensberatung* (Konstanz: Konstanz University Press, 2015), 267. On the 1915 typewriting contest *The Rotarian* writes: 'It is [...] the one event that gives a real indication of the machine's part in the development of speed in typewriting. The question of typewriter merit is not determined by what the exceptional operator of exceptional training can do, *but by what the average operator can do*' (1916, 59, emphasis added). In that respect, the winner of the contest was not so much Miss Stollnitz, as it was a Model 10 Remington Typewriter. *The Rotarian. Magazine of Service,* vol. 8, no. 1 (January 1916).
11 Frank B. Gilbreth & L.M. Gilbreth, *Applied Motion Study. A Collection of Papers on the Efficient Method to Industrial Preparedness* (New York: Sturgis & Walton Company, 1917).
12 Miss Stollnitz came second (Hoof 2015, 267).
13 The six contestants who ranked higher than Miss Stollnitz all used an Underwood typewriter (Hoof 2015, 267).

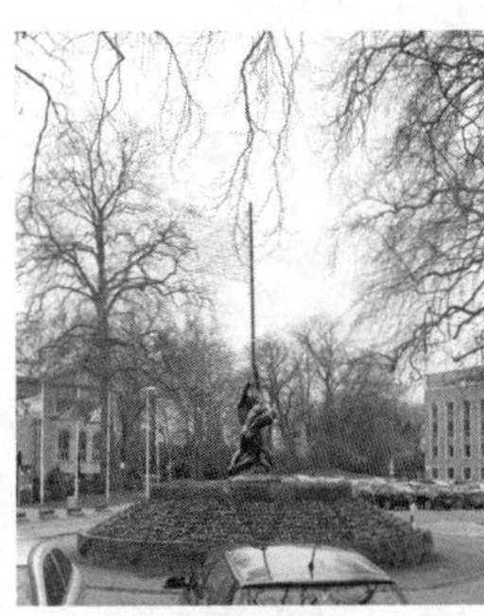

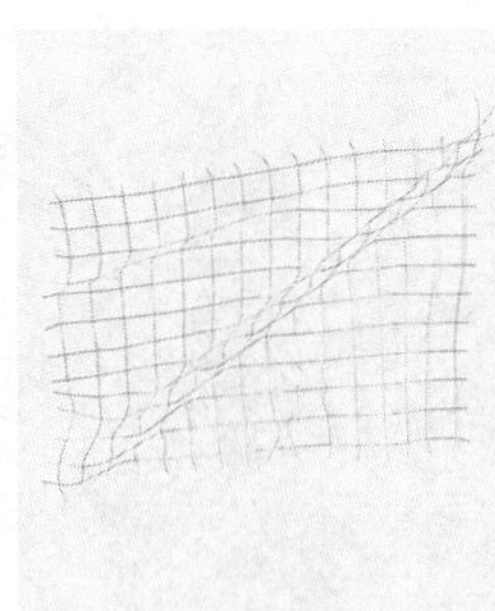

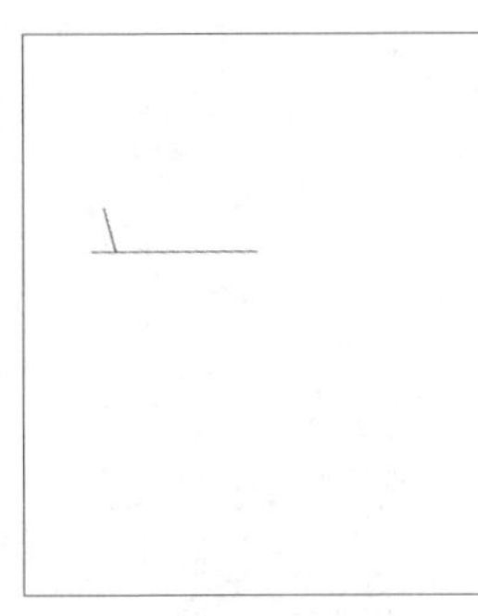

F#13